Detaining the Immigrant Other

Detaining the Immigrant Other

Global and Transnational Issues

EDITED BY RICH FURMAN, DOUGLAS EPPS,
and
GREG LAMPHEAR

OXFORD
UNIVERSITY PRESS

OXFORD
UNIVERSITY PRESS

Oxford University Press is a department of the University of Oxford. It furthers the University's objective of excellence in research, scholarship, and education by publishing worldwide. Oxford is a registered trade mark of Oxford University Press in the UK and certain other countries.

Published in the United States of America by Oxford University Press
198 Madison Avenue, New York, NY 10016, United States of America.

First Edition published in 2016

Library of Congress Cataloging-in-Publication Data
Names: Furman, Rich, editor. | Epps, Douglas, editor. | Lamphear, Greg, editor.
Title: Detaining the immigrant other: global and transnational issues /edited by Rich Furman, Douglas Epps, & Greg Lamphear.
Description: Oxford ; New York : Oxford University Press, [2016] |
Includes bibliographical references and index.
Identifiers: LCCN 2015030021 | ISBN 9780190222574 (alk. paper)
Subjects: LCSH: Emigration and immigration—Social aspects. | Emigration and immigration law. | Refugees—Legal status, laws, etc.
Classification: LCC JV6225 .D48 2016 | DDC 325/.1—dc23
LC record available at http://lccn.loc.gov/2015030021

1 3 5 7 9 8 6 4 2
Printed by Sheridan, USA

Rich's Dedication:

To Sugs,
Eat the world baby. Eat the world.

Doug's Dedication:

To my family,
Especially Marie, for supporting me even when you didn't want to,
Liam, for inspiring me from day one (Daddy loves you),
and all who've encouraged me to keep pushing on.

Greg's Dedication:

To my sons Everett and Theodore

CONTENTS

CONTRIBUTORS

Alissa R. Ackerman, Ph.D., is an assistant professor of criminal justice at the University of Washington Tacoma. Her research on the management of sexual offenders has appeared in *Criminal Justice & Behavior, Journal of Criminal Justice,* and *Justice Quarterly*.

David Androff, Ph.D., is assistant professor in the School of Social Work at Arizona State University, where he chairs the Policy, Administration, and Community Program and teaches classes in community practice, social policy, and global social welfare. He has published widely on immigration-related issues.

Nurcan Ozgur Baklacioglu, Ph.D., is associate professor in international relations, at Istanbul University, Faculty of Political Science. During the 1990s she studied minority issues, migration politics, cross-border politics, and dual citizenship issues in Macedonia, Kosovo, Turkey, and Bulgaria.

Dafney Blanca Dabach, Ph.D., is an assistant professor at the University of Washington's College of Education. Her research is situated in the field of immigration and education, with particular attention to examining secondary-school-based contexts that immigrant youths encounter in U.S. schools.

Mary Bosworth, Ph.D., is Professor of Criminology and Fellow of St Cross College at the University of Oxford and, concurrently, Professor of Criminology at Monash University, Australia. She is Assistant Director of the Centre for Criminology and Director of Border Criminologies, an interdisciplinary research group focusing on the intersections between criminal justice and border control.

Janet Cleveland, is a member of the Équipe de recherche et d'intervention transculturelles (ERIT) CSSS de la Montagne, McGill University. Since 2003, she has conducted research on the impact of Canadian and Quebec public policies on the rights and health of asylum seekers and refugees.

Azadeh Dastyari is a lecturer in the Faculty of Law at Monash University and an associate of the Castan Centre for Human Rights Law.

Douglas Epps, M.S.W., is one of the editors of this volume and a former immigration detention officer. His scholarship and research centers on the criminalization of immigration.

Andriani Fili is a research associate and the Leverhulme International Network Facilitator at the Centre for Criminology, University of Oxford. With master's degrees in criminology and criminal justice (University of Oxford) and gender and social policy (London School of Economics), she has a range of experience working in the nonprofit sector, mainly in Greece, with migrants and refugees.

Rich Furman, Ph.D., is a professor of social work at the University of Washington Tacoma and one of the editors of this volume.

Susanna Jones, Ph.D., is a professor of social work at Long Island University Brooklyn. Her most recent scholarship examines immigration policy and transnationalism and its impact on social welfare policy and practice.

Shahram Khosravi is an associate professor of social anthropology at Stockholm University. He is the author of the book *The Illegal Traveler: An Auto-ethnography of Borders.*

Carolina Kobelinsky is an anthropologist and researcher at the French Center for Scientific Research (CNRS). Her work focuses on asylum and migration policies, border studies, and the anthropology of the state. Her current research deals with the deaths of migrants at Europe's southern borders. She has recently published together with a research team *At the Heart of the State: The Moral World of Institutions.*

Mieke Kox, M.A., is a Ph.D. candidate at the Criminology Department of Erasmus University Rotterdam, the Netherlands. Her Ph.D. research focuses on the legal consciousness of unauthorized migrants in the Netherlands who are confronted with apprehension, immigration detention, or deportation. In her previous work, she addressed the experiences of Belgian prisoners in a Dutch prison setting, the experiences and the return intentions of immigration detainees, and the living conditions of rejected asylum seekers.

Rachel Kronick is a psychiatrist working with children, adolescents, and families at the Centre for Addiction and Mental Health, Department of Psychiatry, University of Toronto. Her research focuses on Canadian migration policies affecting children and families, particularly detention.

Sasagu Kudo is a Ph.D. candidate at the Graduate School of International Relations at Ritsumeikan University, Japan. He received his B.A. and M.A. in law also from Ritsumeikan University. His current research focuses on the nexus of security and politics, particularly in Malaysian immigration policy.

Greg Lamphear works as an editor, journalist, and teacher and is one of the editors of this volume.

Stefan Le Courant is an anthropologist and member of the Laboratoire d'ethnologie et de sociologie comparative, University of Paris Ouest Nanterre La Défense. His publications include "What Can We Learn from a 'Liar' and a 'Madman'? Serendipity and Double Commitment During Fieldwork" (*Social Anthropology/Anthropologie sociale,* 2013) and "Le poids de la menace: l'évaluation quotidienne du risque d'expulsion" (*Ethnologie française,* 2015).

Arjen Leerkes is an associate professor of sociology at Erasmus University Rotterdam and researcher at the Research and Documentation Center (WODC) at the Dutch Ministry of Security and Justice. He has written extensively on immigration control and the position of unauthorized immigrants in Europe and the United States, as well as on issues of transnationalism, neighborhood safety, and crime.

Melody Loya, Ph.D., is an associate professor of social work at West Texas A&M University. She has led an innovative international social work course to Costa Rica and has published widely on a variety of issues related to social work practice and education.

Ċetta Mainwaring is an assistant professor in the Sociology and Legal Studies Department and the Balsillie School of International Affairs at the University of Waterloo. She completed her D.Phil., "Centring on the Margins: Migration Control in Malta, Cyprus and the European Union," at the University of Oxford in 2012. Her work has been published in various academic journals, including *Population, Space and Place* and the *Journal of Immigrant and Refugee Studies.*

Gordon Mathews teaches anthropology at the Chinese University of Hong Kong. He has written about asylum seekers in his book *Ghetto at the Center of the World: Chungking Mansions, Hong Kong* and has been teaching a weekly class of asylum seekers in Chungking Mansions for the past ten years.

Antje Missbach is a research fellow at the Department of Anthropology at Monash University in Melbourne. Her current research interests include transit migration, diaspora politics, and border and mobility studies. Her latest publications include *Troubled Transit: Asylum Seekers Stuck in Indonesia* and *Linking People: Connections and Encounters Between Australians and Indonesians* (edited with Jemma Purdey).

Tania Penovic is a senior lecturer in the Faculty of Law at Monash University and a deputy director of the Castan Centre for Human Rights Law.

Cécile Rousseau has researched the impact of migratory politics on refugee and migrant mental health in the last 15 years, at McGill University, Division of Social and Transcultural Psychiatry.

Rebecca Sutton is a barrister and solicitor (Law Society of Upper Canada), juris doctor (University of Toronto), master of science (University of London, School of Oriental and African Studies), and bachelor of arts and science (McMaster University). Her current affiliation is as a Ph.D. candidate at the London School of Economics and Political Science with a Trudeau Foundation Doctoral Scholarship.

Shana Tabak is a practitioner in residence at the American University Washington College of Law, and has an L.L.M. from George Washington University, a J.D. from Georgetown University Law Center, and B.A. from Macalester College.

Chee Wai-chi is currently a research assistant professor at the School of Modern Languages and Cultures of the University of Hong Kong. She received her Ph.D. in anthropology from the Chinese University of Hong Kong. Her research interests include migration, education, youth, globalization, and culture and identity, about which she has published a number of journal articles and book chapters.

Sonja Wolf holds a Ph.D. in international politics from Aberystwyth University. She has held postdoctoral fellowships at the ITAM and the UNAM in Mexico City, where she carried out research on transnational street gangs, organized crime, and security assistance programs in Central America. Subsequently, she worked at the Mexico City–based Institute for Security and Democracy, where she conducted a comprehensive assessment of Mexico's National Migration Institute. She is currently a researcher with the Drug Policy Programme at the Centre for Economic Research and Teaching in Aguascalientes, Mexico.

Detaining the Immigrant Other

1

Introduction

Global and Transnational Issues

RICH FURMAN, DOUGLAS EPPS, AND GREG LAMPHEAR

Illegals. Wetbacks. Aliens. These are some of the words we use to describe undocumented immigrants. The terms reflect a distancing, a discounting, a labeling that clearly delineates an *us* and a *them* (Gonzales, 2010; Mehan, 1997). As powerfully repressive as these monikers are, they pale when compared to the actions taken against those who are on the wrong end of the social forces that create and are created by these dehumanizing names (Furman, Ackerman, Loya, Jones, & Negi, 2012). The current discourse around undocumented immigrants in the United States, and indeed in numerous countries, reflects the confluences of various social forces: post–9/11 xenophobia and racism, the securitization of borders, a general climate of fear and moral panic, as well as the economic turmoil of the last decade and a half. According to this discourse, the United States and the Global North have suffered and someone must be to blame. Enter the other, the generalized, amorphous, nefarious immigrant other.

Power and privilege necessitate the creation of "an other" (Gil, 1992). The most horrifying crimes against humanity, war and genocide, are rationalized and perpetuated by a systematic othering that not only creates false separations between human beings but also seeks to strip the humanity from them (Sekhon, 2003). Dehumanizing a group makes it far easier to impose your will on them, to discount them, to separate them, to strip away their human rights (Fanon, 2004; Grygier, 1954). Othering human beings allows you to separate yourself from them (Mehan, 1997); it shifts blame from us to them. Throughout time, one of the most effective ways of separating "the other" from those deserving of freedom and full rights is to imprison them. This is one of the important subtexts of this book; the imprisonment of vulnerable immigrants around the world is not merely a consequence of their having consciously broken "the laws of the land." It is part and parcel of a history of systematic oppression of vulnerable people throughout the world.

On a fundamental level, on the level of lived experience and the impact on the lives of real people and their families, the term *immigration detention* is purely a euphemism. Immigration detention is imprisonment (Wexler, 2007). As readers will come to understand, in many instances, and in many countries, immigration detention is far worse than standard imprisonment. Detained immigrants frequently reside outside of the laws and protections of the country in which they are located. Immigration detention is largely a liminal state outside of borders, outside of normal protections (Welsh, 2000). Detained immigrants are often not afforded legal counsel and can often be held without due process. They exist between worlds, neither in their country of origin nor in their country of destination. They are imprisoned for attempting to survive. Yet, this fundamental truth is not part of the humanizing discourse. Consider the term *illegal alien*. It conjures images not of a courageous person seeking to provide for a family within the context of a capricious and often cruel transnational global economy but of a nonhuman landing on our soil to destroy the fabric of a world this nonhuman has invaded—parasitic, hurtful, and evil.

In this introduction, as we have already begun to do, we will paint a brief picture of some of the most important issues that will be explored throughout the book. We seek not to provide easy definitions to complex concepts but instead to set a context that will help the reader contextualize and understand how the various chapters in this book use these concepts. Therefore, we start with a brief discussion that situates immigration detention within a globalizing, transnational world. This is then followed with an elucidation of key notions regarding immigration detention, including how immigration detention fits within these global, transnational dynamics.

Finally, as we wrote each chapter introduction, we became conscious of how difficult it is to describe, in only a few words, the richness of the chapter and the lived experiences of those actually detained. We therefore ask you to treat these chapter introductions as mere hints of what is to come: the tragic stories of detained immigrants throughout the world.

The Transnational World and Immigration Detention

Why a book that views immigration detention though a global and transnational lens? This section will answer this question and situate immigration detention within the large movement toward globalization and the encroachment of corporate, global capitalism into the detention industry.

Globalization is a phenomenon as complicated as it is ubiquitous (Reitan, 2012). It is frequently cited as the cause and cure for a wildly disparate array of phenomena (Le Mare, 2012). As complex as globalization may be, what it refers to, on a basic level, is a dynamic congruent with an understanding of ecosystems theories insights about the interdependence of various levels of social systems (Negi & Furman, 2010).

Globalization in this sense can be viewed as the increasing interconnectedness of nation states, financial sectors, nongovernmental organizations, communities, and the many other institutions in an increasingly interconnected world (Furman & Negi, 2007). In a globalizing world, governments seek to understand and contend with the economic and security factors that are no longer directly under their control (Levitt, 2013). In this sense, globalization has weakened the power of nations to directly control, through national policy, various domains that were once viewed as domestic policy. The notion of *border* has been transformed. Goods and services more easily flow from country to country, and events that happen in one part of the world have an impact on the lives of those in another. Paradoxically, borders have become more permeable, just at a time when nation states, for security reasons, are viewing secure borders as essential in a post-9/11 world.

In part fueled by various technological innovations that permit rapid communications across nation states, this interconnectedness disproportionately benefits those who most fully control these systems and technologies. As such, corporate capitalism and the rise of neoliberal politics are key features of our current form of globalization (Kaseke, 1998). The agenda of neoliberal policies, promulgated by corporate elites, the World Bank, and the International Monetary Fund, is the privatization of various sectors of social welfare, broadly defined (Danaher, 1994 and 2001).

By controlling access to loans and investment, the proponents of neoliberal policies compel developed nations to make radical cuts in social welfare and income maintenance programs as a means of ostensibly reducing public debt and forcing the poor into the labor economy (Kaplinsky, 2005). Such policies create increasing disparities between the haves and the have-nots, in part creating some of the "push" factors that lead to undocumented immigration (Guevarra, 2010).

Other factors, of course, also byproducts of increasing globalization, create additional push factors. For instance, multinational treaties, economic crises, and political upheavals all highlight our increasing interconnectedness and often lead to rapid changes in the market economy. Without the social service or income maintenance safety net, the poor and the displaced look for opportunities for work simply to survive (Ackerman & Furman, 2014).

Although undocumented immigration is not a new phenomenon, globalization creates not only new factors that compel the poor of the developing world to leave their family, their home, and often their safety and well-being behind (Portes, 1997), but also new streams of information and support that facilitate their movement (Pries, 2004). The internet, inexpensive cellular telephones, and social networks allow undocumented people to move through transnational spaces far more efficiently and with more knowledge than ever before (Madianou & Miller, 2011). Just as the U.S. border has become increasingly militarized and this has made it much more difficult to cross our southern border, the drug wars of Mexico have exacerbated the involvement of organized crime in the smuggling of the poor from the Global South. As such, the border has become more violent and traumatic, yet more in need of crossing (Nevins, 2010).

These various technological, economic, and social transformations have changed how people move across and between nations. Prior waves of immigrants tended to discontinue frequent back-and-forth movement between nations (Pries, 2004). This was not always true, but traditional migrants tended to establish strong, permanent ties to their receiving countries. New immigrants would maintain their prior cultures, develop complex new cultural expressions, become bicultural, or assimilate into the dominant cultural milieu of their own state. Still, their lives, over time, were primarily lived in their new country (Nieswand, 2011). These traditional patterns have been altered by globalization and have created patterns of transnational migration and a rapidly growing group: the transmigrant.

Transmigration has existed throughout human history, but globalization has greatly accelerated this pattern of immigration (Kim, 2015). Transmigration is a pattern of migration where people live lives across nation-state boundaries. They maintain familial, economic, social, political, and geographic ties as they move physically, emotionally, and electronically between two countries (Montes, 2013). This new pattern of immigration is now accepted by scholars as a pattern of movement that reflects the nature of globalization, capital movement, and technological change. The world is truly smaller. Borders are more permeable, and people naturally adapt to their system's changes.

Sadly, the governments of their world and the manner in which borders are constructed have not adapted as well. Instead, they have dug in their heels and attempted to restrict this transnationalism in various ways. Immigration detention is one such mechanism, which we shall explore more in the following section.

Understanding Immigration Detention

Although we previously argued that *immigration detention* is, in terms of the human cost, a euphemism for incarceration, there are distinctions between immigration detention and traditional incarceration that should be understood. Immigration detention is typically viewed as different from incarceration in that it is conceptualized for "administrative" reasons rather than as detention of one who committed, or allegedly committed, a crime (Sampson & Mitchell, 2013). In the United States, for example, as in many countries, entering the country without proper authorization is not considered a crime but is an administrative offense, as is paying taxes late, for example.

The Global Detention Project (2009), an organization that maps immigration detention globally, uses the term *administrative detention* to highlight this distinction. In their definition, they point out the realities of immigration detention as it is used for

> deprivation of liberty in the absence of a criminal charge. Although the Global Detention Project focuses uniquely on migration-related detention, which is generally administrative in nature, administrative detention can also include detention for security reasons; internment of persons with mental illness; administrative detention or confinement on public or health grounds; and administrative detention in the context of an armed conflict. Domestic legal systems are often not as detailed regarding these detention situations, which can result in administrative detainees facing legal uncertainty. Among the difficulties these detainees can face are lack of access to the outside world (including to legal counsel), inadequate or no possibilities of challenging detention through the courts, and lack of limitations on the duration of detention.

The exact number of people in immigration detention globally is unknown. Yet, given that international immigration has increased rapidly and the movement toward the criminalization of immigration has followed, the number of people in immigration detention is also likely to grow rapidly. Since 1990, the number of international migrants went from 154 million to 232 million in 2013 (UNDESA, 2013). As an example of proliferating detention practices, the United States has nearly tripled its daily detainment of immigrants since 1996 to more than 33,000 individuals (Detention Watch Network, 2012), a similar trend can be observed throughout a multitude of nations around the globe (Sampson & Mitchell, 2013). For example, the Netherlands has increased detention capacity from 45 in 1980 to more than 3,000 in 2006 (Broeders, 2010). Mexico, in spite of a professed capacity of only 3,500 beds, detained more than 90,000 in 2012 (Global Detention Project, 2009) .

The exact number of detained immigrants around the world is unknown; the consequences of immigration detention for real people are not. The specifics differ from nation to nation, as you will soon read, yet the dynamics are similar. Undocumented immigrants, who were at one point usually perceived as a solution to labor force problems or were refugees from untenable conditions in their sending countries, become constructed as a problem of security, safety, or economic well-being (Abramsky, 2004). By criminalizing key aspects of their lives and heightening profiling within their communities, a greater number will wind up detained (Aman & Rehrig, 2011). A common dynamic in many Western nations, this is played out perhaps most powerfully in the United States. The conflation of security, terrorism, and undocumented immigration has led to a proliferation of state policies that have criminalized key aspects of the lives of undocumented people (Coleman & Kocher, 2011).

As one example, take the state of Alabama in the American South. For undocumented people there, engaging in a "contract" with the state government, which includes registering a mobile home or signing up for utilities, is a criminal offense according to the state's anti-immigration law (Werner, 2011). This trend has accelerated in the United States over the last decade, with nearly every state legislature having at least initiated some social policy that seeks to criminalize immigration. Although state advocacy against undocumented immigration has led to the criminalization of immigration and subsequent immigration detention, the enforcement and expansion of federal policy has expanded immigration detention and deportation. This policy accelerated and was fueled by the xenophobic rhetoric of the Bush administration, but it is the Obama administration that has detained and deported a record number of undocumented immigrants (Medina, 2012). In 2009 alone, the Obama administration deported approximately 395,000 immigrants, and in 2010 another 387,000 were removed from the United States (Department of Homeland Security, 2011). This example from the United States greatly mirrors many of the worldwide trends readers will discover throughout this book.

In theory, detaining immigrants in specialized facilities is for their benefit. For example, in such facilities they are separated from a general prison population, which may be infinitely more violent, and can be "processed" by specialist immigration courts that can resolve their immigration issues in a timely and efficient manner. Sadly, the realities, as you will soon read, can be far different. Immigrant detention for many is a demoralizing, degrading experience that retraumatizes people who have previously been victims of oppression, violence, and state abuse (Androff & Tavassoli, 2012). Immigration detention rips families apart, and it frequently harms children and dependent spouses who no longer have their primary income earner working. It can lead to desperate family members not even knowing the whereabouts of their loved ones, wondering if they have indeed been detained, deported, or worse. It can leave lasting psychological trauma on adults, and especially on children (Androff et al., 2011; Bess, 2011; Jones, 2012). Immigration detention denies the transnational nature of many families; many undocumented residents in the United States and other countries have children who are citizens in what are called "mixed-status" families (Hilfinger Messias, Morris McEwen, & Clark, 2015). Some undocumented people have not been to their country of birth since they were very young children, and they may not even know their native language (Zayas & Bradlee, 2014).

Chapter Introductions

As immigration detention is global and transnational, so are the chapters in this book. We are honored and proud to introduce you to the chapters in our book written by some of the leading scholars in the field. The authors, as you will see, use an array of methodologies to portray how immigration detention is lived and performed in an increasingly transnational, global world.

The chapter by Dafney Blanca Dabach and colleagues, "The Northwest Detention Center: A Nexus of the Immigration Debate," is the only one in this book with an explicit focus on the United States. Tacoma, Washington, is not an immigration receiving site that is frequently explored in the literature, but it has a notorious place in this history of immigration and immigration detention. It is the birthplace of "the Tacoma Method," a name given to when and how a group of Tacoma's leaders forcibly expelled Chinese immigrants from the city in 1885. In an expression of extreme fear and xenophobia, a group of white citizens rounded up the legal Chinese residents of the city and marched them through the driving rain to board trains to Portland, Oregon. More than a century later, Tacoma has again become a lightning rod of the immigration debate. On Tacoma's soil exist two dichotomous expressions of our country's values vis-à-vis immigration: the Chinese Reconciliation Park and the Northwest Detention Center, one of the largest immigration detention centers in the nation. A cruel irony not lost on local advocates, this paradox provides the context for Chapter 5's powerful illustration of many of the current dynamics of immigration detention expressing themselves around the world.

The Netherlands, known widely as a tourist hub for its liberal drug and prostitution laws, is discussed in Chapter 2 for its less-than-welcoming position toward immigrants. "Pressured into Deportation? Detainees' (Un)willingness to 'Return' and the Moderating Influence of International Relations," by Arjen Leerkes and Mieke Kox, examines the implications of Dutch immigration detention and deportation policy. Despite the supposed administrative purpose of immigration detention, the confinement of human beings is undeniably punitive in nature. The authors explore reality through in-depth interviews with detained migrants. Their chapter helps readers gain an understanding of the Netherlands' use of detention and deportation policy as a method of deterrence. Leerkes and Kox skillfully analyze respondent data, interpreting the effectiveness of Dutch policy as a form of coerced self-deportation and intimidation for preventing migrants from returning. Both practical and ethical questions naturally arise in regard to the use of immigration policy as a deterrent, a practice that the authors suggest is far more prevalent than one would hope.

Of the various marginalized groups, LGBTI (lesbian, gay, bisexual, transsexual, and intersex) immigrants face particularly complex and painful challenges. As tenuous as the lives of heterosexual undocumented immigrants are, the few laws that protect them and their families have no counterparts for LGBTI populations. In fact, they often face a double criminalization, first for their sexual orientation/identity in their host country and then through the process of undocumented immigration. Tragically and ironically, many LGBTI immigrants are actually refugees fleeing oppressive conditions at home or an unsafe community context where they have been victims of domestic violence and abuse. Yet, their refugee status is frequently unrecognized, or at best not quickly recognized, thereby leading to their being imprisoned in immigration detention. Shana Tabak's evocative Chapter 3 explores the various psychosocial dilemmas that LGBTI immigrants face within immigration detention. She presents a portrait of how LGBTI immigrants are revictimized, thereby perpetuating a cycle of abuse and human rights violations. Her chapter deftly explores UN conventions and other relevant policy considerations.

Malaysia's geography, cultural diversity, and ascendancy as one of the "Asian tiger" economies have made it a prime candidate for receiving immigrants. By 2013, more than two million undocumented workers joined almost the same number of documented foreign workers. Because Malaysia was not a signatory of the 1951 UN Convention on Refugees, any irregular immigrant entering the country is not considered eligible for refugee status; as such, many vulnerable immigrants are at risk. Sasagu Kudo's Chapter 4, "Immigration Detention in Malaysia: The State Monopoly of (In)security," explores the criminalization of undocumented immigration and its relationship to state policy and security. The author traces this securitization to global and transnational trends and also to local and regional dynamics that make potential solutions complex. A chapter such as this demonstrates the need for advocates and policy makers to develop analytical tools that enable us to truly think and act simultaneously locally and globally.

Sonja Wolf's Chapter 6, "Migration Detention in Mexico: Human Rights Denied," relates one of the underexplored immigrant stories, the dynamics of immigration and immigration detention to and through Mexico. Frequently viewed only as nation of departure whose citizens disproportionately end up in immigration detention, Mexico's geographic and geopolitical position between Mexico and the rest of Latin America has led it to develop its own immigration detention apparatus. In less than a year during 2014, more than 100,000 undocumented immigrants were detained within Mexico, and 95 percent were from the northern Central American countries of Guatemala, Honduras, and El Salvador. Not coincidentally, these are countries that have been racked with violence and social upheaval due to the profound maldistributions under globalization and the growing problems of transnational gang violence and drug cartels. In order to understand immigration detention in the United States, we must understand how many of these immigrants were previously detained within Mexico. Their journeys are long and painful; immigration detention serves as a systematic vehicle for retraumatizing the poor from the Global South.

Exploring immigration detention from a transnational perspective in one country is difficult enough, but presenting a cogent exploration of the phenomenon in two countries presents additional challenges. Mary Bosworth and Andriani Fili, in their Chapter 7, "Immigration Detention in Greece and the UK," deftly explore the experiences of immigration detention staff and detainees. They explore findings with a broad array of implications, yet with a special focus on the alleged deterrence of immigration detention, one of the key rationales that governments use to justify immigration detention as well as what the authors refer to as the "incongruous internal character" of immigration detention. Using a criminological lens, the authors begin their exploration with a discussion of "fortress Europe" and extend this metaphor to the lived experiences of refugees and immigrants in detention. The authors present numerous quotes and anecdotes that put faces on what policy makers often portray as anonymous and dehumanized beings. The authors demonstrate how the project of immigration detention dehumanizes not only immigrants but workers in the system as well. This is typified by the words of the head of the Hellenic Police (Greece), who admitted, "We have to make their lives miserable; otherwise they will be under the impression that by coming to Greece they will be free to do what they want."

The world's fourth-most-populated country, Indonesia, is also the largest majority-Islamic nation in the world. It is diverse, consisting of thousands of islands, including dozens of highly populated archipelagos in a region of growing industrialization yet profound and entrenched poverty and maldistribution of wealth. Chapter 8, "Detaining Asylum Seekers and Refugees in Indonesia," by Antje Missbach, explores the dynamics of, and conditions within, immigration detention in this complex, fascinating, diverse, and important nation. Missbach analyzes the political dynamics of Indonesia's relationship with Australia as a supporter of the latter's growing detention system. She presents the lived experience of detained asylum seekers from the Middle East, many of whom struggle to maintain their sense of dignity and cultural traditions as they navigate the complexities of asylum in an increasingly transnational world. Missbach examines the resistance of detained asylum seekers as they seek agency in the context of an often violent, isolating existence.

Too frequently, scholars select research questions or study populations that confirm the findings they wish to obtain. Sometimes, the actual nature of the population or context studied contributes to a seeming uniformity in findings. This is largely the case in this book; immigration detention is largely a horribly abusive institution that greatly disrupts and traumatizes. In their Chapter 9, "Detaining the Immigrant Other in Hong Kong," Gordon Mathews and Chee Wai-chi present findings that show an alternative view of immigration detention. In their interviews with formerly detained immigrants in Hong Kong, we come to see that immigration detention can be far more humane and less disruptive than it often is. Of course, viewing detention of any sort in a favorable light is perhaps more suggestive of oppressive and depriving environments outside of the walls of detention centers than a glowing endorsement of said centers. Still, this chapter stands in sharp contrast to many other narratives of immigration detention and demonstrates that immigration detention can be, at the very least, made more humane.

Ċetta Mainwaring's Chapter 10, "Transnational Migration and Control: Immigrant Detention on the Edge of Europe," successfully explores the rise of immigration detention as a mechanism for contending with powerful geopolitical changes through impeding movement of undocumented immigrants through transnational spaces. Malta is a small island nation that joined the European Union in 2004. Just prior to its entry, unauthorized immigrants and refugees began to arrive in great numbers, establishing Malta as a key transit stop for the poor from the Global South into the EU. Malta has also chosen immigration detention policies sharply criticized by various human rights and immigrant advocacy organizations. This includes detaining undocumented immigrants for up to 18 months, a period of time that certainly has deleterious effects on immigrants and their families. Mainwaring intelligently explores how Malta's position in the EU is implicated in its creation of an immigration detention infrastructure.

"Trapped to the Local: The Effects of Immigration Detention in France," by Stefan Le Courant and Caroline Kobelinsky, presents powerful vignettes of mostly African detained immigrants. Their Chapter 11 weaves together narratives that demonstrate the movement from immigrant to criminalized other. The authors explore the impact of various laws and policies and trace how changes in France's immigration laws have not only affected immigrants but has also shifted the very fabric of French society and what it means to be French. The authors demonstrate how "immigration detention and border politics weaken migrants' possibilities of having an ordinary life, always wiping the slate clean, confining them to the local and perpetuating the present." The first author's position as a legal advocate providing pro bono assistance to detained immigrants affords us with a powerful, inside view of the detention system and its damaging effects.

In our previous chapter on Indonesia, you were introduced to some of the dynamics involved with immigration detention in Australia. Tania Penovic and Azadeh Dastyari's Chapter 12, "Harm and Accountability in Transnational Detention Environments: The Case of Australia's Extraterritorial Processing and Detention of Asylum Seekers," delves deeper into the unique methods of Australia's use of "outsourcing" for the purpose of detaining refugees and asylum seeking immigrants. The authors effectively analyze the harmful effects of extraterritorial processing from a policy perspective and also from the perspective of its often unseen human costs. Penovic and Dastyari expertly connect the implications of such practices with international relations, human rights, and global ethics; the end product is an informative, big-picture look into an ethically dubious practice.

Turkey is a nation that straddles two worlds; it is typically conceptualized as existing within and between Asia and Europe and rife with passages through the border of the European Union. Nurcan Ozgur Baklacioglu's Chapter 13, "From 'Guesthouses' to Removal Centers: Europeanization of Immigrant Detention in Turkey," accurately depicts Turkey's place in the global trend toward criminalizing migrants by documenting the nation's radical departure from providing migrant "guesthouses" to a harsher focus on removal. The author shows how growing xenophobic trends have encouraged Turkey to adopt immigration policies and procedures similar to those of its European neighbors. For example, the pending Readmission Agreement between Turkey and the EU has resulted in more than 1.5 million Syrian refugees being stuck in refugee camps—rejected from the EU yet unwanted in Turkey. Baklacioglu's investigation of Turkey's immigration policy not only uncovers the human implications, but also portrays the transnational spread of anti-immigrant sentiment.

Chapter 14, "Deportation as a Way of Life for Young Afghan Men," written by scholar Shahram Khosravi, paints a startling picture of the revolving door of deportations Afghan men face. To use the author's own words, "...Afghan men are stuck on one side of a powerful transnational apparatus that forcibly excludes and expels them from the Global North." Many are deported to multiple countries, awaiting their fate in destinations that are completely alien to them. Khosravi explores these experiences through detailed interviews with those men most experienced in forced detention, expulsion, and repatriation.

South Africa has a long and troubled history of racial and ethnic relationships. For many, the concept and implementation of immigration detention is an all-too-painful reminder of the abuses that took place during the apartheid era. Rebecca Sutton's Chapter 15, "Immigration Detention in South Africa: The View from Inside Lindela," presents a rare and thought-provoking exploration of the only detention center for foreign migrants in all of South Africa. Sutton's ethnographic approach investigates the "illegal foreigner" label to explore how detainees interpret such an unwelcomed label given to them. The author vividly portrays, through in-depth qualitative interviews, how confined migrants "make sense" of their experiences at Lindela by exploring interactions with officials and the realizations of how confinement has an impact on "life outside."

Chapter 16, by Rachel Kronick and her coauthors, "'They Cut Your Wings over Here . . . You Can't Do Nothing': Voices of Children and Parents Held in Immigration Detention in Canada," is another meaningful account in which a specific population is the focus of analysis. In this stimulating piece, the author weaves together real-life narratives from fathers, mothers, and children marooned in Canadian detention centers. Kronick shows the impact of detention on families, highlighting the incongruences behind such a practice, where spouses are separated and fathers are removed from their paternal role. The author explores several stages of the detention process, from pre-migratory experiences and arrest to life in detention, and to the difficulties of navigating legal processes. Perhaps most heartbreaking, Kronick necessarily delves into the emotions of family members mandatorily separated from their loved ones, painting a sorrowful picture of the family for those unfortunately entangled in immigration detention.

As you can see, the chapters represent examples of the marginalizing effect of detaining immigrants on several continent. Through your reading all the chapters together, we hope you will come to appreciate the global and transnational nature of immigration detention, and how these detentions are lived by real, breathing human beings. We understand that emotionally this is not an easy book to read. While working with the authors on their chapters, we all experienced anger, frustration, sadness, and at times hopelessness. Yet we are struck by the resilience of people, their capacity to overcome, and their striving to transcend even the most oppressive of social structures. We hope that you too will have a transcendent experience and feel compelled toward action as a means of honoring those who have lived the horrible injustice that is immigration detention.

References

Abramsky, S. (2004, July 19). Incarceration, Inc. *Nation, 279*(3), 22–25. Retrieved July 14, 2008, from Academic Search Premier database.

Ackerman, A., & Furman, R. (2014). The criminalization of immigration and the privatization of immigration detention: Implications for justice. *Contemporary Justice Review, 16*(2), 251–263.

Aman, A. C., & Rehrig, G. (2011). *The domestic face of globalization: Law's role in the integration of immigrants in the United States.* Legal Studies Research Paper, no. 196, Indiana University School of Law. Bloomington: University of Indiana.

Androff, D., Ayon, C., Becerra, D., Gurrola, M., Salas, L., Krysik, J., Gerdes, K., & Segal, E. (2011). U.S. immigration policy and immigrant children's well-being: The impact of policy shifts. *Journal of Sociology & Social Welfare, 38*(1), 77–98.

Androff, D., & Tavassoli, K. (2012). Deaths in the desert: The human rights crisis on the U.S.-Mexico border. *Social Work, 57*(2), 165–173.

Bess, A. (2011). *The impact of immigration and detention on children and families: Human rights update.* Washington, DC: National Association of Social Workers, Human Rights and International Affairs Division.

Broeders, D. (2010). Return to sender? Administrative detention of irregular migrants in Germany and the Netherlands. *Punishment & Society, 12*(2), 169-186.

Coleman, M., & Kocher, A. (2011). Detention, deportation, devolution and immigrant incapacitation in the US, post 9/11. *Geographical Journal, 177*(3), 228–237.

Danaher, K. (2001). *Ten reasons to abolish the IMF and World Bank.* New York: Seven Stories Press.

Danaher, K. (1994). *50 years is enough: The case against the World Bank and the International Monetary Fund.* Boston, MA: South End Press.

Department of Homeland Security. (2011). *Annual Report, Immigration Enforcement Actions: 2010.* Retrieved Apr. 6, 2015, from www.dhs.gov/xlibrary/assets/statistics/publications/enforcement-ar-2010.pdf.

Detention Watch Network, (2013). Detention Watch Network Supports Border Communities on Day of Action Against Militaration. Retrieved March 30, 2015 from http://www.detentionwatchnetwork.org/node/3536.

Fanon, F. (2004). *The wretched of the earth.* New York: Grove Press.

Furman, R., Ackerman, A., Loya, M., Jones, S., & Negi, N. (2012). The criminalization of immigration: Value conflicts for the social work profession. *Journal of Sociology & Social Welfare, 29*(1), 169–185.

Furman, R., & Negi, N. (2007). Social work practice with transnational Latino populations. *International Social Work, 50*(1), 107–112.

Gil, D. (1992). *Unraveling social policy*. New York: Schenkman.

Global Detention Project. (2009). GDP glossary. Retrieved Nov. 17, 2014, from http://www.globaldetentionproject.org/resources/glossary.html.

Gonzales, R. G. (2010). On the wrong side of the tracks: Understanding the effects of school structure and social capital in the educational pursuits of undocumented immigrant students. *Peabody Journal of Education, 85*, 469–485.

Grygier, T. (1954). *Oppression: A study in social and criminal psychology*. New York: Routledge.

Guevarra, A. (2010). *Marketing dreams, manufacturing heroes: The transnational labor brokering of Filipino workers*. New Brunswick, NJ: Rutgers University Press.

Hilfinger Messias, D. K., Morris McEwen, M., & Clark, L. (2015). The impact and implications of undocumented immigration on individual and collective health in the United States. *Nursing Outlook, 63*(1), 86–94.

Jones, S. (2012). Working with immigrant clients: Perils and possibilities for social worker. *Families in Society, 93*, 47–53.

Kaplinsky, R. (2005). *Globalization, poverty and inequality: Between a rock and a hard pace*. Malden, MA: Polity Press.

Kaseke, E. (1998). Structural adjustment programmes and the problem of urban poverty: An African perspective. *International Social Work, 41*, 311–320.

Le Mare, A. (2012). Show the world to women and they can do it: Southern Fair Trade Enterprise as agents of empowerment. *Gender & Development, 20*(1), 95–109.

Levitt, P. (2013). Social welfare in an era of transnational migration. *Tikkun, 28*(3), 44–46.

Kim, A. M. (2015). An introduction to international migration studies: European perspectives. *Ethnic and Racial Studies, 38* (3), 499–501.

Madianou, M., & Miller, D. (2011). *Migration and new media: Transnational families and polymedia*. New York: Routledge.

Medina, M. I. (2012). The challenges of facilitating effective legal defense in deportation proceedings. 53(3), *South Texas Law Review*, available on Social Science Research Network, http://ssrn.com/abstract=2000979.

Mehan, H. (1997). The discourse of illegal immigration debate: A case study in the politics of representation. *Discourse & Society, 8*(2), 249–270.

Montes, V. (2013). The role of emotions in the construction of masculinity: Guatemalan migrant men, transnational migration, and family relations. *Gender & Society, 27*(4), 469–490.

Negi, N. J., & Furman, R. (Eds.). (2010). *Transnational social work practice*. New York: Columbia University Press.

Nevins, J. (2010). *Operation Gatekeeper: The rise of the "Illegal Alien" and the making of the U.S.-Mexico boundary*. New York: Routledge.

Nieswand, B. (2011). *Theorising transnational migration: The status paradox of migration*. New York: Routledge.

Portes, A. (1997). Immigration theory for a new century: Some problems and opportunities. *International Migration Review*, 31(3): 799–825.

Pries, L. (2004). Determining the causes and durability of transnational labour migration between Mexico and the United States: Some empirical findings. *International Migration*, 42(2): 3–39.

Reitan, R. (2012). Theorizing and engaging the global movement: From anti-globalization to global democratization. *Globalizations, 9*(3), 323–325.

Sampson, R., & Mitchell, G. (2013). Global trends in immigration detention and alternatives to detention: Practical, political and symbolic rationales. *Journal on Migration and Human Security (1)*3, 97–121.

Sekhon, V. (2003). The civil rights of "others": Anti-terrorism, the Patriot Act, and Arab and South Asian American rights in post–9/11 American society. *Texas Journal on Civil Liberties & Civil Rights, 8*(1), 117–148.

Welsh, M. (2000). The role of the immigration and naturalization service in the prison-industrial complex. *Social Justice, 27*(3), 73–88.

Werner, D. (2011). SPCL ready for long legal battle over Alabama's harsh anti-immigrant law. *Southern Poverty Law Center.* Retrieved Apr. 1, 2015, from http://www.splcenter.org/get-informed/news/.

Wexler, L. (2007). The non-legal role of international human rights law in addressing immigration. *University of Chicago Legal Forum*, (2007) 359–404.

Zayas, L. H., & Bradlee, M. H. (2014). Exiling children, creating orphans: When immigration policies hurt citizens. *Social Work, 59*(2), 167–175.

2

Pressured into Deportation?

Detainees' (Un)willingness to "Return" and the Moderating Influence of International Relations

ARJEN LEERKES AND MIEKE KOX

In most countries, immigration detention is an administrative measure that ensures migrants can be located and will not abscond while the deportation is prepared (Cornelisse, 2010). Although the detention is formally not a punishment, and does not require conviction for a crime, governments do seem to use it for deterrence purposes, i.e., as a means to deter unwanted immigrants from the territory (Kalhan, 2010; Leerkes & Broeders, 2010, Martin, 2012; Mainwaring, 2012). In the Netherlands, for instance, the then-minister of immigration and asylum has said that immigration detention is meant to "incite to departure". The underlying assumption seems to be that if detainees experience the detention as sufficiently severe, and if the duration is long enough, they may eventually reveal their identity, hand over identification documents, and/or give up their claims to legal status. This should facilitate their deportation since identification and documentation of detainees are, in principle, a sine qua non for their expulsion, as no country of origin accepts undocumented returnees (cf. Ellermann, 2008).

The punitive elements in administrative detention warrant the question of whether immigration detention actually coerces detainees to become willing to leave the country, and by extension whether such processes increase the probability of detention resulting in deportation. The logic of deterrence echoes claims by the classical school in criminology, which argues that rule violation—in this case, continued stay as a deportable or unauthorized migrant—ceases to exist provided that the state ensures the costs of rule violation become higher than its benefits. Various sociological and criminological studies have, however, shown that the reasoning of the classical school is too simplistic in the context of *criminal* imprisonment, if only because it is wrongfully assumed that the consequences of punishment are determined by just two actors: the punishing state and the individual "deviant."

In reality, such consequences depend on various other actors, such as fellow prisoners, or employers who may or may not be willing to offer employment to ex-prisoners. As a result, imprisonment may exacerbate crime problems rather than reducing recidivism via deterrence. In this chapter, we confront the neoclassical specific deterrence logic in the context of immigration detention to a more relational sociological viewpoint that recognizes that social outcomes are the result of complex social interactions in complex figurations. More specifically, we examine the influence of immigration detention on migrants' willingness to leave the country, and we study whether such willingness contributes to the deportation of migrants.

Our analysis is based on data collected for two research projects conducted in the Netherlands in 2003 (Van Kalmhout & Van Leeuwen, 2004) and 2011 (Kox, 2011). For both studies, interviewers conducted semistructured interviews with detainees in their first or second language. Topics covered included their personal situation in the country of origin and the Netherlands, their stay in immigration detention, and their attitude with regard to staying in, or departing from, the Netherlands. In the 2011 study, respondents were also explicitly interviewed about the possible consequences of their stay(s) in immigration detention for their migration preferences. For both studies, the Dutch government provided data on whether the respondents were deported or released at the end of the detention period. Random sampling was used for both studies. The results are discussed in the chapter sections "Pressured into Willingness to Depart?" and "Pressured into Deportation?" The next section first provides some contextual information about the Dutch detention regime since there are notable differences between countries in how immigration detention is organized.

The Dutch Immigration Detention Regime

There are two main immigration detention types: (1) pre-admission detention at the border involving foreigners not admitted to the territory, and (2) pre-expulsion detention of foreigners whose stay in the territory is or has become unauthorized. The second type is more common in the Netherlands, and both the 2003 and 2011 study focused on it. The Dutch government has recently proposed to introduce a milder detention regime, but in 2003 and 2011 the Dutch regime for pre-expulsion immigration detention closely resembled criminal imprisonment: it was modeled after the regime for suspects of serious felonies who are detained before trial. Detainees could leave their cells (mostly two-person cells) eight hours a day, i.e., between 8:00 a.m. and 12:00 noon and between 1:00 and 5:00 p.m. When out of their cell, they were to spend time in a recreational room with cooking facilities, television, table tennis, and parlor games. There were programs, including airing (one hour per day), sports (45 minutes, twice a week), recreational activities (six hours a week), library visits (one hour per week), religious ceremonies (one hour per week), and visits (two hours per week). There were no "re-integration" facilities like education or trainings. In 2003, immigration detainees had access to labor facilities but in 2011 that was no longer the case.

Under Dutch law, a foreigner can be held in immigration detention if a number of conditions are met. These include that there is a realistic prospect for deportation. If this is no longer present or if the government has made insufficient progress toward deportation, the detention has to be ended. The European Return Directive, implemented in the Netherlands in 2011, stipulates that immigration detention may last for six months, unless the detainee is considered uncooperative in revealing his or her identity or has been convicted of certain crimes, in which case the detention may be extended to 18 months. In 2011, pre-expulsion detention lasted 74 days on average, varying from less than a week to 18 months. In 2003, there was no preset maximum detention duration, but largely similar time periods were generally used. If detainees cannot be deported and the detention has to be terminated, they are generally released with a day train ticket and an order to leave the country immediately. Those who stay, and do not obtain legal stay (which is the rule), can be redetained when there is a "new fact," such as new information about the migrant's identity, or when at least a year has passed since the previous detention period (Van Dokkum, 2010). In case of repeated detention, the cumulative detention duration can exceed 18 months. A final specificity of the European context is that part of those released because of a failed deportation procedure may migrate (illegally) to neighboring countries; illegal onward migration is not impossible since land borders are hardly policed within the EU.

In 2003 and 2011, the total inflow in the Dutch immigration detention centers amounted to about 12,000 and 6,000 persons respectively (Van Schijndel and Van Gemmert, 2012). The decrease in immigration detainees is in line with estimated decreases in the unauthorized population in the Netherlands as a whole. For example, in the 2003–2011 period, illegal labor migration was increasingly being replaced by *legal* labor migration. This substitution was not due to changes in labor immigration policy; rather, various countries in Central and Eastern Europe became EU member states in 2004 (including Poland) and 2007 (Bulgaria and Romania). This legalized unauthorized workers from these countries overnight—they obtained legal stay as EU citizens—and gave employers much less restricted access to cheap labor. The number of rejected asylum seekers was probably also higher in 2003 than in 2011, because of both a decrease in asylum applications and an amnesty for rejected asylum seekers in 2007. In 2010, 27 percent of the detainees had been in immigration detention before (Kox, 2011), and such "recidivists" filled an even larger share of the total detention capacity since they are detained for relatively long periods of time. According to a 2011 government survey conducted among 460 immigration detainees (the response rate was 39 percent), 60 percent of the detainees were experiencing their first detention period, 18 percent their second, and 18 percent had been in immigration detention at least twice before (5 percent did not answer the question; Van Alphen et al., 2013).

Pressured into Willingness to Depart?

As was explained in the previous section, immigration detention in the Netherlands has three main migration outcomes: (1) deportation, or in some cases assisted voluntary return from detention (see the next section), to a country where the migrant's admission is guaranteed, usually the country of origin; (2) continued unauthorized stay in the detaining state's territory; and (3) illegal onward migration to another European country. To the extent that immigration detention has a deterrent effect among detainees, we should observe that the detention experience changes their migration preferences from continued stay to going to the country of citizenship, or from continued stay to onward migration to a different European country, and that it does so because detainees want to end their exposure to such detention or evade repeated detention.

In line with deterrence theory, two aspects of the immigration detention experience may potentially pressure detainees into willingness to leave the country. First, let's consider the *perceived severity* of the detention experience. Much like regular prisoners, immigration detainees are subjected to various forms of deprivation, or what Sykes (1958) famously called the "pains of imprisonment": deprivation from liberty, autonomy, social relationships, goods and services, and security. However, these classic pains of imprisonment, though still relevant today, represent only a part of detention's painfulness. Additionally, immigration detainees may be subjected to what Crewe (2011) calls the "pains of uncertainty and indeterminacy," as they do not know in advance how long they will be detained, while it is often unclear whether they will be deported or not, and whether they will be redetained. An additional "pain of immigration detention" may be that the legitimacy of immigration detention is more problematic than in case of criminal imprisonment; detainees often do not see detention as a deserving response to violation of migration rules (cf. Leerkes & Broeders, 2010; Bosworth, 2013).

Second, being detained may alter the perceived certainty of being redetained. The detention experience implies that one has been "caught," and that one's unauthorized status is known to the authorities. Research suggests that personal or vicarious experiences of an event, in this case being detained, tend to increase the perceived probability of such events (Piquero & Pogarsky 2002; Matsueda, Kreager, & Huizinga, 2006). Immigration detention may produce willingness to depart to the extent that the detention experience leads to a higher perceived probability of being caught in the case of continued unauthorized residence.

To understand immigration detention's potential deterrent effects among detainees, it is useful to divide the immigration detainee population into three main groups. First, there are family migrants who immigrated, at least in part, because of family ties with legal residents in the Netherlands. Among such detainees in particular, there are a notable number of former residence permit holders who lost their permit because they committed a deportable crime. Compared to the United States, however, the number of such former residence permit holders is limited, mostly due to legal differences in what constitutes a deportable crime. Second, there are asylum migrants who no longer have a right to stay in the country, both rejected asylum seekers and asylum seekers who received temporary residence permits that were withdrawn or not renewed. Part of them had weak claims to asylum; others experienced difficulties in proving a well-founded fear of persecution or fled unsafe conditions that are not officially recognized as grounds for asylum. Third, there are unauthorized labor migrants from non-EU countries all over the world. In the past, such migrants worked in a relatively large number of sectors of the Dutch economy, but as policies with respect to illegal residence grew more restrictive, unauthorized workers largely came to depend on the informal labor market, in sectors such as construction, hospitality, and domestic work.

The potential deterrent effects among immigration detainees have been analyzed on the basis of the 2011 study, as the 2003 study did not explicitly examine this. Table 2.1 provides an overview of respondents' migration preferences at the time of the interview and—retrospectively reported—before the detention period.

In some cases, an eventual preference to leave the Netherlands was unrelated to detention. For example, a number of family migrants were in the process of

Table 2.1 **Migration preferences during and before the detention period(s) (2011)**

	Continued Stay	*Return Migration*	*Onward Migration*	*Undecided*
All respondents				
At the time of the interview	41	14	15	11
Before this detention	54	9	13	5
Repeatedly detained respondents				
At the time of the interview	12	7	2	4
Before this detention	14	6	2	2
Before the first detention period	19	4	1	1

arranging a temporary return to the country of citizenship in order to submit a request for legal immigration from there; Dutch migration rules stipulate that a residence permit for family migration must be applied for in the country of origin. Similarly, asylum migrants in particular were already in the process of preparing onward migration to another European country after their asylum claim had been rejected. However, eventual changes in detainees' migration preferences during the detention were mostly detention-related.

Among the 81 detainees interviewed in 2011, nine indicated that they already preferred to go to their country of citizenship before they were detained. Fourteen respondents (not necessarily the same ones) held that migration preference at the time of the interview during detention. The number of respondents preferring onward migration to a new European country also increased somewhat (from 13 to 15) as well as the number of undecided respondents (from 5 to 11). Among the 81 respondents, 41 still had a preference to stay in the Netherlands in spite of being detained.

A significant number of the respondents (N = 36) had been detained repeatedly—the maximum detention tally was no less than eight—and their migration preferences just before the detention period during which they were interviewed had sometimes been produced by previous detention periods (see Table 2.1, lower panel). When previous detention periods are taken into account, 7 out of 81 respondents seemed to have been coerced into willingness to go to the country of citizenship; (14–9) + (6–4) = 7. This also applied to a man from Pakistan who was being detained for the third time and had spent about a month and a half in a detention center when he was interviewed:

> I only began to think about return when I was in detention the first time. But I didn't know what to do. I've nothing there and I didn't want to return. Now I want to go back because I'm afraid that this will keep going on. I don't want to get into that carousel [be re-detained again and again]. Your life passes by and you can't do anything, you can't build up anything. It's wasted time, and I'm 36 already. [The man's third detention period was ended because there was insufficient prospect for deportation.]

It should be mentioned, however, that eventual changes involving several detention periods were sometimes, at least in part, reported to be the result of other factors. For example, repeatedly detained respondents sometimes changed their mind about return owing to the difficulties they had encountered after previous detention periods ended, for instance, the difficulty of finding work without papers (some detainees also lost their employment because of the detention).

Although immigration detention was generally experienced as painful and distressing, the deterrent effects of immigration detention among detainees seemed moderate. Most respondents had even stronger reasons to try to stay in the Netherlands. The types of reasons, however, varied by detainee category. Family migrants generally did not want to give up their local family ties and the associated ambition to settle in the Netherlands permanently, which is shown by the interview with a Surinamese man who had been in the Netherlands for ten years and was being detained for the second time:

> Everyone at a certain age thinks about return, but I've never returned. If I reached the point that it has been enough, then I'll return. I've been here for so long. I've built my social relations here. My wife and daughter are here. Return is only possible if we're all ready for that, because over there, we have to adapt again. I want my daughter to choose when she's old enough so that she can decide where to live and where to be. [The respondent was released with an order to leave the Netherlands.]

Asylum migrants, by contrast, often had insufficient confidence that it would be safe enough to go to their country of citizenship, and a significant number also reported socioeconomic objections as they had migrated to Europe with the intention to settle permanently, or for an indefinite period of time and seemed to have left little in the country of citizenship to return to. The suffering in immigration detention and reluctance to return was also evident in the story of an Iranian Kurd who had spent four and a half months in detention (he had fled Iran when the authorities supposedly found out that he was financing Kurdish rebels):

> It's hard to be locked up. The guards bang on the door with their keys when they come to get you. My cellmate uses four tranquilizers a day, and I'm afraid that he'll get nuts. Or that I'll get nuts. I sometimes smell kerosene [the detention center is next to an airport] and am afraid that I'll be poisoned. Some guards make racist jokes. One guard said the other day that an African guy here had arrived with the banana boat. I would love to go to Iran: I speak the language, my family is there, I had a good life, but the Mullahs [here: a derogative term for fundamentalist Muslims] have ruined it. If I return, I risk being imprisoned for 10–15 years. Other Iranians even risk being sentenced to death, for example because they are Christians. There are just real problems in countries where people must return to. [The respondent was deported to a country that he had transited en route to the Netherlands.]

Compared to family and asylum migrants, labor migrants seemed somewhat more likely to develop willingness to leave the country. They usually had migrated with the intention to return to their country of origin after having earned a certain amount of money (and some were close to reaching that amount) or lacked a clear plan about how long they would be away for, but intended to return eventually. Their immigration detention sometimes made them bring their return intentions forward, as was indicated by an interview with a woman who had spent a month and a half in detention:

> I originally planned to return in 2012 since my passport expires at the end of 2012. I didn't want to apply for an extension or a new passport. Since I'm in detention, I want to return home as soon as possible. If I don't go home, I would die in here. [The respondent eventually went to China via assisted voluntary return from detention (AVRD).]

Thus, even though most family migrants and asylum migrants were immigrants with a strong orientation toward permanent stay in the country (or continent) of destination, most labor migrants were temporary migrants, some of whom were willing to bring pre-existing return plans forward.

Pressured into Deportation?

In this section, we examine whether the migration outcome of the detention depends on migrants' willingness to go to their country of citizenship, or receiving states' positions toward the readmission of deportees from the Netherlands. Here, we use data from the 2003 and 2011 studies. For both years, we made an effort to distinguish states that were relatively cooperative in readmitting their citizens through forced return from the Netherlands and states that were relatively uncooperative. There are some notable differences between these years, however. Compared to 2003, by 2011 few countries were still in the process of becoming EU member states and relations with Surinam, a former Dutch colony, had chilled considerably. Besides, the International Organization for Migration (IOM) has had a regular presence in the Dutch detention centers since 2007, which provided detainees in 2011 with the option to leave the Netherlands via assisted voluntary return from detention (AVRD) instead of being deported. This happened under a number of conditions, among them that the "removal" was not being delayed. In the case of AVRD, the detainee is taken to the airport, is released after having passed immigration, and meets an IOM employee in the departure hall.

In 2003—just before the 2004 and 2007 EU enlargements—relatively cooperative states were defined as countries aspiring to EU membership, and Surinam, a former colony that—at the time—had good international relations with the Netherlands. For 2011, we used information on EU readmission agreements and previously classified information on the extent to which states issue temporary travel documents to undocumented migrants, i.e., for whom the Dutch authorities can show only an expired travel document, a copy of a travel document, or no ID at all. Temporary travel documents can be divided into laissez passers (a temporary travel document issued by an embassy or consulate) and so-called EU staten, which are issued by the Dutch authorities. In case of an EU state, a deportee is flown to his or her country of assumed citizenship, assuming the deportee will be accepted there on the basis of that document. Using this information, we defined relatively "cooperative" states as those that (1) had concluded readmission agreements with the EU by 2011, or (2) were honoring at least 15 percent of the requests by the Dutch authorities to provide laissez passers, or (3) were, according to the Dutch government, regularly readmitting undocumented deportees on the basis of the EU state.

Table 2.2 shows detention outcomes by detainees' migration preferences and category of receiving state (the upper panel shows data on 2003; the lower panel pertains to the 2011 study). It turns out that detainees' stated migration preferences are a poor predictor of the migration outcome of detention in terms of release in the Netherlands, deportation, or AVRD. The differential willingness among states to readmit nationals seems to be more influential. In 2003, for example, respondents from countries aspiring to EU membership or Surinam had an 84 percent probability of deportation, and it did not matter much whether detainees personally wanted to go to these countries; those who wanted to go there had a 91 percent probability of deportation, against 81 percent among those who were reluctant to go. Among respondents originating from other countries, the deportation rate was considerably lower (49 percent). We found that a preference to go to the country of citizenship seemed to make a somewhat larger difference among the latter nationals but still reduced the probability of deportation only from 68 to 50 percent.

For 2011, deportation rates were lower than in 2003, but largely similar patterns were observed. (Some caution interpreting the 2011 figures is in order because numbers are relatively small when cross-tabulated by migration preference and country of origin.) Nineteen of the 37 respondents originating from relatively "cooperative" countries were eventually released in the Netherlands (51 percent). Just as in 2003, that share was much larger among respondents from relatively uncooperative countries (84 percent in 2011). Furthermore, as in 2003, eventual willingness to go to the country of citizenship did not seem to make much of a difference for detention migration outcomes, especially among nationals from "cooperative" states. In fact, among the latter, 4 out of 6 individuals (67 percent) who wanted to go to their country of citizenship were released, against 15 of 31 respondents (48 percent) who wished to stay in the Netherlands or in Europe more generally. Among those from relatively uncooperative states, 3 out of 8 respondents who wanted to go to the country of citizenship eventually left through AVRD, thereby apparently reducing the probability of a failed removal procedure among such nationals, but still only from 89 percent to 63 percent (Cramer's V = .28; p = .06).

Table 2.2 **Probability of immigration detention resulting in deportation or AVRD by country and detainees' willingness to return**

	Released	*Deported*	*AVRD*	*Total*
	2003 study			
Countries aspiring to EU membership[a], and Surinam				
Wants to return	1 (9%)	10 (91%)	Na	11 (100%)
Does not want to return	4 (19%)	17 (81%)	Na	21 (100%)
Total	5 (16%)	27 (84%)	Na	32 (100%)
Other countries				
Wants to return	18 (32%)	38 (68%)	Na	56 (100%)
Does not want to return	96 (50%)	97 (50%)	Na	193 (100%)
Total	114 (46%)	135 (54%)	Na	249 (100%)
	2011 study			
Relatively "cooperative" countries[b]				
Wants to return	4 (67%)	1 (17%)	1 (17%)	6 (100%)
Does not want to return	15 (48%)	15 (48%)	1 (3%)	31 (100%)
Total	19 (51%)	16 (43%)	2 (5%)	37 (100%)
Relatively "uncooperative" countries[c]				
Wants to return	5 (63%)	0 (0%)	3 (38%)	8 (100%)
Does not want to return	32 (89%)	4 (11%)	0 (0%)	36 (100%)
Total	37 (84%)	4 (9%)	3 (7%)	44 (100%)

[a] This category includes all countries that became EU member states in the period 2004–2007 (Bulgaria, Cyprus, Czech Republic, Estonia, Hungary, Latvia, Lithuania, Malta, Poland, Romania, Slovakia, and Slovenia).

[b] This category includes Afghanistan, Albania, Belarus, Bosnia, Cameroon, Democratic Republic of Congo, Gambia, Georgia, Iraq, Lebanon, Liberia, Morocco, Nepal, Nigeria, Pakistan, Russia, and Turkey.

[c] This category includes Algeria, Armenia, Azerbaijan, Benin, Burkina Faso, China, Ecuador, Egypt, Ethiopia, India, Iran, Ivory Coast, Niger, Sierra Leone, Sudan, Surinam, Syria, and Uganda.

These patterns underline the importance of international relations in shaping the migration outcomes of immigration detention. Readmission agreements with the EU, for example, are mostly signed by states that want to keep the door to EU membership open, or that expect other benefits in cooperating with the EU, such as trade, technical collaboration, or development aid (Cassarino, 2010).

Differences between states in the extent to which requests to provide laissez passers were honored, and whether or not undocumented deportees were admitted on the basis of the EU state criterion, also seem to depend, at least partly, on international relations. For example, in 2011, among the countries of citizenship reported by our respondents, Iraq and Afghanistan were the only states "regularly" readmitting citizens on the basis of an EU state. In both countries, there was a significant military presence by the "coalition forces" at the time, which, for several years, included Dutch troops. One respondent explained:

> Even for people with copies of their passport, the Dutch government cannot do a thing. The Dutch have not built up a good relation with the Chinese. There are lots of people who really want to return, but cannot. My suggestion is: put more effort in the relationship with the Chinese embassy instead of putting us in detention. [Anonymous respondent.]

Conclusion

Immigration detention is formally not a punishment, but governments do seem to use it for deterrence purposes. In this chapter, we analyze whether the detention experience pressures immigration detainees into willingness to leave and whether eventual willingness to go to the country of citizenship raises the probability of deportation (or assisted voluntary return from detention). We find that the Dutch detention regime is capable of coercing a minority of the detainees into willingness to go to their country of origin. In the 2011 study, 14 of 81 respondents preferred to go to their country of citizenship, and in seven cases the preference seemed to have been coerced, at least in part, by detention, including repeated detention.

The deterrence logic overlooks that the deterrent effects on the level of detainees' migration preferences—which are already limited there—are considerably diluted by embassies and consulates. Differential willingness on the part of states to admit deportees seems to be much more influential in shaping detention migration outcomes than detainees' migration preferences. Detainees who are undocumented are very much at the mercy of relevant embassies and consulates. Although additional research on the role of embassies and consulates is urgently needed, international relations and the stakes that states have in maintaining friendly relations with the deporting state are clearly crucial (cf. Ellermann, 2008). We expect, however, that a perceived legitimacy deficit of deportation and immigration detention on the part of countries of origin is also among the reasons for noncooperation. "Uncooperative" states occasionally accept the repatriation of detainees who want to go to their country of citizenship, but the very factors that pressure a minority of the detainees into willingness to leave may actually reduce the willingness of states to comply with deportation in general.

Our findings raise questions of principle as well as pragmatic questions. One of the former is whether it is acceptable that states use immigration detention as a deterrent. There are clearly punitive elements in the detention experience that are not required by the detention's administrative function, which is to ensure that individuals cannot abscond while their removal is being prepared. The more pragmatic question is whether it is actually wise for governments to try to pressure detainees into deportation, as detention often perpetuates the state of deportability among detainees, who, as a rule, seem to exit the detention centers in worse shape than how they entered them.

References

Bosworth, M. (2013). Can immigration detention be legitimate? In K. F. Aas & M. Bosworth (Eds.), *The borders of punishment: Citizenship, crime control, and social exclusion* (pp. 149–165). Oxford: Oxford University Press.

Cassarino, J. (2010). Dealing with unbalanced reciprocities: Cooperation on readmission and implications. In J. Cassarino (Ed.), *Unbalanced reciprocities: Cooperation on readmission in the Euro-Mediterranean area* (pp. 1–30). Washington, DC: Middle East Institute.

Cornelisse, G. (2010). *Immigration detention and human rights: Rethinking territorial sovereignty.* Leiden and Boston: Martinus Nijhoff.

Crewe, B. (2011). Depth, weight, tightness: Revisiting the pains of imprisonment. *Punishment and Society, 13*(5), 509–529.

Ellermann, A. (2008). The limits of unilateral migration control: Deportation and interstate cooperation. *Government and Opposition, 43*(2), 168–189.

Kalhan, A. (2010). Rethinking immigration detention. (Sidebar.) *Columbia Law Review, 110*, 42–58.

Kox, M. (2011). Leaving detention ... A study on the influence of immigration detention on migrants' decision-making processes regarding return. The Hague: International Organization of Migration.

Leerkes, A., & Broeders, D. (2010). A case of mixed motives? Formal and informal functions of administrative immigration detention. *British Journal of Criminology, 50*(5), 830–850.

Mainwaring, C. (2012). Constructing a crisis: The role of immigration detention in Malta. *Population Place and Space, 18*(6), 687–700.

Martin, L. (2012). Catch and remove: Detention, deterrence, and discipline in U.S. noncitizen family detention practice. *Geopolitics, 17*(2), 312–334.

Matsueda, R., Kreager, D., & Huizinga, D. (2006). Deterring delinquents: A rational choice model of theft and violence. *American Sociological Review, 71*(1), 95–122.

Piquero, A., and Pogarsky, G. (2002), Beyond Stafford and Warr's reconceptualization of deterrence: Personal and vicarious experiences, impulsivity, and offending behavior. *Journal of Research in Crime and Delinquency, 39*(2), 153–186.

Sykes, G. (1958). *The society of captives: A study of a maximum security prison.* Princeton, NJ: Princeton University Press.

Van Alphen, B., Molleman, T., Leerkes, A., & Van den Hoek, J. (2013) *Van bejegening tot vertrek. Een onderzoek naar de werking van vreemdelingenbewaring*, Den Haag: Boom Lemma.

Van Dokkum, B. (2010). *Kernthema's Vreemdelingenbewaring.* Nijmegen, Netherlands: Ars Aequi.

Van Kalmthout, A., & Van Leeuwen, K. (2004). *Terugkeermogelijkheden van vreemdelingen in de vreemdelingenbewaring.* Nijmegen: Wolf Legal.

Van Schijndel, C., & Van Gemmert, N. (2012). *Vreemdelingenbewaring in getal 2007-2011.* The Hague: DJI.

3

LGBTI Migrants in a Global World

SHANA TABAK

Recently, the unique vulnerabilities faced LGBTI migrants have drawn much attention as more and more of them have been placed in immigration detention (Tabak & Levitan, 2014). As the practice of detaining migrants for immigration-related purposes has increased globally, so too has concern that immigration detention disproportionally jeopardizes the rights of already-vulnerable populations, including children, women, the elderly, LGBTI people, and the mentally disabled. As the Special Rapporteur on Torture to the UN Human Rights Council encapsulated it well: "Within detention facilities, there is usually a strict hierarchy, and those at the bottom of this hierarchy, such as children, the elderly, persons with disabilities and diseases, gay, lesbian, bisexual and trans-gender persons, suffer double or triple discrimination" (2010).

This chapter focuses on the special concerns of lesbian, gay, bisexual, transgender, and intersex (LGBTI) detained migrants, a subgroup of vulnerable detainees that has largely remained invisible in detention systems around the globe. According to guidance from the UN High Commissioner for Refugees (2013), LGBTI asylum seekers are to be recognized as refugees under art 1(A)(2) if they suffer persecution on the ground of "membership of a particular social group."

Every year, national migration policies in states across the globe dictate that millions of migrants be detained in places of immigration detention. Yet the practice of immigration detention presents numerous problems, most significantly from a human rights perspective. As states have expanded the practice of immigration detention, it has become critical that state governments and the international community devote attention and resources to upholding the human rights of migrants in detention. Although sovereign states have the authority to regulate migration flows within their borders, this regulation must not come at the cost of violations of international human rights law (Office of the UN High Commissioner for Human Rights, n.d.). Detention in and of itself can constitute a violation of international refugee and human rights law, as has been well documented (Goodwin-Gill & McAdam, 2007). Despite states' legal obligations under human rights and refugee law, violations of detainees' rights abound across the globe (UN Representative of the Working Group on Arbitrary Detention, 2010). These violations include such concerns as physical and sexual violence perpetrated both by facility staff and by other inmates, indefinite or arbitrary detention of migrants, social isolation, high incidence of mental illness, and severe lack of access to medical care (ibid.; Parliamentary Assembly of the Council of Europe, 2010; UN General Assembly, 2012; UN High Commissioner for Human Rights, 2009).

Yet despite the prevalence of detention, it is unclear that detention meets the presumptive goals of states that choose to detain, namely, deterring migrants from crossing their borders without authorization (Edwards, 2011). Furthermore, it appears that irregular migration is increasing globally, despite the attempts of governments to secure their borders against irregular migrants (ibid.).

In exploring the multiple ways in which the transnational phenomena of state detention of migrants intersect with the lives of LGBTI migrants, this chapter seeks to briefly respond to three primary questions. First, who are LGBTI immigrant detainees and why do they migrate? Second, if LGBTI migrants are detained, should they be identified as LGBTI in order to receive specific protections, and if so, who is responsible for that identification? Third, if LGBTI migrants are detained, what type of harm might they face in detention? In discussing these three central questions, this chapter concludes that whereas no vulnerable populations should ever be detained unless they pose a clear security risk, and although the multiple alternatives to detention should always be first rigorously examined by states, if LGBTI migrants are detained, precautions must be taken by states to protect their most basic rights.

Who Are LGBTI Migrants?

The term *LGBTI migrant* encompasses incredibly heterogeneous groups of migrants. Some of these individuals may have been out in their home countries for years, working as human rights defenders for LGBTI rights; some may have never acted on their gender identity or sexual orientation but may be targeted as such regardless. Still others may leave their home countries for reasons having nothing to do with their sexual orientation or gender identity, but if detained, they may face more vulnerability than others in detention. Thus, a variety of push or pull factors lead to the choice for LGBTI migrants to depart their home countries. In some cases, the decision to emigrate is explicitly motivated by persecution suffered as a result of a migrant's gender identity or sexual orientation. In other cases, an LGBTI migrant's decision to emigrate is rooted in more general desires, such as for a better economic situation or freedom of political opinion or religious beliefs. In either case, however, LGBTI individuals who migrate have likely lived through human rights violations in their home countries related to sexual orientation or gender nonconformance.

Sexual minorities worldwide continue to face severe discrimination and persecution at the hands of both private and state actors. Criminalization of same-sex relationships is still widespread. In 76 nations, engaging in consensual same-sex sexual activities between adults is a criminal act (Itaborahy & Zhu, 2013)—often for both sexes, though sometimes only for men (Jansen & Spijkerboer, 2011). Although such criminalization is specific to nonconforming sexual orientation and does not normally refer to or otherwise criminalize transgender or intersex gender identity, oftentimes the criminalization of same-sex sexual activity acts as an indicator that those with nonconforming gender identity may be persecuted as well (ibid.). Nonconforming gender identity may also be specifically prosecuted under laws targeting cross-dressing, or punished under other nongender-specific legal doctrines (ibid.).

Even in countries that do not criminalize same-sex relationships, pervasive social stigma and deeply held biases against sexual minorities may lead to severe identity-based violence, including murder (Human Rights Watch, 2011). These experiences of persecution, discrimination, criminalization, and social and familial stigma may become important considerations in evaluating the choices that sexual minorities face, and the behaviors they exhibit, if and when they are detained by other states once they have left their home countries.

These "push" factors may motivate LGBTI migrants to leave their home countries in search of more accepting conditions; "pull" factors may also influence the choice to migrate. A recent uptick in reporting on attention paid to LGBTI rights, especially in the West, and notable rights advancements made in these legal systems there potentially attract migrants to the significant protections for LGBTI rights outside of an individual's home country (Gettleman, 2011; Brooks & Smith, 2012; Fiss, 2012).

Whatever the cause of the migration, LGBTI people are a significant part of the global migration stream, and consequently they are, like other migrants, subject to state detention of irregular migrants.

How Are LGBTI Migrants Identified in Detention?

Prior to identifying the failings of detention for LGBTI migrants, it is necessary to answer a number of threshold questions: Who exactly are LGBTI detainees? At what point in the detention process should a person be identified as LGBTI? Finally, who should make this determination of detainee identity?

The rights of all migrants who are detained in immigration detention are jeopardized, and yet for certain vulnerable groups detention may be even more dangerous thanks to particularized needs. For example, women in detention may have specific physical and mental health needs, such as maternal health services (Burton & Goldstein, 1993), assistance with the aftereffects of rape (ibid.), or protection from sexual violence while detained (Townsend, 2013). Similarly, children face unique challenges if they are deprived of education or appropriate mental health treatment (Martin & Hutchinson, 2005), are detained with juvenile offenders irrespective of whether they themselves are offenders (Benfer, 2004), or are put into solitary confinement (ibid.). Migrant detainees who suffer from mental illness face especially difficult circumstances as they may be unable to advocate for themselves, and "may be punished for behavior they cannot control" (Hing, 2009). Further, they may be denied medical treatment for mental disabilities if the disabilities are not made known to detention staff.

One challenge that distinguishes LGBTI detainees from these other vulnerable populations is the difficulty of identifying individual members of this group. Because the characteristics associated with membership in groups are for the most part more obvious, reports and analyses on the protection gaps faced by vulnerable populations such as women, children, and the mentally ill do not generally address the issue of identification (UN High Commissioner on Refugees, 2012; *Matter of Toboso-Alfonso*, 1990; *Canada v. Ward*, 1993; *R v. Immigration Appeal Tribunal*, 1992; *Refugee Appeal No. 1312/93*, 1995; Millbank, 2009; *J v. Secretary of State for the Home Department*, 2006; *Appellant S395/2002 v. Minister for Immigration & Multicultural Affairs*, 2003; *HJ v. Secretary of State for the Home Department*, 2010; UN High Commissioner for Refugees, 2008). On the other hand, within the diverse group of LGBTI migrants, no standards exist to classify LGBTI detainees as such. Furthermore, sexual minorities may have varying abilities to "pass" or "cover," choosing not to identify, visibly or otherwise, with a vulnerable group. This potential for invisibility presents both opportunities and challenges for LGBTI detainees.

Sexual minorities are incredibly heterogeneous within the LGBTI umbrella. The term *LGBTI* encompasses a variety of people, some of whom may easily "pass" as gender-conforming, such as lesbian women or gay men whose outward expression and behavior conform to culturally heteronormative presentations of gender. These people may never be identified by others as LGBTI unless they choose to be, or they may be out and present as such. Others may not have the option of concealing their gender identity while in detention. For instance, transgender individuals in the earlier stages of transition through hormonal therapy or other treatments may be particularly visible within a detained population. Thus, within the LGBTI group, visibility varies greatly, as does the likelihood of experiencing identity-based targeting due to an individual's visibility as nonconforming in sexual orientation or gender.

Even within the group of LGBTI detainees who have the ability to "pass" and do not obviously present as belonging to a vulnerable subgroup of detainees, multiple subtle issues regarding LGBTI self-identification and expression arise.

Although some LGBTI people may make conscious choices about how to present or not present, depending on where the person is in the coming out process, not all may be self-aware enough to articulate their identity as such. Scholars who have explored the psychological complexities around the process of self-identifying as LGBTI have commented that "in the absence of a safe environment, many LGBT individuals are not able to work through the internal processes necessary to allow them to integrate the multiple aspects of their sexuality" (Shidlo & Ahola, 2013). Thus, processes by which individuals determine how or even whether to self-identify as LGBTI are enormously complex.

LGBTI migrants are faced with a unique challenge if detained: public expression of their sexual orientation or gender identity while detained may result in increased protection, if it is recognized appropriately. Yet, to claim LGBTI status more often than not exposes LGBTI people to heightened violations of their basic human rights. The dilemma that revealing one's sexual orientation or gender identity may either lead to greater protection or more rights violations highlights the difficulty in determining whether LGBTI migrants in detention should be compelled to reveal their LGBTI status. The higher likelihood of abuse no matter how LGBTI migrants present themselves also suggests that although obfuscation of LGBTI status may be deemed acceptable to some LGBTI detainees, the elimination of choice regarding how to express one's sexual orientation or gender identity is an imperfect solution in the detention context.

Absent some means of identification of LGBTI populations, it is very difficult for such facilities to address the special vulnerabilities of these detainees. States may either develop mechanisms within their detention facilities to identify and classify LGBTI detainees or create mechanisms for self-identification by LGBTI detainees, or take a hybrid approach between these options. A subsequent question then arises of whether those individuals prefer to receive protection specific to sexual orientation or gender identity. Either approach creates problems, however, since forcibly outing LGBTI migrants would violate their human rights, yet relying on self-identification can exacerbate already acute protection gaps.

Although leaving LGBTI migrants to self-identify may be preferable in some ways, in a detention context this approach can contribute to the protection gap that such migrants face. Relying on detained LGBTI individuals to self-identify to determine eligibility for special protection does little to protect those who decide not to identify themselves at all once they are placed in detention facilities. Indeed, in many cases, expecting LGBTI detainees to self-identify may be unrealistic. LGBTI detainees may never have experienced being out before they are placed in immigration detention. Some individuals may have always concealed their sexual orientation or gender identity in their home country because they feared harm from others, including their family members, friends, neighbors, society generally, or state authorities. Once placed in detention, it may be unreasonable to expect that these individuals would willingly self-identify as LGBTI.

These same individuals, however, may still find themselves experiencing discrimination or abusive treatment at the hands of other inmates or detention personnel, even though they have not outwardly identified themselves as nonconforming in sexual orientation or gender.

Given these tensions, states should avoid detaining LGBTI migrants entirely if at all possible. This approach ensures that states do not force LGBTI detainees to conceal their identity or risk facing persecution while detained. If states decide, however, that LGBTI migrants must be detained, they must be ready to grapple with the difficulty of LGBTI detainee identification. First, states must create opportunities for migrants to self-identify, and must grapple with those whose perception of self-identity is complicated by multiple layers of persecution, trauma, internalized homophobia, and other mental health-related concerns. Second, states must take into account that the presentation of sexual orientation and gender identity can be manipulated consciously or unconsciously, and that identity exists on a spectrum of varying externalized presentations and internalized feelings of self that do not fit neatly into Western notions of nonheteronormative sexual orientation or gender identity. Finally, detention centers must provide adequate training for detention staff regarding these complexities.

What Challenges Do LGBTI Detainees Face in Detention?

Although all detainees are vulnerable to human rights abuses, the challenges that LGBTI detainees face may be particularly pronounced with regard to (1) physical violence and sexual violence, (2) social isolation and segregation of LGBTI detainees, (3) adequate access to medical care, and (4) mental health concerns (Tabak & Levitan, 2014).

Physical violence and sexual violence. Although best practices suggest that immigration detention facilities should be segregated by sex, such sex-segregated facilities do not typically provide safe accommodations for LGBTI migrants (UN High Commissioner for Refugees, 2012). LGBTI detainees are vulnerable to abuse from both other detainees and from facility staff, which can include identity-based physical and sexual harassment and violence (EU Agency for Fundamental Rights, 2009), as well as verbal abuse, including harassment and threats of rape (Jansen & Spijkerboer, 2011). Research indicates that LGBTI detainees, particularly transgender individuals and gender-nonconforming gay men, are more vulnerable to sexual violence in detention than heterosexual, gender-conforming inmates (Stop Prisoner Rape, 206; Leon, 2012). Transgender women, who are usually housed with men in sex-segregated immigrant detention facilities (Lieberman, 1990), are perhaps the most vulnerable to this abuse; in the

United States, for instance, one in five transgender women prisoners have been sexually assaulted by prison staff or other inmates (Grant, 2011).

Sexual violence against LGBTI detainees, as common as it may be, often go unreported or undetected. Detention facility officials may interpret any outward signs of homosexual orientation or transgender identity as evidence of "consent to rape" and ignore complaints of sexual violence brought by sexual minority detainees (Stop Prisoner Rape, 2004). Yet reports on detention-based violence against sexual and gender minorities suggest that LGBTI detainees are reluctant to complain of sexual violence for fear of deportation (ibid.) or retribution from staff or other detainees (ibid.), compounding their vulnerability to physical and sexual abuse. Overcrowding and a general lack of governmental oversight or civil society monitoring of these facilities also leads to increased vulnerability in this realm (ibid.).

Isolation and segregation of LGBTI detainees. LGBTI migrants in detention may be segregated from the general population, and may suffer social isolation as well (UN High Commissioner for Refugees, 2010). Physical isolation may be implemented as a matter of policy. Officials at facilities where migrants are detained sometimes proactively isolate LGBTI individuals from the general population, allegedly for their own protection. In the United States, for instance, LGBTI detainees are often placed in administrative segregation—an allegedly nonpunitive form of isolation (U.S. Immigration & Customs Enforcement, 2013a)—because of their actual or perceived vulnerability to sexual violence (National Immigrant Justice Center & Physicians for Human Rights, 2012). Detaining states may thus cite safety, security, or public health as the basis for segregating sexual minorities from other detainees (U.S. Immigration & Customs Enforcement, 2013a). These reasons, however, are neither acceptable under international law nor justified in practice. In reality, such practices are detrimental to migrants' safety, security, and health.

Social isolation can occur for any of several reasons. Other detainees may isolate LGBTI migrants because of prejudice. Conversely, many LGBTI migrants isolate themselves from other detainees from their home countries in order to avoid potentially negative consequences of disclosing their sexual orientation (EU Agency for Fundamental Rights, 2009). This social isolation in detention mirrors what many sexual minorities experience in their country of origin and may exacerbate feelings of depression, PTSD, and other mental health consequences. All of these potential abuses are compounded in the context of detention by frequent and severe stigmatization, isolation, and even solitary confinement of LGBTI individuals.

Inadequate access to medical care. Another significant problem faced by LGBTI migrants in immigration detention is lack of access to adequate medical care. Many migrants may not seek medical treatment for longstanding issues until they arrive in countries of first asylum. In many immigration detention facilities, only urgent medical care is provided, interpreters are rarely present during medical procedures, and medical expenses are often borne by the detainees (UN High Commissioner for Human Rights, 2013b).

These factors stand in the way of appropriate medical care, and can seriously impair detainees' health (Masmas, 2008). These problems are exacerbated by the unhealthy environment within many detention facilities—including crowded conditions and substandard hygiene (Special Rapporteur on Torture to the Human Rights Council, 2012), which may increase the spread of communicable diseases and worsen the physical state of detainees with preexisting medical conditions.

The unhealthy nature of many detention facilities and the barriers to adequate medical care that often exist are especially problematic for LGBTI detainees, in particular for those who either need specialized medical attention based on exposure to or treatment of HIV/AIDs, or for transgender LGBTI migrants receiving hormonal treatment in order to maintain their gender identity. Thus, LGBTI asylum seekers and migrants may enter detention with specific medical needs and have particular vulnerabilities relating to their physical health. These health needs must be adequately addressed by state authorities detaining these individuals.

Mental distress and posttraumatic stress syndrome. Lastly, there is an incredibly high incidence of mental distress and PTSD for LGBTI detainees. Many asylum seekers who are detained are sufferers of past trauma; this past persecution, indeed, is requisite for an asylum claim to be valid. In general, migrants throughout the world, particularly asylum seekers, report a high level of mental illness, including depression, PTSD, and other such mental health difficulties, compared with the population at large (Steel et al., 2004). Despite this, when asylum seekers are detained, oftentimes states inadequately prepare for the need to provide counseling and medical services to detained migrants to address these psychological needs.

LGBTI migrants, like other migrants generally, may suffer significant mental health impacts from their experiences in their home country, in transit, and once they arrive in their destination, particularly when they end up detained. LGBTI asylum seekers and refugees report trauma-related mental health problems as a result of the persecution experienced based on their sexual orientation or gender identity often experienced repeatedly over a lifetime (Shidlo & Ahola, 2013). This harm includes physical and sexual violence, and various forms of harassment and discrimination, experienced in a variety of both private and public settings, carried out by wide-ranging perpetrators, including family, peers, employers, and strangers (ibid.). The relentlessness of persecution in the lives of LGBTI people is extremely common; as noted by Ariel Shidlo and Joanne Ahola,

> Lesbian, gay, bisexual and transgender . . . forced migrants around the world report a history of multiple traumatic events across their lifespan.

> . . . . Many suffer from significant mental health consequences as a result of a lifetime of cumulative trauma. (ibid., p. 9.)

The psychological consequences of this often unremitting harm include depression, panic and anxiety, traumatic brain injury, and substance abuse (ibid.). Sexual minority migrants may also suffer from both PTSD, which is characterized by the "re-experiencing of traumatic events, numbing and avoidance of thinking about these events, and hyper-arousal," and complex PTSD, which is characterized by "self-destructive behavior, amnesia, intense shame, difficulties with intimacy, experiencing bodily pains in response to psychological distress, and despair about finding loving relationships" (ibid., p. 9.). In addition, the sexual violence that is prevalent in many detention settings may retraumatize LGBTI rape survivors (Dumond, 1992). Since LGBTI migrants so often experience sexual violence in their country of origin, they may be entering detention facilities with more severe mental aftereffects of rape and suffer greater trauma if sexually abused in detention.

Conclusion

LGBTI migrants, if they are detained by states, face severe risks to their physical and mental well-being. As this chapter has detailed, LGBTI detainees face increased sexual and physical violence, mental health concerns, social and physical isolation, and a lack of appropriate health care suited for individuals with nonconforming gender identity or sexual orientation. Whether these abuses are perpetrated by state officials or by other detainees, it is the responsibility of states to prevent these human rights violations.

To remedy these acute problems associated with the detention of LGBTI migrants, states—if they determine that detention is indeed the only option—must take immediate action. Because of the potential difficulties of adequately identifying and protecting LGBTI migrants, these detainees may face increased vulnerabilities associated with their invisibility. States that detain these migrants must draw attention to this invisible group in order to ensure that detention facilities do not perpetuate human rights violations against LGBTI detainees.

The simple act of state acknowledgment of diverse need among migrant populations is crucial. This recognition demands that states develop express recommendations regarding how best to identify these vulnerable populations and prevent their exposure to specific types of abuse and discrimination. For example, states must ensure the safety and well-being of LGBTI detainees, and they must end discrimination and abuse in detention, by prison officials and by other detainees. Finally, it is crucial that all detainees be afforded access to appropriate health care, welfare services, and contact with legal counsel and external LGBTI support systems.

Most simply: detention should never be applied to the most vulnerable populations. States that are committed to safeguarding the human rights of all detainees, including LGBTI detainees, must explore alternatives to detention as they seek politically viable means to approach noncitizen populations within their borders.

References

Appellant S395/2002 v. Minister for Immigration & Multicultural Affairs. (2003) 216 CLR 473. 78 HJ (Iran).

Benfer, E. A. (2004). Note, in the best interests of the child: An international human rights analysis of the treatment of unaccompanied minors in Australia and the United States. *Indiana International and Comparative Law Review, 14*(2004), 729–745.

Brooks, X., & Smith, E. (2012). Call me Kuchu: Nobody expected David Kato to be killed. *The Guardian*. Retrieved from http://www.guardian.co.uk/film/video/2012/nov/05/call-me-kuchu-david-kato-video.

Burton, E. B., & Goldstein, D. B. (1993). Vietnamese women and children refugees in Hong Kong: An argument against arbitrary detention. *Duke Journal of Comparative and International Law, 4*(1), 71–92.

Canada (Attorney General) v. Ward, [1993] 2 S.C.R. 689 (Can.).

Dumond, R. W. (1992). The sexual assault of male inmates in incarcerated settings. *International Journal of the Sociology of Law, 20*(2): 135–157.

Edwards, A. (2011). Methods of first resort: Alternatives to immigration detention in comparative perspective. *Equal Rights Review*, 7(2004) 117–142.

EU Agency for Fundamental Rights. (2009). Homophobia and discrimination on grounds of sexual orientation and gender identity in the EU member states: Part II—The social situation. 99–100. Retrieved from https://fra.europa.eu/sites/default/files/fra_uploads/397-FRA_hdgso_report_part2_en.pdf.

Fiss, J. (2012). The murder of David Kato: One year later. *Human Rights First*. Retrieved from http://perma.cc/0b1KxJEpZSY.

Gettleman, J. (2011). Ugandan who spoke up for gays is beaten to death. *New York Times*. Retrieved from http://perma.cc/0Yn6rADaxVt.

Goodwin-Gill, G. S., & McAdam, J. (2007). The refugee in international law. *The International Journal of Refugee Law, 20*(3), 483–485.

Grant, J. M., et al. (2011). Injustice at every turn: A report of the National Transgender Discrimination Survey. National Gay & Lesbian Task Force & National Center for Transgender Equality. 168. Retrieved from http://perma.cc/0rNsNYHDNiv.

Hing, B. O. (2009). Systemic failure: Mental illness, detention, and deportation. *University of California Davis Journal of International Law and Policy, 16*(2009), 341–364.

HJ (Iran) v. Sec'y of State for the Home Dep't (HJ and HT), [2010] UKSC 31, [2011] 1 A.C. 596 (appeal taken from Eng. & Wales).

Human Rights Watch. (2011). We'll show you you're a woman: Violence and discrimination against black lesbians and transgender men in South Africa. 1–2, 13–14. Retrieved from http://perma.cc/0qXeikfC9dh.

Martin, F. & Hutchinson, T. (2006). Mental health and human rights implications for unaccompanied minors seeking asylum in Australia. *Journal of Migration and Refugee Issues, 1*(1), 1–24.

Itaborahy, L. P., & Zhu, J. (2013). *State-sponsored homophobia: A world survey of laws: Criminalization, protection and recognition of same-sex love.* International Lesbian Gay Bisexual Trans & Intersex Association. 22. Retrieved from http://perma.cc/0jDfQVnNVej.

J v. Secretary of State for the Home Department, [2006] EWCA (Civ) 1238, [2007] Imm. A.R. 73 (appeal taken from Asylum & Immigr. Trib.) (Eng.).

Jansen, S., & Spijkerboer, T. (2011). *Fleeing homophobia: Asylum claims related to sexual orientation and gender identity in Europe.* Available at: http://www.refworld.org/docid/4ebba7852.html.

Leon, E. (2012). The plight of LGBT immigrant detainees. *Feet in 2 Worlds.* Retrieved from http://fi2w.org/2012/02/15/the-plight-of-lgbt-immigrant-detainees/.

Lieberman, A. (1990). Complaints by transgender detainees quantify abuse. *Women's ENews.* Retrieved from http://womensenews.org/story/lesbian-and-transgender/130902/complaints-transgender-detainees-quantify-abuse.

Masmas, T. N. (2008). Asylum seekers in Denmark: A study of health status and grade of traumatization of newly arrived asylum seekers. *Torture, 18*(2), 77–86.

Matter of Toboso-Alfonso, 20 I&N Dec. 819 (B.I.A. 1990) (U.S.).

Millbank, J. (2009). From discretion to disbelief: Recent trends in refugee determinations on the basis of sexual orientation in Australia and the United Kingdom. *International Journal of Human Rights, 13*(2–3), 391–414.

National Immigrant Justice Center & Physicians for Human Rights. (2012). Invisible in isolation: The use of segregation and solitary confinement in immigration detention 9. 19–20. Retrieved from http://perma.cc/0BG7QwezzEq.

Office of the UN High Commissioner for Human Rights. (n.d.). Administrative detention of migrants 1. Retrieved from http://perma.cc/0VTTnXrLSMt.

Parliamentary Assembly of the Council of Europe. (2010). Detention of asylum seekers and irregular migrants in Europe. *Resolution 1707.* 3–4, 6–7. Retrieved from http://perma.cc/0Mhuf7v3iS.

R v. Immigration Appeal Tribunal, ex parte Shah, (1992) 2 A.C. 629 (U.K.).

Refugee Appeal No. 1312/93 Re GJ (unreported) Refugee Status Appeals Authority, Aug. 30, 1995 (N.Z.).

Shidlo, A., & Ahola, J. (2013). Mental health challenges of LGBT forced migrants. *Forced Migration Review, 42,* 9–11.

Special Rapporteur on Torture to the UN Human Rights Council. (2010). Study on the phenomena of torture, cruel, inhuman or degrading treatment or punishment in the world, including an assessment of conditions of detention. *A/HRC/13/39/Add.5.* par. 231.

Steel, Z., Frommer, N., & Silove, D. (2004). Part I—The mental health impacts of migration: The law and its effects: Failing to understand: Refugee determination and the traumatized applicant. *International Journal of Law and Psychiatry, 27*(6), 511–528.

Stop Prisoner Rape. (2006). In the shadows: Sexual violence in U.S. detention facilities. 12, 14. Retrieved from http://perma.cc/06ckvFLngTc.

Stop Prisoner Rape. (2004). No refuge here: A first look at sexual abuse in immigration detention. 1–2, 8. Retrieved from http://perma.cc/0EyyT57ggjM.

Tabak, S., & Levitan, R. (2014). LGBTI migrants in immigration detention: A global perspective. Report for Center on American Progress on Detention and LGBT.

Townsend, M. (2013). Detainees at Yarl's Wood Immigration Center facing sexual abuse. *The Guardian.* Retrieved from http://perma.cc/07Ym3XS5Eea.

UN General Assembly. (2012). G.A. Res. 67/172. *U.N. Doc. A/RES/67/172.*

UN High Commissioner for Refugees. (2008). UNHCR guidance note on refugee claims relating to sexual orientation and gender identity. Retrieved from http://perma.cc/03H9B8zd57n.

UN High Commissioner for Human Rights. (2009). Opening remarks to the panel discussion on human rights of migrants in detention centers. Retrieved from http://perma.cc/0UtcEVKnmol.

UN High Commissioner for Refugees. (2010). The protection of lesbian, gay, bisexual, transgender and intersex asylum-seekers and refugees: Discussion paper. Retrieved from http://perma.cc/0YGryZSUg9o.

UN High Commissioner for Refugees. (2012). Guidelines on international protection no. 9: Claims to refugee status based on sexual orientation and/or gender identity within the context of Article 1A(2) of the 1951 Convention and/or its 1967 protocol relating to the status of refugees. *HCR/GIP/12/09.*

U.S. Immigration & Customs Enforcement. (2013a). Directive 11065.1: Review of the use of segregation for ICE detainees. Retrieved from http://perma.cc/0ruDsRgHPkG.

U.S. Immigration & Customs Enforcement. (2013b). Performance-based national detention standards 2011. 181. Retrieved from http://perma.cc/0htKpdoCV1X.

UN Representative of the Working Group on Arbitrary Detention. (2010). *Human Rights Council 13th session. U.N. Doc. A/HRC/13/30* (pp. 59–65).

4

Immigration Detention in Malaysia

The State Monopoly of (In)security

SASAGU KUDO

Malaysia, home to the third-largest economy in Southeast Asia, has long been a major host country of both regular and irregular migration in the region. In a parliament session held on October 23, 2013, it was revealed that the number of foreign workers with valid working permits amounted to 2,116,998 in June 2013 (Dewan Rakyat, 2013). In addition, the authorities have been roughly estimating the existing total of undocumented migrants (locally called Pendatang Asing Tanpa Izin, or PATI) to amount to approximately 2 million, which demonstrates extremely high dependence on a foreign workforce relative to the country's population of about 28.2 million. The largest group comes from neighboring Indonesia owing to the geographical and cultural proximity of the countries, although workers from other countries such as Myanmar, the Philippines, Bangladesh, and Nepal are also seen in various working sectors.

For the last two decades, the direction of policy formation against undocumented migrants has increasingly been influenced and defined with the narrative of security in Malaysia. By bringing in the logic of security to the field of policy making, undocumented migrants in the country have been represented not only as criminals who can defy everyday public order, but also and more accurately as an overt threat undermining the national security. In other words, going well beyond the term *criminalization*, securitization of undocumented migration has been under way as observed in many of the receiving countries (Watson, 2008; Bourbeau, 2011).

However, as maintained by scholars who support a critical approach to security studies, it should be emphasized that speaking of security is never neutral or innocent. In reality, as Aradau accurately notes, pursuing one's security will inevitably engender insecurity against others (2008). In much of a similar vein, Bigo and Tsoukala (2008) have elucidated that even though the practice of security is about survival, it is simultaneously about sacrifice.

Studies have been done to examine the mainstreaming process of securitization in Malaysian policy response toward undocumented migration (for example, Liow, 2006); this chapter will examine the synchronistic nature of (in)security by particularly focusing on the immigration detention measures. To gain a deeper understanding of the present immigration detention policy and the source of its legitimation, the political system ruled by the steadfast party coalition Barisan Nasional (National Front), which has been allowing the state to intensely concentrate its authority and marginalize the influence of civil society, must be taken into account. The study tries to demonstrate how the political setting featuring the far-reaching influence of the state, which is often described by analytical concepts such as semidemocracy, quasi-democracy, or illiberal democracy, has formulated immigration detention policy in line with the securitization process, and how it has affected the plight of undocumented migrants in the country. The focus of the chapter also extends to the reaction of civil society to pursue immigration detention reform.

Undocumented Migrants in Malaysia: The Many Faces

In Malaysia, the incursion of undocumented migrants is, and has been, constantly rampant in both Peninsular and East Malaysia. In Peninsular Malaysia, immigration policies come under the purview of the Immigration Department, while in Sabah and the Federal Territory of Labuan, the function is administered by the Federal Special Task Force for Sabah and Labuan (Pasukan Petugas Khas Persekutuan Sabah dan Labuan, PPKPS/L) which was set up in April 1989, under the National Security Council in the prime minister's department.

Whereas rapid industrialization and economic development since the 1970s generated inflows of foreign workers to fulfill the demands of a low-skill labor force in a variety of sectors such as plantations and construction, it was not until the mid-1980s that the government of Malaysia began to officially arrange a policy framework seeking to control the economic migration. Despite the attempt to deter unauthorized border crossings, which was not effective, the Malaysian response toward irregular migration has been significantly framed in the context of security from the early 1990s onward.

Countries of origin vary, but the majority of economically driven undocumented migration has been attempted by Indonesians residing particularly in rural areas, accelerated by the geographical and cultural proximities as well as the economic gap between the two countries. For many, rather than bear financial costs and time-consuming procedures to obtain official work permits, undocumented migration remains certainly an alluring option, which is not only limited to illegal entry but also includes illegal departure and reentry. Thus, the task of tracing informal outflows has also been a thorn for the Indonesian government as a main sending country (author's interview with an officer in the Ministry of Foreign Affairs in Indonesia, August 2012). The same goes for the situation in the state of Sabah in East Malaysia, where an enormous amount of illegal settling of people from the Philippines is more significant.

Law enforcement against undocumented migration rests primarily on the Malaysian Immigration Act 1959/1963, which stipulates persons entering the country without valid documents can be punished by a fine not exceeding RM 10,000 and/or imprisonment of up to five years and also liability to a whipping of not more than six strokes. Let alone the legal aspect, the porous borders of Malaysia, both land and sea, have been important a factor in variation in undocumented migration in the country. That is, aside from the undocumented economic migration, Malaysia has also long been facing an influx of refugees and asylum seekers.

As is evident from the case of Vietnamese boat people's arrival, which began in the mid-1970s, the influx of refugees and asylum seekers is not a new issue in Malaysia. The inflow of Acehnese from Indonesia was a constant salient issue throughout the 1990s and 2000s, while various ethnic minorities from Myanmar have been the majority in more recent years. At the end August 2014, the number of those regarded as persons of concern by the UN High Commissioner for Refugees amounted to 149,027 in Malaysia, and of these, 137,788 were arrivals from Myanmar (UNHCR, 2014). Although UNHCR has been allowed to operate in the country since 1975, Malaysia still lacks ratification of the 1951 UN Convention Relating to the Status of Refugees as well as its 1967 Protocol. With the lack of a sufficient legal framework to protect refugees and asylum seekers, the government has been condemned for its lukewarm stance in handling those in asylum.

Therefore, despite the efforts of UNHCR in issuing UN identification cards through the process of refugee status determination (RSD), the sojourn of refugees in Malaysia pending resettlement to a third country can be highly unpredictable. In particular, the distributed UN cards are occasionally devalued by law enforcement agencies at the grassroots level and have been predisposed to face extortion, or in the worst cases a precursor to being sent to a detention center.

In the next section, I consider the institutionalizing process of security response against undocumented migrants and how it has had an impact on the differences in identity within the single category of "illegals."

Institutionalization of Security Response

The impact of applying a security discourse on policy agendas can vary. On the one hand, security discourse, among others, paves the way for government agencies to increase the allocation of budgets and human resources. On the other hand, formulating policies oriented in the logic of security can be problematic, for it easily stipulates legal constraints and thus entails the risk of resulting in draconian responses. With these multifaceted effects of applying the logic of security in mind, this section will briefly outline the institutionalization process of security response against the influx of undocumented migrants in Malaysia.

Since the early 1990s, facing the limitations on policy effectiveness for controlling undocumented migration, the government was quick to shift its modus operandi along with the context of security. This shift was accentuated by the implementation of nationwide crackdowns (locally referred as *operasi*). In particular, the shifting mode was commenced by the introduction of Operasi Nyah I and II in 1991, which tried to prevent illegal entry by tightening border security as well as to root out those already settled illegally in the country. Following the introduction of nationwide raids, in July 1992, as a cornerstone of establishing ground for the government's strong initiative, the Cabinet Committee on Foreign Migrants (Jawatan Kuasa Kabinet Mengenai Pekerja Asing, later renamed Jawatan Kuasa Kabinet Mengenai Pekerja Asing dan PATI) was set up as the central locus of policy making to encounter undocumented migration at the national level. Chaired by the deputy prime minister, the Cabinet Committee is constituted from a range of government institutions such as the Ministry of Home Affairs, the Ministry of Foreign Affairs, and the Ministry of Manpower. Whereas the two states of Sabah and Sarawak were given high autonomy to define the direction of their immigration policies, it is mainly under this clandestine environment that the government has been allowed to monopolize the management of (in)security against undocumented migrants in the country until today.

Repeatedly articulated as "public enemy number two" (number one being circulation of illicit drugs), the government adopted even tougher measures of punishment throughout the 2000s. In August 2002, undocumented entry to Malaysia was subjected to judicial caning of not more than six strokes, as mentioned in the previous section. Although the details of this judicial process remain unspecified, a total of 34,923 undocumented migrants were said to be caned during 2002 to 2008 (Amnesty International, 2010). Moreover, since late 2005, special judicial courts (known as Mahkamah PATI) were established inside or in the vicinity of detention facilities in order to speed up prosecution procedures against those captured through security operations.

The process of securitization was further bolstered by frequent mobilization of the general population during crackdowns. This is particularly marked by the presence of the People's Volunteer Corps (Jabatan Sukarelawan Malaysia, or more commonly RELA), a longstanding security apparatus comprising ordinary citizens under the purview of the Ministry of Home Affairs. With approximately three million citizens registered (though not all registrants are actively engaged), RELA has been performing an extensive role within an institutionalized security framework against undocumented migrants. Prior to the launch of nationwide raids (Operasi Tegas) begun in 2005, the volunteer force was granted authority to search private premises without warrant and arrest those deemed to be illegal. This provoked numerous cases of misconduct, which even caused diplomatic tension between sending countries (most notably Indonesia) until the authority to solely practice operations was extinguished in 2011. Although security operations are carried out constantly, aggressiveness tends to increase especially in the aftermath of amnesty programs, which are implemented periodically (the most recent took place in 2011) and give illegal migrants an opportunity to legalize their status to remain and work, or return to their home countries without facing legal prosecution.

Other than the direct mobilization of citizens in conducting raids, the security discourse, which spreads threat perception socially, has also gained momentum through the media (which are under strong government censorship) as they correlate the inflow of irregular migration and other social problems, most notably exaggerating the spread of infectious diseases and the rise in criminal activities. Furthermore, public legitimacy of securitization has been further reinforced by everyday reports of the process and the outcome of raids, which are frequently publicized not only by government agencies but by a variety of local media outlets. Seen in this light, as Nah asserts, one can understand the peculiarity of crackdowns as "specifically designed to be *public spectacles*" (2011, p. 138).

Regardless of the intensification of a tougher response, the efficacy of policies particularly in terms of deterring irregular inflow remains open to question. This is mostly evident in the government's continuing heavy dependence on large-scale crackdowns. In September 2013, massive raids codenamed Operasi Bersepadu (Integrated Operation) were launched with the aim of apprehending those who remained in illegal status after implementation of the amnesty program. On the first day of the operation, the authorities arrested 2,433 undocumented migrants, and by December of the same year the number of implemented raids was 2,278, with approximately 16,800 arrested in total (*Sun Daily*, Jan. 21, 2014). During the second phase (Jan. 21–Apr. 16, 2014) of the operation, a total of 10,399 undocumented migrants were apprehended through 1,644 operations throughout the nation (*Bernama*, Apr. 18, 2014). The scope of operations is explicitly reflected in the number of deportations. Between January 21 and November 20, 2014, a total of 59,765 (made up of 24,614 Indonesians, 6,834 Bangladeshis, 6,483 Filipinos, and many more from other countries) had been repatriated to their home countries (*New Straits Times*, Nov. 21, 2014).

In parallel with these domestic policy developments, ASEAN (Association of Southeast Asian Nations) began to address the issue of transnational crimes (including undocumented migration) in terms of a potential threat to regional stability since the mid-1990s. Reflecting this trend, regional declarations were adopted (notably the ASEAN Declaration on Transnational Crime in 1997) while leaving the formulation of a concrete policy response in the hands of all member states (Emmers, 2003). A particular problem is the traditional weakness inherent in ASEAN diplomacy in dealing with human-rights-related issues. With the absence of an official regional framework to sufficiently protect the rights of undocumented migrants, it helps a receiving country like Malaysia that it can pursue measures in its own harsh manner without facing much direct interference from neighboring sending countries.

It is precisely under these circumstances that implementation of raids as well as subsequent detention is socially embedded as everyday routine practices, and thus the social distribution of insecurity is ubiquitous among undocumented migrants. As we have already seen, the insecure position of refugees and those seeking asylum, notably facing imminent risk of detention, becomes more precarious, especially when massive crackdowns are carried out. In 2014, through the activities of UNHCR including visits to detention centers, court actions, and hotline interventions, 3,723 persons of concern were freed from immigration detention sites as of August (UNHCR, 2014).

Closely entangled with the introduction of nationwide security operations directed toward undocumented migrants, since the early 1990s the Malaysian government began construction of immigration detention centers to hold massive numbers of people captured through raids. In the next section, which focuses on the perimeter of immigration detention sites, we examine the outcome of the aforementioned government reaction against undocumented migrants; that is, insecurity and sacrifices emanating from institutionalized security responses.

Immigration Detention and the State Monopoly of (In)security

As with the implementation of massive raids and its institutionalization, the detention policy of undocumented immigrants has been an issue of controversy since the early 1990s. In Malaysia, management of immigration detention centers is governed by the Immigration (Administration and Management of Immigration Depots) Regulations of 2003. In the Peninsular states and Sarawak, administration of the detention centers (known as *depot*) has seen some shifts involving the Prison Department, Immigration Department, and Depot Department (Jabatan Depot), which was established in 2010 to exclusively take charge of detention and deportation processes; the role was again taken over by the Immigration Department after a temporary period. By contrast, in the state of Sabah, immigration detention centers are called Temporary Detention Centers (Pusat Tahanan Sementara, PTS) and are managed by the Federal Special Task Force in tandem with the broader immigration policy framework. In any case, unlike the Western host countries of undocumented migrants in which one observes the rise of private security companies in administration of immigration detention centers (Doty & Wheatley, 2013), it is the state that has been overwhelmingly taking the helm of managing the detention facilities in Malaysia.

In April 2014, the Immigration Department reported that a total of 11,043 individuals (8,896 male adults, 1,549 female, and 598 children) were detained in twelve detention centers operating in Peninsular Malaysia (*Harian Metro*, Apr. 20, 2014). Detainees imprisoned at PTS in Sabah numbered 3,662 as of April 2, 2014 (Dewan Negara, 2014). According to information released by the National Human Rights Commission of Malaysia (SUHAKAM, 2014), from January to October 2013 a total of 1,406 children were detained in depots. The period of imprisonment tends to become protracted, particularly when dealing with those in asylum or uncertain nationality.

It cannot be denied that, as alleged by the authorities on occasions, the financial cost of managing detention facilities is a fiscal burden for the government. For instance, between January and August 2012, the government budget was RM4.233 million (US$1,326,930) to provide food to detainees (Depot Department, 2012). In April 2014, the Minister of Home Affairs, Ahmad Zahid Hamidi, revealed that the government spent RM2 million (US$600,000) per month or RM24 million annually for operating detention centers in the country, thus revealing the need to speed up detention and deportation procedures (*New Straits Times*, Apr. 18, 2014).

The constrained budget, combined with institutionalization of the security response, has had a profound impact regarding the features of detention sites. For example, Semenyih Detention Center, established in 1992, located at the outskirts of Kuala Lumpur, is one of the largest immigration detention facilities, with a capacity of approximately 1,200 inmates. Bounded by electric fences with broadly installed surveillance cameras, the building structure of the depot is largely akin to that of a prison. Similar to the situation in exercising security operations, personnel at RELA are deployed to undertake security monitoring to complement a chronic deficiency of manpower in the Immigration Department. Detainees, including children as mentioned above, are roughly divided into gender-segregated groups and imprisoned in large camps in which bedding is not provided. Hence, detainees are compelled to sleep on hard wooden floors (see Fig. 4.1). Visitation of inmates by relatives or friends is allowed under certain conditions.

Moreover, several disturbing aspects that can directly impose insecurity on detainees, such as limited access to clean water and the spread of dysentery, have been constantly pointed out (e.g., Human Rights Commission of Malaysia, 2014). Additionally, as symbolized by the massive crackdowns, misappropriate use of security discourse has clearly been a factor in overcrowded conditions in detention sites. Regarding this situation, in January 2008 SUHAKAM even suggested that the arrested immigrants should immediately be deported without going through the

Figure 4.1 Inside a detention camp at Semenyih Depot (photo by Sasagu Kudo).

courts, to avoid detention due to insecure conditions (*Bernama*, Jan. 28, 2008). In December of the same year, a commissioner of SUHAKAM, N. Siva Subramaniam, commented that there were 1,300 deaths of illegal foreigners deaths under detention in sites during the past six years, adding that most of the deaths were caused by lack of access to sufficient medical treatment (*The Star*, Dec. 18, 2008).

Such a condition clearly uncovers the specific instance of sacrifices inflicted under the banner of security, and immediately raises a concern regarding the fact that detainees also include children, as already stated. A study by a local NGO revealed that traumatic symptoms were observed among former juvenile detainees (Verghis and Pereira, 2009) .

Owing to the practice of immigration detention, which clearly reflects the influence of (in)security logic, the many faces of undocumented migrants have largely been undermined by the single identical category of "illegals." As a result, the uncertainty that binds prisoners has been a decisive factor in triggering defiance, taking the form of hunger strikes and riots. For instance, on March 26, 1998, an extensive riot was provoked by detainees from Indonesia, resulting in the deaths of an officer of the Federal Reserve Unit and three Indonesian inmates as well as causing injury to 41 policemen. Reportedly, the riot was attempted by Acehnese in asylum and on the verge of deportation.

However, the riot did not bring about an easing of the quandary, but rather led to the consequence of reproducing the discourse of security and further justified the authorities in tightening the security provisions. The following allegations made by the then-Inspector-General of Police Abdul Rahim Noor in the wake of the disturbance well illustrate this aspect:

> Repatriating the illegal immigrants is a step towards cutting down on the expenditure involved in running the detention camps and reducing the crime rate. We are learning through experience, in dealing with hardcore illegal immigrants who are serious in their bid to resist deportation.
>
> —*New Straits Times*, Mar. 28, 1998

Regardless of the "lesson" for the government, riots continued to erupt throughout the 2000s and 2010s. After more turmoil broke out at Lenggeng Immigration depot in April 2011, which resulted in the escape of 109 detainees (though many were later rearrested), the state police chief confirmed that some of them had been detained for three to 12 months awaiting resettlement to third countries (*Malaysiakini*, Apr. 5, 2011). Furthermore, indistinctive detention became evident when 16 detainees from Afghanistan and Myanmar who were victims of human trafficking absconded from a depot located at Kuala Lumpur International Airport in June 2010. All of the 88 service officers who had been in charge of the KLIA depot were said to be later transferred when a similar escape occurred again in August of the same year.

Although then-Home Minister Hishammuddin Hussein accentuated that the number of fugitives consisted of a "mere 0.06 percent of all detainees nationwide" (*The Star*, Oct. 28, 2010), the incident paved the way to reinforcing security management inside the detention facilities. Soon after the escape occurred, RM100 million was approved to pursue a tougher security environment (*New Straits Times*, Oct. 28, 2010). This included installing electric fences and surveillance cameras in detention centers. Also in April 2012, an anti-riot special squad (Pasukan Kawalan Khas, PKK) of specially trained personnel from the Immigration Department and RELA was formed to suppress any disturbances within the detention facilities.

As these transitions underscore, along with the state's authority to monopolize (in)security, the impact of securitization is diffused by managing immigration detention. It is in this respect that demands have been made, both domestically and internationally, for amelioration of the detention environment. In the next section, I examine how the state's overwhelming authority in managing immigration detention was met by counteractions by Malaysian civil society.

Decline of the State Monopoly?

The state monopoly of managing (in)security within the field of immigration detention is not only maintained by the influence of security discourses and practices, which is backed by the limited capability of ASEAN's official diplomacy to a certain extent, but also by the constrained influence of civil society associated with the extensive authority of the Malaysian state.

Here, it should be emphasized that from an early stage of the securitization process, the severe conditions facing foreign detainees have been recognized by local civil society, and thus, advocacy movements have been organized echoing international society. At the forefront of the movement was a local advocacy group, Tenaganita (Women's Force). In 1995, the group's director, Irene Fernandez (1946–2014) published a memorandum titled "Abuse, Torture and Dehumanized Conditions of Migrant Workers in Detention Centers," which reported the insecurity conditions surrounding inmates, with information obtained from her interviews with dozens of ex-detainees.

Even though civil society's bid to delegitimize the state monopoly was potentially an opportunity to carry out reforms in immigration detention, the state authority swiftly intervened with rigorous pressure. Fernandez was subsequently claimed to be publishing "false information," and in 1996 she was charged under the draconian Printing Presses and Publications Act of 1984. At the initiative of the Ministry of Home Affairs, in order to investigate the allegations of Tenaganita, the Independent Board of Visitors (IBV), led by Zulkifli Mahmood (former director-general of the Anti-Corruption Agency), was formed in 1995. From the beginning, the "independence" of IBV came into question from members of opposition parties and NGOs who were designated as board members, contrary to claims made by the deputy home minister during the early stages. Because of this, extreme secrecy underlying immigration detention was highlighted when cases of prisoner deaths (from India, Indonesia, Myanmar, and the Philippines) in the Semenyih depot during 1992 and 1994 were brought to light; diplomatic missions of the four countries denied receiving any notification from the Malaysian authorities (*New Straits Times*, Aug. 25, 1995). Despite the government's reaction, intended to overshadow the circumstances inside the detention milieu through a "legal" approach, a number of facts substantiated claims raised by Fernandez and were exposed by ex-detainee witnesses in the judicial process. Although Fernandez was sentenced to a one-year prison term in 2003, after appealing she was finally acquitted by the High Court in November 2008.

The prosecution of Fernandez, notwithstanding the fact that it turned out to be a long-term hindrance for the grassroots movement in advocating immigration detention reform, has played a crucial role in boosting civil society's anticipation of disseminating the plight of detention sites. This is partially expressed by the gradual change observed in the conventionally closed circumstances of detention sites. Few human rights groups have been granted access to these detention centers. Certainly the International Committee of the Red Cross (ICRC) and SUHAKAM have routinely carried out visits to exercise monitoring activities. However, other than UNHCR, which has been allowed regular visits for implementing refugee identification, only the international human rights group Amnesty International was granted access to three detention centers in 2009 (Amnesty International, 2009).

Following these grants of access, discussions have proceeded in efforts to review detention conditions with the initiative of SUHAKAM. In November 2013, at a roundtable consultation organized by SUHAKAM with officers in the Immigration Department, detention of children became a topic. At the discussion, the possibility of introducing the idea of alternatives to immigration detention (ATD), in the case of Hong Kong in particular, was also raised as a subject (Human Rights Commission of Malaysia, 2013). Moreover, the necessity of improving the detention environment has at least been openly stated by enforcement agencies. In October 2013, local media featured a comment by the head of the Enforcement Division in the Immigration Department mentioning the necessity of placing medical staff at immigration detention facilities so as to enable daily medical checks (*New Straits Times*, Oct. 29, 2013).

Even though these moves can be regarded as a positive sign that might lead to a decline in state monopoly of (in)security, which has long maintained legitimacy in the name of security, it should also be emphasized that the development is only in the early stages. In this context, it should be stressed that entry of local human rights advocacy groups to the immigration centers is still much restricted. Regarding transnational efforts, even though ASEAN came to agreement on its Declaration on the Protection and Promotion of the Rights of Migrant Workers in January 2007, which stipulates the protection of basic human rights of migrant workers as an obligation of receiving states, the underlying principles of noninterference that define the regional body have been a hindrance to delegitimizing the (in)security monopolized by the Malaysian state authority. To ease insecurity stemming from the current situation within the immigration detention sites, it is obvious that there is still more room for the Malaysian authorities to forge deeper collaboration with a variety of stakeholders.

Conclusion

We have examined how immigration detention systems developed in line with the broader trend of securitization of undocumented migration in Malaysia since the early 1990s. As this chapter highlighted, institutionalized security response with the state's monopolizing power to socially determine others has undoubtedly allowed the authorities to legitimize (in)security deeply, and perhaps thoroughly embed it in the management of immigration detention. Amid the emerging development of discussions for detention policy reform, it is imperative to note that the government's continuous desire to maintain the issue of undocumented migration within the context of security is clear.

Against this backdrop, for further progress it will be indispensable for the government to eschew relying on the conventional idea tied up with the security mode mindset of it being nonterminating in nature, and to revise the traditional approach, which is evidently characterized by state-centricity in the policy field of immigration detention. To put crudely, it is thus clear that the possibility of immigration detention policy reform will largely rest on a more fundamental transformation in the current political environment, which has been largely undermining the potential role of local civil society. Without undergoing this process, which inevitably requires a certain degree of improvement in the conventional relationship of the state and civil society, effectively reforming immigration detention in Malaysia is likely to remain a daunting task.

References

Amnesty International. (2009). *Abused and abandoned: Refugees denied rights in Malaysia.* London: Amnesty International.

Amnesty International. (2010). *A blow to humanity: Torture by judicial caning in Malaysia.* London: Amnesty International.

Aradau, C. (2008). *Rethinking trafficking in women: Politics out of security.* New York: Palgrave Macmillan.

Bigo, D., & Tsoukala, A. (2008). Understanding (in)security. In D. Bigo & A. Tsoukala (Eds.), *Terror, insecurity and liberty: Illiberal practices of liberal regimes after 9/11.* (pp. 1–9). New York: Routledge.

Bourbeau, P. (2011) *The securitization of migration: A study of movement and order.* New York: Routledge.

Depot Department. (2012). Jumlah Tuntutan Bayaran Perkhidmatan Pembekalan Makanan di Depot-Depot Tahanan Imigresen di Seluruh Malaysia pada Bulan Januari hingga Ogos Tahun 2012 (Total financial cost of food in immigration depots in Malaysia from January to August 2012). Unpublished document.

Dewan Rakyat. (2013). Parlimen Ketiga Belas Penggal Pertama Mesyuarat Ketiga, Oct. 23, 2013 [DR 23.10.2013].

Dewan Negara (2014). Parlimen Ketiga Belas Penggal Kedua Mesyuarat Pertama, May 6, 2014 [DN 6.5.2014].

Doty, R. L., & Wheatley, E. S. (2013). Private detention and the immigration industrial complex. *International Political Sociology,* 7(4), 426–443.

Emmers, R. (2003). ASEAN and the securitization of transnational crime in Southeast Asia. *Pacific Review, 16*(3) 419–438.

Human Rights Commission of Malaysia. (2013). *Roundtable on alternatives to immigration detention.* Retrieved Sept. 23, 2014, at http://www.suhakam.org.my/wp-content/uploads/2013/12/Report-on-Roundtable-on-ATD-Malaysia.pdf.

Human Rights Commission of Malaysia. (2014). *Annual report 2013.* Retrieved on Oct. 3, 2014 from http://www.suhakam.org.my/pusat-media/sumber/laporan-tahunan/.

Liow, J. C. (2006). Malaysia's approach to Indonesian migrant labor: Securitization, politics, or catharsis? In M. Caballero-Anthony, R. Emmers, & A. Acharya (Eds.), *Non-traditional security in Asia: Dilemmas in securitization.* (pp. 40–65) Aldershot, UK: Ashgate.

Nah, A. M. (2011). Legitimizing violence: The impact of public crackdowns on migrant workers and refugees in Malaysia. *Australian Journal of Human Rights, 17*(2) 131–157.

UNHCR (2014). Malaysia fact sheet, March 2014. Retrieved on Oct. 11, 2014, from http://www.unhcr.org/5314928e9.html.

Verghis, S., & Pereira, X. V. (2009). Health concerns of refugees and asylum seekers in Malaysia. Retrieved Oct. 3, 2014, from http://www.healthequityinitiatives.com/wp-content/uploads/2012/06/HEALTH-CONCERNS-OF-REFUGEES-AND-ASYLUM-SEEKERS-IN-MALAYSIA.pdf

Watson, S. D. (2008). *The securitization of humanitarian migration: Digging moats and sinking boats.* Oxon, UK: Routledge.

5

The Northwest Detention Center

A Nexus of the Immigration Debate

RICH FURMAN, DAFNEY BLANCA DABACH, ALISSA R. ACKERMAN, DAVID ANDROFF, DOUGLAS EPPS, SUSANNA JONES, AND MELODY LOYA

Tacoma, Washington, is a city with a notorious past regarding our nation's historical treatment of immigrants. During the last half of the 19th century, Chinese railroad workers were drawn to the area to work on the great transcontinental railroad. As in other periods in American history, immigrants were recruited when labor shortages threatened essential, developing industries. As the national economy took a downturn in the 1870s, lukewarm feelings on the part of many of Tacoma's citizens turned xenophobic. In 1878, a meeting of the first literary society, filled with city leaders, voted to affirm a resolution: that Chinese immigration has been an injury to the United States (Hunt, 1916). This was not the first indication of the antipathy people from Tacoma had toward the Chinese, but the number of local leaders who voted for the resolution, and their political and social clout, marked a key moment in the city's relationship to its Chinese population.

> In the early 80s [1880s], white labor began to be heard in earnest. California had set a righteous pace. In Tacoma, idle men who wanted work reviled and hated the yellow competitor who had employment when he wanted it because he labored for a less wage and was more servile. Yet, even among the whites who wanted work, there was developing an inclination to regard as menial anything that a Chinaman could do. Honest labor, in short, was losing its dignity. White women disliked to take employment as maids because it put them in a class with the Chinese. A servant class, or menial class, was being developed, and this was the real serious aspect of the Chinese problem, and it could be cured only by ousting the Chinese. The cure came with a drastic remedy. (p. 356)

In 1885, a group of native Tacomans engaged in what was soon to be known as the Tacoma Method (Allerfeldt, 2003). A mob of citizens took to the streets and knocked on all the doors of Chinese business and homes. The Chinese were told to pack up their things, and meet at a central location; they would have to leave the city. Within a day, the remaining several hundred of the approximately 700 Chinese immigrants who worked and lived Tacoma were marched through the mud and driving rain to a train station in the southern part of town. There, they were loaded on a freight car and taken to Portland, where they would have to begin anew, or return to China.

Slightly over 100 years after this notorious event, the Northwest Detention Center (NWDC) opened, marking a continuation of Tacoma's history of being front-and-center in our nation's mistreatment of immigrants. The face of immigration may have changed over the last century, but the treatment of immigrants has remained relatively the same. The various participants and players enact, often unwittingly, nativist and xenophobic scripts that are emblematic of their particular era. Exploring this history and its continuation illuminates national and global trends in the movement and treatment of vulnerable populations. The Tacoma Method and the NWDC both represent important historical, global phenomena, and demonstrate how they are performed within the same geographic context.

The purpose of this chapter is to explore the Northwest Detention Center as representing a nexus of key aspects of the immigration debate. The NWDC is a private, for-profit immigration detention center in the city of Tacoma, Washington. In this chapter, we will explore how the NWDC, symbolically and in practice, represents a poignant expression of key dynamics of the "immigration debate" in the United States today. To meet these aims we explore several interlocking areas. First, we present a brief description of the NWDC itself, providing the reader with context about its purpose and development. Second, we present the NWDC as representative of widespread trends toward the privatization of prisons, and immigration detention more specifically. Third, we explore the NWDC as being a powerful expression of the increased movement toward the criminalization of immigration. Fourth, we show how these trends have led to various micro- and macro-level human rights violations, and how these are perpetrated by the NWDC. Fifth, we explore how advocacy and human rights groups have responded to the center and the realities it embodies.

About the Northwest Detention Center

At first glance, the NWDC appears to be an out-of-place government office building with an unimposing manicured lawn and patriotic flags flying above the structure. The razor wire that lines the internal fence, however, gives a clue that this building is off-limits and used for incarcerative purposes. Designed to hold a maximum of 1,000 immigrant detainees, the NWDC opened its doors in April 2004. In 2009, the center expanded its capacity to 1,579 people and now must maintain a daily population minimum to be in compliance with its current private contract (U.S. Department of Homeland Security, 2012b). Correctional Services Corporation (CSC) originally constructed the first section of the now-227,000 square-foot institution, which in 2005 was purchased by an international private corrections conglomerate, the Geo Group (Geo Group, 2013b).

The facility resides in the industrial area of Tacoma's tide flats, situated among railroad tracks and a local propane distributor. It rests on the soil of a former toxic waste dump and an EPA Superfund cleanup site (Seattle University School of Law & OneAmerica [SUSLO], 2008). This land, according to the preliminary environmental impact statement issued by the Immigration and Naturalization Service (INS), was found to be "an undefined risk with the redevelopment of the site resulting in liability concerns for the INS" (Immigration & Naturalization Service, February 2001, p. 2). However, because of pressure from local government officials, including a personal joint letter from two congressmen and persistence from CSC lawyers, INS eventually withdrew their reluctance (Kamb, 2012; Immigration & Naturalization Service, December 2001). The lure of incoming jobs and boosts to future local taxes proved too enticing, despite the well-identified risks laid out before them.

The Geo Group is publically traded and operates 95 correctional, detention, and reentry services globally, totaling 72,000 beds and employing 18,000 staff (Geo Group, 2012). According to a 2012 annual report for shareholders, corrections and detentions account for approximately two-thirds of the $1.5 billion of revenue for the fiscal year (ibid.). The NWDC is the fourth-largest federal detention center in the country (Gavett, 2011), making it an extremely lucrative endeavor. Immigration and Customs Enforcement pays the Geo Group approximately $100.65 per person per day for detention (U.S. Department of Homeland Security, 2012b). By meeting their basic daily contractual requirements, Geo would gross approximately $119,000 per day. The commodification of undocumented immigrants has become a booming business within America.

The NWDC detains people from more than 80 countries, and the average length of stay is about 35 days (International Law Clinic, University of Seattle School of Law, 2008). The center houses all classifications of detainees, from low-security to high-security individuals (Geo Group, 2013b). Level 1 detainees are considered nonviolent, have little or no criminal history, and are not allowed to commingle with the high-risk level 3 detainees, who likely have previous acts of violence on their records (Immigration & Customs Enforcement, 2008). A January 2012 report from an internal compliance inspection provides a snapshot of the population held at the NWDC. According to this report, NWDC housed a total of 1,358 ICE detainees, including 665 level 1 males, 396 level 2 males, 118 level 3 males, 145 level 1 females, 33 level 2 females, and 1 level 3 female (U.S. Department of Homeland Security, 2012b, p. 1). At the time of this report, the majority of the population was low- or medium-risk, with a significant portion of nonviolent detainees (n = 810). Less than 9 percent of the population was classified as level 3 or high-risk. The majority of detainees have never been incarcerated and as such, the correctional methods of confinement embodied by the NWDC may come as quite a shock to the immigrant detainees.

In 2012, ICE removed 409,849 people from the United States (Immigration & Customs Enforcement, n.d.). This is important to note, as the NWDC remains a big player in deportation, ranking in the top 3 percent nationally for detainees leaving ICE detention. More than four-fifths (81 percent) of those who leave the facility either are deported or have signed voluntary departure orders. An additional 13 percent are released on bond or orders of recognizance (OR) while they continue immigration proceedings (TRAC Immigration, 2010). A voluntary departure is an agreement by a foreign national to voluntarily return to his or her country of citizenship (U.S. Citizenship & Immigration Services, n.d.). Persons released on bond or ORs may eventually be deported as their cases with the immigration court conclude. A disconcerting 2 percent of immigrants who chose to fight their cases ended with no grounds to deport (TRAC Immigration, 2010). This statistic paints a clear picture of the most likely outcomes once an individual is detained at the NWDC.

As a Nexus of Privatization

The movement toward the privatization of prisons has been rapidly increasing. This trend is not an isolated phenomenon, but represents part of the global neoliberalist agenda (Danaher, 1994, 2001), and its proponents believe strongly in the privatization of most government services (Dorwart & Epstein, 1993; Kaseke, 1998). Although most associate the neoliberal agenda and the push toward privatization with the structural adjustment policies of the World Bank and International Monetary Fund, this movement has been closely aligned with the social and economic policies of both parties since the 1980s. Ackerman and Furman (2013) contend that:

> A natural consequence of this strong advocacy of neoliberal policies, along with the agenda of the political right and the response to the growing federal budget deficit, has been for privatization to become viewed as a key means of meeting the social obligations toward providing custodial and care oriented service. (p. 254)

The privatization of prisons and the prison industrial complex are said to have influenced the sharp increase in the overall U.S. prison population over the last several decades. Indeed, privatization has allowed private companies to profit from keeping individuals behind bars. Privatization is not a new issue, however; Schlosser (1998) suggested that the lure of big money tainted the U.S. criminal justice system because public service has been abandoned for the sake of higher profit.

Several private entities currently operate correctional and detention facilities. The two largest entities are the Corrections Corporation of America (CCA) and the GEO Group (Ackerman, Furman, Judy, & Cohen, 2014). Together, the two companies own 174 facilities. These companies contract with the Federal Bureau of Prisons (BOP), the U.S. Marshals Service, and Immigration and Customs Enforcement (ICE), as well as half of the U.S. states. If CCA were a state corrections department, it would be the fifth largest in the United States.

Recently, U.S. state prison populations have seen the first decrease since the 1970s (Justice Policy Institute, 2011; West, Sabol, & Greenman, 2010). Private prison companies obtain the most revenue from state prison contracts and as such they have developed strategies to ensure future profit (Justice Policy Institute, 2011). The CEO of the GEO Group has acknowledged, during a call with investors, that future profit will stream from detention of undocumented immigrants. The detention of undocumented individuals in private facilities has been a smart venture as related to profit. Immigration and Customs Enforcement detains around 33,000 people on any given day, with 17 percent of them housed in contract detention centers (Immigration and Customs Enforcement, 2012). As noted, the NWDC is one of the facilities that ICE contracts with to detain the undocumented.

As a Nexus of Criminalization

The last twenty years have witnessed what is referred to as the criminalization of immigration, or "crimmigration" (Ackerman & Furman, 2014). There have been several key factors increasingly criminalizing the lives of immigrants. Perhaps the most significant shift in immigration policy and practice occurred not in response to the events after 2001 but to legislation passed in 1996, the Illegal Immigration and Immigration Reform Act (IIIAIRA). This act allowed the U.S. government to deport people for minor law infractions, whereas prior to the act only individuals who committed felonies publishable by more than five years in prison could be deported. The act was retroactively applied to individuals who had been convicted of deportable offenses (Carter, 2002). In addition, Section 287(g) of the act allows the federal government to enter into agreements with states and local governments to engage in immigration law enforcement functions. By mid-2013, ICE had entered into agreements with 36 law enforcement agencies in 19 states and trained almost 1,300 local and state law enforcement officers to enforce immigration laws. Since September 11, 2001, the act has been applied much more forcefully. The ability of the U.S. government to deport people was only amplified in 2011 by the Office of Detention and Removal Services, situated within the Department of Homeland Security, and developed Operation Endgame as its strategic plan (U.S. Department of Homeland Security, 2003). The expressed goal of this new policy was to deport all undocumented immigrants by the year 2012.

Various states have passed laws that increasingly criminalize many aspects of what immigrants must do in daily living to survive. The Arizona legislature enacted the Support Our Law Enforcement and Safe Neighborhoods Act, also known as S.B. 1070. This law requires all residents of the state to carry identification; failure to comply could result in fines or imprisonment. Additionally, the law makes it illegal to pick up passengers for work. Similarly, any undocumented individual who seeks to gain employment is in violation of the act (Jones, 2014). Shortly after the enactment of S.B. 1070, Alabama passed the Beason-Hammon Alabama Taxpayer and Citizen Protection Act, commonly known as H.B. 56. This law required schools to determine whether students had been born outside of the United States. It also disqualified undocumented students from enrolling or attending public institutions of higher education in the state (Alabama Code, 2011). In addition to these examples, the Immigration Policy Center (2011) notes a drastic increase in state-level immigration bills from 2005 to 2009. Primarily, this is in response to the inability of the U.S. Congress to pass comprehensive immigration reform.

Although these factors have all greatly contributed to the expansion of immigration detention, the largest factor was the Secure Communities Program, which provided the administrative mechanism to increase detention. Started under President George W. Bush in 2008, Secure Communities originally encouraged (and now nationally mandates) that fingerprints sent to the FBI be routed to the Department of Homeland Security if immigration violations are found. The program was originally conceptualized as a tool to detain and deport only those offenders who placed the public at most risk, but the vast majority of those arrested are not for violent offenses (Kohni, Markowitz, & Chavez, 2011). The long-term consequences of state-level immigration laws and federal policies such as Secure Communities remain to be seen, but in the short run, the state laws have had detrimental effects on citizens and noncitizens alike.

A Nexus of Human Rights Violations

Escalating trends in the privatization of prisons, criminalization of immigrants, and militarization of the U.S.-Mexico border have contributed to the mistreatment of immigrants in the United States. Discrimination and dehumanization are masked by anti-immigrant rhetoric and stereotyping that stigmatizes immigrants and obscures violations of their rights (Androff et al., 2011). The term *detention* conceals the true nature of the action: imprisonment without the normal due process and rights afforded to others. By constructing immigration violations as an administrative violation, caged persons, known as detainees, are subjected to many human rights violations.

There are more than 34,000 people held daily in more 250 immigration detention facilities, many of which are private prisons (U.S. Department of Homeland Security, 2012a). The total detainee population was 429,247 in 2011, 18 percent more than 2010 and almost double from 2005 (Simanski & Sapp, 2012). Eighty-eight percent of detainees are Latino, from Mexico, Guatemala, Honduras, and El Salvador. This population, at the center of the criminalization of immigration, is increasingly at risk for human rights violations in privatized prisons. With an incarceration rate of 1 in 100 Americans, the United States has a disproportionate 25 percent of the world's prisoners with only 5 percent of the world's population (Chazaro, 2012). The privatization of immigration detentions like the NWDC is an extension of the national reliance on incarceration that has traumatized communities of color while enriching private corporations (ibid.).

Immigrants in the United States are entitled to the same universal human rights as everyone else. International human rights law recognizes the status of "migrant" as especially vulnerable and in need of extra protections against discrimination (Androff, 2014). The human rights of people in countries other than their own are specifically addressed in several international human rights agreements, notably the International Covenant on Civil and Political Rights; the International Covenant on Economic, Social, and Cultural Rights; the International Convention on the Elimination of All Forms of Racial Discrimination; the Convention on the Elimination of All Forms of Discrimination Against Women; the Convention on the Rights of the Child; and the International Convention of the Rights of All Migrant Workers and Their Families. These primarily promote migrants' right to safe and equitable working conditions and to accessing health care, education, and social services. They also call for equal treatment of noncitizens by prohibiting discrimination on the basis of nationality or unfair or arbitrary treatment of migrants. The human rights of migrant workers' families are also protected, because they are entitled to the highest attainable standards of physical and mental health and education. The children of migrants have the right to registration documents (Suárez-Orozco, Suárez-Orozco, & Katsiaficas, 2014). These rights pertain to the entire process of migration, including preparation, transit, period of stay, and return.

Unfortunately, many of these agreements have a low rate of ratification, and enforcement of migrant rights remains weak. Immigrants continue to be an extremely vulnerable group; the UN Special Rapporteur on the Human Rights of Migrants notes that migrants are experiencing a "continuing deterioration in their human rights" (Wexler, 2007, p. 5). These violations include death, lack of due process, physical and sexual abuse, deprivation, inhumane conditions, and separation from family members. It is estimated that more than 5,000 people have died during their migration to the United States since 1994 (Androff & Tavassoli, 2012); the Government Accounting Office or GAO (2006) has attributed this preventable loss of life to U.S. immigration policy. Federal prosecutions of apprehended migrants, through a program known as Operation Streamline, consist of mass hearings of up to 80 people, depriving them of their due process and access to adequate legal representation (Androff & Tavassoli, 2012).During President Obama's first term, 1.5 million people were deported, 409,849 in 2012 alone. The manner in which people are deported is often especially inhumane, as family members are separated and deposited across the border at different locations, and violations of human rights such as physical assaults by border patrol agents have been reported.

Immigrants' human rights have been violated in private immigration detentions centers. There have been at least 110 deaths in immigration detention reported by ICE since 2003. Human rights groups such as No Más Muertes (or NMM; 2008) have documented violations of immigrants' human rights by inhumane treatment. These include hundreds of cases where immigrants, including pregnant women, were denied food, water, medical care, and access to bathroom facilities. Immigrants in detention have suffered physical, sexual, and verbal abuse and been denied access to legal counsel. Immigrants in detention have been subjected to extreme temperatures in their holding cells, and women and children in detention have been denied blankets (ibid.; Southwest Institute for Research on Women [SIROW], 2009).

The NWDC has been the site of numerous human rights violations against immigrants. Ninety percent of people held in the NWDC do not have legal representation (Chazaro, 2012). Research by the Seattle University School of Law and OneAmerica (SUSLO, 2008) documents further lack of due process, violations of attorney-client privilege, failures to share information with families and attorneys when people are transferred, and detainees being pressured to sign documents even if they did not understand them. Human rights violations stemming from incidents of mistreatment include episodes of physical and verbal abuse, humiliating and degrading treatment, and denial of food and access to restrooms. Detainees at NWDC also have reported denial of medical and mental health care, including seizures suffered from an untreated cancerous brain tumor. Inhumane conditions documented include overcrowding and unhygienic facilities (ibid.).

Despite these violations, the Geo Group has a global human rights policy (Geo Group, 2013), which has been called the first human rights policy in the private prison industry. The policy references international human rights documents and relates to training of employees so as to minimize risks to human rights. According to the Geo Group, the NWDC scored 99.2 percent on its most recent accreditation by the American Correctional Association. However, what is on paper does not seem to reconcile with the reality that detainees live with every day.

As a Nexus of Human Rights Activism

In response to the various human rights implications of immigration detention in general, and specifically in response to the presence and operations of the NWDC, several important advocacy groups engaged in considerable advocacy in the Puget Sound region. It would not be accurate to say that all of these groups began after the development of NWDC, yet the presence of the prison most certainly has served as a touchstone of activism. In this section, we briefly explore activism and human service responses to immigration detention. Although we highlight two national-level responses as means of demonstrating the overall scope of responses, we will focus primarily on local responses.

The Detention Watch Network (DWN) is a national coalition of organizations and affiliation groups that focuses on immigration detention reform and the rights of immigrants. Its platform is based on three areas of advocacy (Detention Watch Network, 2013). First, they seek to end mandatory immigration detention; ICE officials currently are compelled to retain 70 percent of those detained without due process, owing to policy and enforcement protocol. They are pursuing a repeal of the laws that mandate detention while seeking administrative policy shifts in the interim that provide more flexibility and discretion, and increase due process rights. Second, they want to eliminate what has been interpreted as a quota for immigration detention, which is currently over 33,000 detainees. They wish Congress to clarify previous reports that appear to ICE to set this number as a minimum, not as a maximum, for the number of detained persons. Third, they desire to end the relationship between for-profit prisons and immigration detention. To meet the aims of these three goals, the network builds capacity within existing organizations, engages in coordinated and collaborative action, participates in policy advocacy on local and federal levels, and provides significant public education.

The Northwest Immigrants Rights Project (NWIRP, 2013) has been a major player in helping prisoners incarcerated in the NWDC, and is perhaps the most influential group working with this population. The NWIRP started in 1984 to assist refugees of the violent civil wars in Central America. They helped their early refugees seek official asylum, and found other mechanisms for obtaining legal status in the United States. Since then, the organization has provided legal services to immigrants from more than 100 countries. They also have increasingly become involved in advocacy around various immigration issues.

Although laws in some states have attempted to compel human service programs and providers to coordinate with ICE personnel (Kohni et al., 2011), no such laws exist within the state of Washington. As such, providers may offer services to anyone in need of them. One such organization is Tacoma Community House, which provides several types of services: help with immigration status, English language classes, U.S. citizen classes, and case management for assistance in navigating the complex web of social services. It also provides services to victims of crime, an important service for immigrant communities. Given that local jails and law enforcement have increasingly cooperated with Homeland Security, it is essential that immigrant victims have advocates who will assist them in meeting their health and psychological needs.

The NWDC has galvanized activism across the social and political spectrum. The Bill of Rights Defense Committee is an organization that focuses on the rule of law and the upholding of constitutional rights for all people (BORDC, 2013). It views itself as a coalition of diverse people and groups, yet it most certainly espouses a libertarian, constitutionally based philosophy.

> BORDC is guided by the Bill of Rights, which was adopted to limit the power of the state over individuals and to preserve basic human and individual rights for every person under U.S. jurisdiction or control, even in times of war or other national crises, and regardless of who holds elected power. (ibid., para. 3)

The BORDC expresses concern for constitutional rights not being extended to detainees in immigrant detention, and it has highlighted the NWDC. It views immigrant detention as an extension of the spirit of the Patriot Act, which served to inappropriately (against the Constitution) limit individual rights in the name of national security. The BORDC engages in several types of actions. It works to educate the media through bringing attention to the NWDC and other immigration detention centers. It also directly engages in policy advocacy on a federal level to challenge laws and policies that inhibit the immigrants living in the community and those detained from being accorded the same constitutional rights as citizens. The organization has as well created curricular tool kits for teachers to use in classrooms.

Conclusion

In 2010, the City of Tacoma opened the Tacoma Chinese Reconciliation Park to serve as a reminder of past abuses of those different from the majority. The aim of the project is to serve as

> an act of reconciliation and inclusivity toward appreciation of the people of diverse legacies and interests who are part of the city as a dynamic community.
>
> (Chinese Reconciliation Project Foundation, 2013, para. 5)

The creation of the park is a powerful symbol for a city with a long history of human rights violations against immigrants. Yet, as powerful as this symbol is, it is a painful contrast to the ominous presence of the Northwest Detention Center only a few miles away. Immigrant detention centers such as the NWDC operate within a shadowy area outside the normal human rights and due processes that represent the best of our values. They are emblematic of inaccurate and xenophobic conceptions of economic refugees, and are greatly incongruent with the nature of transnational migration in a rapidly globalizing world.

This chapter presents an example of how one immigration detention center is situated at the nexus for the criminalization of immigration and other powerful social dynamics surrounding the immigration debate. Though it is a particularly poignant example, this is but one of many stories of how social institutions can oppress vulnerable populations. It should raise concern that for-profit entities are becoming entrenched within the criminal justice system, setting up the potential dynamic of valuing profit over human rights, often focused on the most vulnerable populations. Social workers, human service workers, and other advocates would be well served to explore how immigration detention centers have an impact on the lives of immigrants, immigrant communities, and all members of their communities. Without understanding the nature of these institutions, it is impossible to fully understand the lives of undocumented as well as documented immigrants in our communities.

References

Ackerman, A. R., & Furman, R. (2013). The criminalization of immigration and the privatization of the immigration detention: Implications for justice. *Contemporary Justice Review, 16*, 251–263.

Ackerman, A. R., & Furman, R. (2014). (Eds.). *The criminalization of immigration: Contexts and consquences*. Durham, NC: Carolina Academic Press.

Ackerman, A. R., Furman, R., Judy, B., & Cohen, J. (2014). Profit over pragmatism: Privatizing immigration detention centers. In A. R. Ackerman & R. Furman (Eds.), *The criminalization of immigration: Contexts and consequences*. (pp. 101–111) Durham, NC: Carolina Academic Press.

Alabama Code. (2011) §§31-13-1—31-13-34 ("H.B. 56").

Allerfeldt, K. (2003). Race and restriction: Anti-Asian immigration pressures in the Pacific Northwest of America during the Progressive Era, 1885–1924. *History, 88*, 53–73.

Androff, D. (2014). Human rights violations in the war on immigrants. In R. Furman & A. Ackerman (Eds.), *Criminalization of immigration: Contexts and consequences*. (pp. 147–159) Durham, NC: Carolina Academic Press.

Androff, D., & Tavassoli, K. (2012). Deaths in the desert: The human rights crisis on the U.S.-Mexico border. *Social Work, 57*(2), 165–173.

Androff, D., Ayon, C., Becerra, D., Gurrola, M., Salas, L., Krysik, J., Gerdes, K., & Segal, E. (2011). U.S. immigration policy and immigrant children's well-being: The impact of policy shifts. *Journal of Sociology & Social Welfare, 38*(1), 77–98.

Bill of Rights Defense Committee [BORDC] (2013). *About the BORDC.* Retrieved Aug. 14, 2013, from http://www.bordc.org/about/.

Carter, M. L. (2002). Giving taxpatriates the boot—permanently: The Read Amendment unconstitutionally infringes on the fundamental right to expatriate. *Georgia Law Review, 36,* 835.

Chazaro, A. (2012). Rolling back the tide: Challenging the criminalization of immigrants in Washington State. *Seattle Journal for Social Justice, 11*(1), 126–148.

Chinese Reconciliation Project Foundation. (2013). *Homepage.* Retrieved Sep. 26, 2013, from http://tacomachinesepark.org/.

Danaher, K. (1994). *50 years is enough: The case against the World Bank and the International Monetary Fund.* Boston: South End Press.

Danaher, K. (2001). *Ten reasons to abolish the IMF and World Bank.* New York: Seven Stories Press.

Detention Watch Network (2013). Advocacy. Retrieved Aug. 16, 2013, from http://www.detentionwatchnetwork.org/sites/default/files/Banking_on_Detention_DWN.pdf.

Dorwart, R. A., & Epstein, S. S. (1993). *Privatization and mental health care: A fragile balance.* Westport, CT: Auburn House.

Gavett, G. (2011, Oct. 18). Lost in detention—map: The U.S. immigration detention boom. *PBS Frontline.* Retrieved Aug. 16, 2013, from http://www.pbs.org/wgbh/pages/frontline/race-multicultural/lost-in-detention/map-the-u-s-immigration-detention-boom/.

Geo Group. (2012). The Geo Group, Inc. 2012 annual report. Retrieved from http://www.geogroup.com/documents/GEO_2012_Annual_Report.pdf.

Geo Group. (2013a). Global human rights policy. Retrieved from http://www.geogroup.com/documents/Human_Rights_Policy.pdf.

Geo Group. (2013b). Northwest Detention Center. Retrieved from http://www.geogroup.com/Maps/LocationDetails/52.

Hunt, H. (1916). *Tacoma, its history and its builders: A half century of activity* (Vol. 2). New York: S. J. Clarke.

Immigration and Customs Enforcement. (2008). ICE/DRO detention standards: Classification system. Retrieved Sep. 1, 2013, from http://www.ice.gov/doclib/dro/detention-standards/pdf/classification_system.pdf.

Immigration and Customs Enforcement. (n.d.). Removal statistics. Retrieved from http://www.ice.gov/removal-statistics/.

Immigration and Naturalization Service. (2001, February). Environmental impact statement for the Tacoma/Seattle area detention center. Retrieved Aug. 16, 2013, from http://www.documentcloud.org/documents/408887-snewsroom-p12081312560.html#document/p2/a67579.

Immigration and Naturalization Service. (2001, Dec. 3). Environmental impact statement: Record of decision. Retrieved Aug. 16, 2013, from http://www.documentcloud.org/documents/408886-snewsroom-p12081312570.html#document/p1/a67580.

Immigration Policy Center (2011, April). Q & A guide to state immigration laws: What you need to know if your state is considering Arizona SB 1070- type legislation. Special Report. Retrieved Apr. 16, 2012, from http://www.immigrationpolicy.org/sites/default/files/docs/Guide_to_State_Immigration_Laws_011211.pdf.

International Law Clinic, University of Seattle School of Law. (2008). *Voices from detention: A report on human rights violations at the Northwest Detention Center.* Seattle: Author.

Jones, S. (2014). Undocumented immigration policy in Arizona. In A. R. Ackerman & R. Furman (Eds.), *The criminalization of immigration: Contexts and consequences.* (pp. 49–58) Durham, NC: Carolina Academic Press.

Justice Policy Institute. (2011). *Gaming the system: How the political strategies of private prison companies promote ineffective policies.* Washington, DC: Justice Policy Institute.

Kamb, L., (2012, Sep. 9). A rare look inside the Northwest Detention Center. *Tacoma News Tribune.* Retrieved from http://www.thenewstribune.com/2012/09/09/2284287/part-i-a-rare-look-inside-tacomas.html.

Kaseke, E. (1998). Structural adjustment programmes and the problem of urban poverty: an African perspective. *International Social Work, 41*(3), 311–320.

Kohni, A., Markowitz, P. L., & Chavez, L. (2011). *Secure communities by the numbers: An analysis of economics and due process.* Research report. Chief Justice Earl Warren Institute of Law and Social Policy, University of California, Berkeley Law School. Retrieved Aug. 25, 2013, at http://www.law.berkeley.edu/files/Secure_Communities_by_the_Numbers.pdf.

No Más Muertes [NMM]. (2008). *Crossing the line: Human rights abuses of migrants in short-term custody on the Arizona/Sonora border.* Tucson: Author.

Northwest Immigrants Rights Project (NWIRP). (2013). *Homepage.* Retrieved Sep. 27, 2013, from www.nwirp.org.

Schlosser, E. (1998, December). http://www.theatlantic.com/magazine/archive/1998/12/the-prison-industrial-complex/304669/

Seattle University School of Law & OneAmerica (SUSLO). (2008). Voices from detention: A report on human rights violations at the Northwest Detention Center in Tacoma, Washington. Seattle University School of Law International Human Rights Clinic, in collaboration with OneAmerica. Retrieved Sep. 18, 2013, from http://www.weareoneamerica.org/sites/default/files/OneAmerica_Detention_Report.pdf.

Simanski, J., & Sapp, L. (2012). Immigration enforcement actions: 2011 annual report. U.S. Department of Homeland Security, Office of Immigration Statistics. Retrieved Sep. 18, 2013, from http://www.dhs.gov/sites/default/files/publications/immigration-statistics/enforcement_ar_2011.pdf.

Southwest Institute for Research on Women (SIROW). (2009). *Unseen prisoners: A report on women in immigration detention facilities in Arizona.* University of Arizona. Retrieved from https://womensrefugeecommission.org/images/zdocs/sirow_executive_summary_final.pdf

Suárez-Orozco, C., Suárez-Orozco, M., & Katsiaficas, D. (2014). Children of the unauthorized: Domains of compromise. In A. R. Ackerman & R. Furman (Eds.), *The criminalization of immigration: Contexts and consequences.* (pp. 239–249) Durham, NC: Carolina Academic Press.

TRAC Immigration. (2010). Detainees leaving ICE detention from the northwest contract detention center. Retrieved from http://trac.syr.edu/immigration/detention/200803/CSCNWWA/exit/.

U.S. Department of Homeland Security, (2003) Operation Endgame. https://aclum.org/sites/all/files/education/ice/endgame.pdf

U.S. Department of Homeland Security, (2006). Detention and Removal of Illegal Aliens. https://www.oig.dhs.gov/assets/Mgmt/OIG_06-33_Apr06.pdf

U.S. Department of Homeland Security. (2012a). ICE total removals through August 25, 2012. Retrieved Sep. 18, 2013, from http://www.ice.gov/doclib/about/offices/ero/pdf/ero-removals1.pdf.

U.S. Department of Homeland Security. (2012b). Office of detention oversight: Compliance report. Retrieved Sep. 1, 2013, from http://s3.documentcloud.org/documents/422280/inspection-report.pdf.

U.S. Government Accountability Office [GAO]. (2006). *Illegal immigration: Border-crossing deaths have doubled since 1995; Border Patrol's efforts to prevent deaths have not been fully evaluated* (GAO-06-770). Washington, DC: Author.

West, H. C., Sabol, W. J., & Greenman, S. J. (2010). Prisoners in 2009. Washington, DC: Bureau of Justice Statistics.

Wexler, L. (2007). The non-legal role of international human rights law in addressing immigration. *University of Chicago Legal Forum*, 359–403.

6

Migration Detention in Mexico

Human Rights Denied

SONJA WOLF

Between January and October 2014, Mexico's National Migration Institute (Instituto Nacional de Migración, INM) apprehended and detained a total of 103,820 undocumented migrants. Seventy-seven percent of these irregular migrants were male, and only 23 percent were female. Adults constituted 81 percent of all undocumented migrants, minors—more than half of them aged 12 to 17—the remaining 19 percent. Mirroring the trends of previous years, the vast majority of all unauthorized entries into the country (95 percent) were made by individuals from the Northern Triangle of Central America (Honduras, Guatemala, and El Salvador). Contrary to the authorities' expectations, detention and deportation often do not deter their protagonists from repeating the perilous journey. Given the clandestine nature of the phenomenon, it is unclear how many deportees transit Mexico as often as is necessary to reach their destination. The available research suggests, however, that many feel compelled to persist in their endeavor because of unchanged community conditions, a family and livelihood in the United States, or the need to repay debt incurred for earlier border crossings (Woodhouse, 2013).

Among the factors prompting Central Americans to embark on an uncertain future is a chronic shortage of dignified job opportunities, aggravated by free trade agreements that consolidated neoliberal economic policies and adversely affected trade and labor rights in the isthmus (Moreno, 2012; WOLA, 2009); generalized violence (CIDH, 2013); street gang harassment, including forced recruitment (Kennedy, 2014), sexual violence (Valencia, 2011), and dispossession of homes and land (Valencia Caravantes, 2014); domestic abuse (Camargo, 2014); desire for family reunification (CIDH, 2013); and attacks on LGBT persons and human rights defenders (IACHR, 2011) by both private and state actors, notably in Honduras (HRW, 2009) and El Salvador (IHRLC, 2012).

The situation in Honduras has been particularly critical since the 2009 coup d'état that ousted President Manuel Zelaya and that gravely affected the economy, security, rule of law, and human rights in the country. Resolution of the political crisis was complicated by the U.S. government's tolerance of the overthrow and attempts to prevent Zelaya from returning to power by pushing for new elections. Efforts to restore a semblance of order and stability not only entailed ruthless repression of social and political dissent (Amnesty International, 2012), but also detracted from the need to curb crime and violence (Ruhl, 2012). The problems that underlie the exodus from Central America—be they social and economic marginalization or violence associated with street gangs and organized crime—are inextricably tied to U.S. policies abroad and the failure to address the domestic roots of transnational issues such as U.S.-born street gangs or drug production, trafficking, and consumption. As this chapter demonstrates, the United States also plays a vital role in shaping migration policy and management in Mexico.

Although Mexico is host to distinct migration dynamics, transmigration has perhaps gained the greatest visibility because of the systematic human rights violations it involves. Their irregular status in the country, combined with increasingly stringent migration enforcement, requires undocumented foreigners to take hazardous routes and makes them vulnerable to multiple aggressions, particularly theft, sexual violence, extortion, kidnapping, torture, homicide, and disappearance. To be sure, ordinary citizens have been known to take advantage of unauthorized migrants by overcharging them for food, lodging, and transportation. Serious abuses, however, are generally perpetrated by criminal groups and state agents—notably police and migration agents—who are corrupted or coerced into colluding with them (CIDH, 2013). This trend toward more (and even more serious) migrant rights violations has unfolded in the context of the drug war launched by President Felipe Calderón (2006–2012) and continued by the current president, Enrique Peña Nieto. In response to the onslaught of the Mexican state, organized crime groups—notably Los Zetas—diversified their criminal portfolios and established brutal control over the migrant smuggling and kidnapping industry (Martínez, 2010). The ill treatment of migrants has become notorious at Mexico's southern border and the Gulf Coast, but it is pervasive throughout the national territory, including in detention facilities. The 2011 Migration Law and its 2012 Regulations, adopted in response to the outcry over the massacre of 72 migrants, were initially hailed as a milestone in the protection of migrant rights. However, the legislation contains a series of loopholes, chief among which are a national security perspective and the automatic confinement of undocumented migrants.

This chapter examines migration detention in Mexico against the backdrop of U.S. politics and border security. It argues that migrant rights violations are affected not only by structural deficiencies within the agency tasked with administering migrant detention centers, but also by U.S. pressure on Mexico to suppress irregular migration northward through swift detection, detention, and deportation. The chapter begins by discussing the U.S. border security policy and its implications for migration management in Mexico, before identifying the attributes and main institutional problems of the INM. Subsequently, it scrutinizes the conditions and treatment of migrants in the INM-administered detention centers. The chapter concludes by exploring the underresearched experience of undocumented migrants in Mexican prisons in order to elucidate the breadth of abuses they suffer.

The Twenty-First Century Border: U.S. Border Enforcement Reaches South

Over the last 20 years, the United States has been progressively closing its southern border through construction of walls and fences, deployment of guards, and use of technology. Behind this security drive lies a series of distinct concerns—most acute in Washington, D.C., and border state capitals—over uncontrolled migration, drug trafficking, spillover violence, and (especially since 9/11) terrorism. To date, however, there is little evidence that Mexico's drug violence seeps across the border or terrorists seek to enter the United States from the south (Isacson & Meyer, 2012). Regardless of how founded these fears may be, the United States has classified all illicit flows of goods and people, including migrants, as potential national security threats. Thus the Border Patrol operates under the assumption that anyone trying to enter the country illegally could be a terrorist (ibid.). In other words, no distinction is being made between unauthorized arrivals seeking safety, economic opportunities, or family reunification and those harboring criminal intent.

Growing U.S. concerns over border security have had major implications for how Mexico patrols its own borders. Stricter policing of the Mexico-Guatemala frontier is of particular relevance given its importance in the regional drug trade and the geographic origin of most northbound migrants. In 2013, more than a third of the migrants the Border Patrol apprehended were from northern Central America, triple the figure for 2011 (Isacson & Meyer, 2014). Unsurprisingly, then, the United States has come to consider migration enforcement at Mexico's southern border an extension of its own border enforcement (Miller, 2014). It is widely believed, though difficult to demonstrate, that Mexico has been receiving strong diplomatic and economic pressures to do its part in stemming the unsolicited transit of people and merchandise. The massive arrival of child migrants at the US-Mexico border in mid-2014, resulting in an overload of detention facilities and immigration courts, perhaps best demonstrates these pressures. Reaction to the "child migrant surge" was swift: whereas the United States expressed strong political disapproval, Mexico orchestrated an unprecedented crackdown on undocumented foreigners, involving in-country checkpoints, operations on cargo trains, and hotel raids.

Nevertheless, Mexico's attempts to assuage its neighbor's disquiet over porous borders have converted the frontier with Guatemala into a first filter for irregular migrants and given rise to an extensive migration enforcement apparatus. Like the United States, since 2001 Mexico has escalated its capacity to control migration and eventually defined as national security threats vulnerable borders, organized crime, armed groups, and terrorism (Isacson & Meyer, 2012). Given that resource constraints and topographical difficulties impede effective patrolling of the frontier with Guatemala, Mexico has established a "vertical border," a dense web of interior checkpoints and detention facilities in the south and center of the country. This migration enforcement is heavily supported by the Mérida Initiative, a U.S. security assistance package initiated in 2008 to support Mexico's fight against drug trafficking.

Initially focused on providing training and equipment for the security forces since 2010, the plan has been emphasizing strengthening of democratic institutions, building of resilient communities, and cooperation on border issues (Ribando Seelke & Finklea, 2013). Control of undocumented migration fits squarely with the objective of creating a 21st-century border structure, which supports the INM in professionalization of its agents, strengthening of internal controls, and use of biometric equipment to track border crossings (Isacson & Meyer, 2012). Indeed, border management assistance has been expanded to cover not only Mexico's northern border but also its southern border, ports, and airports and is developing into the largest of the Mérida Initiative's four pillars (Isacson et al., 2014). This trend toward extended border enforcement is mirrored in the U.S.-sponsored Central America Regional Security Initiative (CARSI), which provides increasing border security assistance to Guatemala (ibid.). The perception of undocumented migrants as a national security threat, combined with the migration management priorities of effective border controls and rapid detection, detention, and deportation of unauthorized foreigners, facilitates human rights violations. These, in turn, are aggravated by structural deficiencies within the INM.

The National Migration Institute emerged from the now-extinct Directorate General of Migration Services (Dirección General de Servicios Migratorios, DGSM) of the Secretariat of the Interior (Secretaría de Gobernación, SEGOB, 2012). Established in 1936, the directorate had managed migration from a police perspective, failed to instill human rights values in its agents, and permitted corruption to flourish. This last matter occurred because hired candidates were not always suitable, and—save rare exceptions—detected wrongdoings went unpunished (Wolf, 2013). In October 1993 the INM was created as a technical (today administrative) autonomous agency within the SEGOB to make migration control more efficient. Incorporation of many DGSM workers into the institute set the ground for the structural problems it experiences today. A development with wide-ranging consequences occurred in 2005 with the INM's designation as a national security agency. The adoption of this approach has had an impact not only on the training of agents, but also access to information and to detention centers. Alleging probable harm to its operational capacity or national security, the institute tends to restrict public data about its personnel and detention facilities. Although it allows state human rights and refugee agencies access to the centers, entry is generally denied to journalists and is complicated for lawyers and nongovernmental organizations (NGOs) that seek to monitor human rights and provide migrants with legal assistance.

The INM is tasked with planning and implementing migration services as well as coordination with other federal agencies that have responsibilities in the area of migration. The institute carries out its work through an administrative structure that comprises 32 federal delegations whose autonomy affords them wide discretion. The actions they take, and how they treat migrants, depend more on the personal style of the delegates and the interpretation of their powers than on a centrally agreed migration management and policy. For this reason their performance and standards vary widely with the jurisdiction. As of March 14, 2013, the INM had a total of 5,875 authorized posts (Wolf, 2013), although, depending on the results of purges and recruitment drives, not all of them are necessarily occupied.

The institute's most serious structural problems are fourfold. In the absence of a professional migration career service, staff selection, recruitment, and appointment are more often based on cronyism and nepotism than on merit. Training is limited to short induction and refresher courses, includes instruction in human rights as well as law enforcement and national security, and does not incorporate systematic participant exams and evaluations. A formal oversight system, which would allow rigorous monitoring of the agents' conduct and implementation of procedures, is nonexistent. Indeed, internal audits have confirmed how shortcomings in oversight and internal controls permit such alarming practices as recruitment of unqualified staff, irregularities in migration procedures, misappropriation of funds, and irregularities in the detention centers (Wolf, 2013). Lastly, the INM lacks an effective sanctions system and in cases of suspected misconduct prefers staff to resign, rather than demand investigations and—if necessary—punishments. Corruption and human rights violations tend to remain unpunished and are thus likely to recur, more so considering that the agents earn low pay, face limited career prospects, and experience difficult working conditions, and that their use of force remains unregulated (ibid.).

Migrant Detention Centers: Safe Havens from Danger?

Migration legislation makes irregular entry into Mexico an administrative violation and contemplates alternatives to detention for unaccompanied minors. Even so, undocumented migrants are generally detained in INM-administered centers in order to prevent their escape and onward journey to the United States. The period of detention is limited to 15 days, but it may be extended for up to 60 days if valid identity and travel documents are hard to obtain. In fact, though, it can be prolonged indefinitely, especially when asylum applications or legal proceedings are initiated. The INM's rhetoric implies that unauthorized migrants are rescued from criminal groups and placed in detention facilities to offer them safety, shelter, and sustenance while preparing their expulsion from the country (Sin Fronteras, 2011). The reality in these centers, however, suggests otherwise. Currently, there exist 58 such installations (Wolf, 2013), geographically clustered in the south and center of Mexico, where migration controls are also concentrated. The regional hubs of Tapachula (Chiapas), Acayucan (Veracruz), and Iztapalapa (federal district) aside, most centers have little or no recreational space, may lack an eating area, and—given their reduced installed capacity—are prone to overcrowding, requiring migrants to sleep on the floor.

The INM's national security status is significant insofar as it determines the physical characteristics of the detention centers, constrains their operation, and curbs access to the installations and information about them. Holding cells and penitentiaries must no longer be used for migration detention, and longstanding criticism of its centers has led the INM to modernize their physical structure, technology, and services. The facilities, however, retain prisonlike features, including high walls and gates, security guards and cameras, and disciplinary measures. Dormitories are generally segregated by sex and, space permitting, also include areas for minors, families, and members of vulnerable groups. On the downside, some centers have inhospitable climate conditions or leave the lights on at night, causing sleeping disorders among some migrants (Sin Fronteras, 2013). Sanitary conditions are variable and worsen in moments of overcrowding, especially in the bathrooms. Garbage collection is deficient in some facilities, producing bad smells and risk of infection. Mattresses and bed sheets are often soiled and reeking, and most centers do not provide towels (CDH Fray Matías de Córdova, 2013). Riots and disturbances ranging from verbal confrontations to burning mattresses have occurred repeatedly for reasons such as uncertainty and frustration about the length of detention, migrants' attempts to claim their rights, and some individuals' aggression profile (Wolf, 2013). Several INM centers, especially in the south and southeast of Mexico, have witnessed periodic escapes. The fortified nature of the premises and the high number of runaways, though, suggest that some of these cases were simulated breakouts that occurred with the complicity of migration agents and security guards (ibid.).

The conduct shown toward the migrant detainee population varies by center and agent. In some facilities the agents are generally considered friendly, attentive, and respectful, and in others they are deemed mostly indifferent. Testimonies suggest that many agents exhibit contemptuous, degrading, and discriminatory behavior toward migrants, particularly when migrants inquire about their situation or make legitimate requests (Wolf, 2013). In the larger facilities, agents commit verbal, psychological, or physical aggression, although this abuse usually goes unreported (INSYDE, 2014). INM agents have also been found to display homophobic and transphobic attitudes toward LGBT migrants, confining them in rooms with mentally sick individuals and soliciting sexual favors in exchange for a better diet or expedited procedures (Ureste, 2014). Complaint procedures are inadequate, since the National Human Rights Commission (Comisión Nacional de los Derechos Humanos, CNDH) conducts only infrequent visits and shows little interest in documenting migrants' grievances (Sin Fronteras, 2013).

Due process infringements are perhaps the most common human rights violation in INM detention centers. Migrants are generally not informed about the estimated length of detention and their rights (including access to legal counsel and consular authorities), and professional interpreter services are unavailable (Wolf, 2013). Access to telephone communication is difficult, as migrants are required to purchase prepaid calling cards but often lack the necessary resources, or is discouraged—as with consular access, medical care, or a change in diet—under threat of extended detention time (INSYDE, 2014). The dissuasion of procedures of any kind—*amparo*, asylum applications, criminal and human rights complaints—under the same warning (Sin Fronteras, 2007) is particularly serious, as it may result in undue hardship and the impunity of ill treatment.

Food standards and quantities vary by center (CDH Fray Matías de Córdova, 2013), and the hot water supply is inconsistent (Sin Fronteras, 2013). Personal hygiene kits are often insufficient or incomplete, requiring migrants to use washing powder as a soap substitute and risk dermatological irritations (CDH Fray Matías de Córdova, 2009; Wolf, 2013). More important, the initial and compulsory medical check-up is conducted unsystematically and superficially (Sin Fronteras, 2013; Wolf, 2013). INM centers offer no 24-hour on-site medical service and often no psychological and psychiatric support for migrants who underwent traumatic experiences at home or in transit or tried to commit suicide in detention (INSYDE, 2014; CDH Fray Matías de Córdova, 2009). Individuals requiring specialized medical attention, for example for hypertension, diabetes, epilepsy, heart problems or tumors, often fail to receive it when prescribed by a doctor (INSYDE, 2014). The stock of medicaments is mostly large and varied, but their available quantity may be limited and doctors are not necessarily available to hand them out to patients (Wolf, 2013). Finally, the detention facilities have become notorious for illicit activities. For example, INM agents often overcharge migrants for phone cards or other items and may collect money transfers, possibly withholding some of the cash from unsuspecting foreigners (INSYDE, 2014; Wolf, 2013). In the largest centers, agents have been found to sell, or permit the sale of, alcohol and drugs (INSYDE, 2014; Sin Fronteras, 2011; Wolf, 2013) and to extort migrants in return for final exit permits (Wolf, 2013).

Convenient Scapegoats: Migrants in the Mexican Criminal Justice System

Mexico's criminal justice system has long been infamous for its corruption, lack of professional investigative capacity, and production of culprits through arrest, prosecution, and incarceration of innocent citizens on trumped-up charges and forced confessions. Under authoritarian rule, the legal apparatus was designed to contain social dissent and subversive threats, rather than controlling what were low crime rates. With the transition to democracy, the justice system retained the institutional routines and flawed procedures that traditionally characterized it (Magaloni, 2012). Arbitrary detentions persist, as do prolonged pre-charge detention, failure to inform defendants of their basic rights, and reliance on defendant and witness testimony, often obtained under torture. These practices tend to go unchecked in the judicial process, because the generalized corruption and mistrust with which they are viewed induces judges to issue blanket convictions—even when presented with doubtful evidence—as proof of their incorruptibility (ibid.). Crime and violence have spiraled with the drug war, yet the justice system remains unable to apprehend and successfully prosecute the real perpetrators, and the Mexican state sees itself compelled to put on a charade of justice. Often this entails torture and false imprisonment, and those most vulnerable to such vindictive behavior are marginalized individuals, including indigenous persons and undocumented migrants.

During Mexico's "dirty war" (1964–1982), torture was widely used against suspected political opponents and guerrillas. Today, torture by police and the military remains widespread and indeed increased a staggering 600 percent between 2003 and 2013 (Amnesty International, 2014), particularly since the beginning of the drug war in 2006. The country has made extensive legal commitments to prevent and punish torture, but these have yet to translate into effective safeguards that would shield people from arbitrary detention and ill treatment. Torture, commonly in the form of beating, water boarding, electric shock, mock execution, and stress positions, is often applied to compel a confession and frame individuals for crimes they did not commit (ibid.). The victims are generally members of vulnerable groups and therefore not at all likely to report the abuse.

The odyssey of undocumented Central American migrants, including that of the Honduran human rights defender Ángel Amílcar Colón, is instructive in this respect.

Foreigners apprehended for irregular entry into Mexico are sent to INM-administered centers reserved for this purpose. However, an important number of (mostly undocumented) migrants are held in state or federal prisons. Although it is unclear how many of them may be unlawfully detained, their situation would be especially alarming given their unfamiliarity with the justice system, difficulties in obtaining consular assistance and legal counsel, and lack of social support in the country. A pioneering study conducted by the human rights NGO Miguel Agustín Pro Juárez sheds some light on the numbers and characteristics of migrants confined in Mexican penitentiaries. According to official statistics, as of October 2013 a total of 1,219 Central Americans—accused or convicted—were in prison, 972 in state prisons and 247 in federal facilities (González Núñez, 2014). The vast majority are male; hail from Guatemala, Honduras, or El Salvador; and at the state level are between 18 and 30 years old (ibid.). Nonetheless, figures on imprisoned migrants vary inexplicably by government agency. The starkest difference concerns Chiapas, where the state security secretariat reported 525 Central Americans in jail, whereas the INM Federal Delegation counted zero (ibid.). The data—available only at the state level—indicate that migrants were mostly accused, often of more than one charge, of theft, homicide, sex crimes, drug-related crimes, firearms offenses, organized crime, migration-related offenses, or human trafficking (ibid.).

Although the subject requires further research, the existing information points to some preliminary patterns and hypotheses. The first indicates that the state prisons with the highest number of Central American migrants are located along migration routes. For example, 54.2 percent of migrant detainees at the state level are held in Chiapas (González Núñez, 2014). The second suggests that the authorities arrest undocumented migrants to pass them off as the perpetrators of unsolved cases and to boost the crime clearance rate. For instance, Quintana Roo state, situated on the Yucatán Peninsula and one of Mexico's premier tourist destinations, has a history of child sex abuse. Central American migrants imprisoned in that part of the country are typically charged with sex crimes (ibid.). Migrant shelters and NGOs have discovered at least 30 cases of migrants who were wrongfully detained, denied adequate legal defense, and (some after torture) incriminated for homicide, drug-related charges, organized crime, or possession of military-grade weapons (ibid.).

The story of Ángel Amílcar Colón illustrates not only the travails of an undocumented migrant, but also the workings of the migrant industry and the failings of the Mexican criminal justice system. Colón, a human rights activist of the Afro-descendent Garifuna community, left his native Honduras in January 2009 to find work in the United States and be able to support his family and pay for his son's cancer treatment. Having been abandoned by his *coyote* (migrant smuggler) in southeastern Mexico, he traveled by himself to Tijuana. A stranger offered to help him cross the border and took him to a safe house, where—unbeknownst to Colón—weapons and drugs were stashed. In March 2009, police raided the residence, arresting the Honduran and ten others. At a military base, Colón suffered racial humiliation and torture before signing a forced confession for a series of federal crimes (González Núñez, 2014). The public defender assigned to him challenged neither the ill treatment nor the validity of the statement. Colón, whose critically ill son died in September 2009, was taken to federal prison, where he would spend more than five years in unlawful detention. Thanks to pro bono legal counsel and a high-profile campaign by Amnesty International, the Garifuna activist was released on insufficient evidence in October 2014. Colón has since returned to Honduras, but through his lawyers he is suing the Mexican state for damages.

Conclusions

Undocumented, mostly Central American, migrants transiting Mexico en route to the United States experience serious and systematic human rights violations. In addition to the crimes and aggressions they suffer along roads and railways, some of them are also subjected to arbitrary arrest and torture in the criminal justice system. Confinement in INM-administered facilities appears designed—through inadequate temperature and lightening conditions—to cause discomfort and discourage individuals from repeating their clandestine journey. More specifically, migration detention is characterized by due process violations, inferior sanitary conditions, and deficient medical and psychological assistance. Adults and minors alike receive indifferent treatment, if not verbal and physical abuse, by INM agents who are underpaid, poorly trained, and evaluated; lack use-of-force regulations; work with insufficient oversight; and face ineffective sanctions for misconduct. Improvements are needed in critical areas such as medical services, respect for due process, and screening of potential asylum seekers or crime victims.

Automatic detention of irregular migrants constitutes a disproportionate measure for an administrative violation. Unnecessary and harmful confinement can be prevented through a case management approach, which would see individuals assessed for vulnerabilities and needs, placed in a community while their migration status is being resolved, and monitored to ensure they remain in migration proceedings (IDC, 2011). Alternatives to detention are challenging to implement in a transit country that borders the United States and—for political, diplomatic, and economic reasons—hesitates to incur the wrath of its powerful neighbor. But Mexico could begin by applying such alternatives to persons in situations of vulnerability, such as unaccompanied minors, pregnant women, elderly migrants, crime victims, and asylum seekers. A comprehensive reform of Mexico's National Migration Institute would go a long way toward achieving significant advances in protection and detention of unauthorized migrants. Nevertheless, for these improvements to be more far-reaching, the United States will need to change the way it addresses migration-motivating factors, views security threats, and conducts border enforcement.

References

Amnesty International. (2012). *Transforming pain into hope: Human rights defenders in the Americas.* London, UK: Author.

Amnesty International. (2014). *Out of control: Torture and other ill treatment in Mexico.* London: Author.

Camargo, A. 2014. *Arrancados de raíz. Causas que originan el desplazamiento transfronterizo de niños, niñas y adolescentes no acompañados y/o separados de Centroamérica y su necesidad de protección internacional.* Mexico City: Alto Comisionado de las Naciones Unidas para los Refugiados.

CDH (Centro de Derechos Humanos) Fray Matías de Córdova. (2009). *Informe sobre derechos humanos y condiciones de detención en la Estación Migratoria Siglo XXI. Tapachula, Chiapas, México.* Tapachula: Author.

CDH (Centro de Derechos Humanos) Fray Matías de Córdova. (2013). *Segundo informe sobre derechos humanos y condiciones de vida de las personas migrantes en el centro de detención de la Ciudad de Tapachula, Chiapas.* Tapachula: Author.

CIDH (Comisión Interamericana de Derechos Humanos). (2013). *Derechos humanos de los migrantes y otras personas en el contexto de la movilidad humana.* Washington, DC: Organización de los Estados Americanos.

González Núñez, D. (2014). *Migrantes en prisión. La incriminación de migrantes en México.* Mexico City: Centro de Derechos Humanos Miguel Agustín Pro Juárez.

HRW (Human Rights Watch). (2009). *"Not worth a penny": Human rights abuses against transgender people in Honduras.* Washington, DC: Author.

IACHR (Inter-American Commission on Human Rights). (2011). *Second report on the situation of human rights defenders in the Americas.* Washington, DC: Organization of American States.

IDC (International Detention Coalition). (2011). *There are alternatives: A handbook for preventing unnecessary immigration detention.* Melbourne: Author.

IHRLC (International Human Rights Law Clinic). (2012). *Sexual diversity in El Salvador: A report on the human rights situation of the LGBT community.* Berkeley: University of California Press.

INSYDE (Instituto para la Seguridad y la Democracia). (2014). *Informe sobre estaciones migratorias del Instituto Nacional de Migración 2013: Iztapalapa, Puebla y Saltillo.* Mexico City: Author.

Isacson, A., & Meyer, M. (2012). *Beyond the border buildup: Security and migrants along the U.S.-Mexico border.* Washington, DC: Washington Office on Latin America.

Isacson, A., Meyer, M., & Morales, G. (2014). *Mexico's other border: Security, migration, and the humanitarian crisis at the line with Central America.* Washington, DC: Washington Office on Latin America.

Kennedy, E. (2014). *No childhood here: Why Central American children are fleeing their homes.* Washington, DC: American Immigration Council.

Magaloni, A. L. (2012). Arbitrariness and inefficiency in the Mexican criminal justice system. In P. Kenny, M. Serrano, & A. Sotomayor (Eds.), *Mexico's security failure: Collapse into criminal violence* (pp. 89–106). New York & London: Routledge.

Martínez, Ó. (2010). *Los migrantes que no importan.* Barcelona: Icaria Editorial.

Miller, T. (2014, Oct. 4). Mexico: The U.S. Border Patrol's newest hire. *Al Jazeera America*. Retrieved from http://america.aljazeera.com/opinions/2014/10/mexico-us-borderpatrolsecurity immigrants.html.

Moreno, R. (2012, Sep. 17). CAFTA-DR a seis años de vigencia en El Salvador. *ALAI, América Latina en Movimiento*. Retrieved from http://alainet.org/active/58008.

Ribando Seelke, C., & Finklea, K. M. 2013. *U.S.-Mexican security cooperation: The Mérida Initiative and beyond*. Washington, DC: Congressional Research Service.

Ruhl, J. M. (2012). Post-coup Honduras: The limits of stabilization. *Security and Defense Studies Review, 13*, 33–47.

Secretaría de Gobernación (SEGOB). (2012). Acuerdo por el que se emiten las Normas para el funcionamiento de las Estaciones Migratorias y Estancias Provisionales del Instituto Nacional de Migración. Published in the *Diario Oficial de la Federación* on Nov. 8.

Sin Fronteras. (2007). *Situación de los derechos humanos de la población migrante en las estaciones migratorias de la Ciudad de México y de Tapachula, Chiapas, 2005–2006*. Mexico City: Author.

Sin Fronteras. (2011). *Perspectiva jurídica y social de la detención de migrantes en Iztapalapa, Distrito Federal y Tenosique, Tabasco*. Mexico City: Author.

Sin Fronteras. (2013). *"Ser migrante no me hace delincuente." Situación de las personas en detención en las estaciones migratorias de Iztapalapa, Distrito Federal, Tenosique y Villahermosa, Tabasco 2011–2012*. Mexico City: Author.

Ureste, M. (2014, May 30). El calvario de un homosexual en una estación migratoria. *Animal Político*. Retrieved from http://www.animalpolitico.com/2014/05/asi-es-el-calvario-de-una-persona-homosexual-en-una-estacion-migratoria/.

Valencia. R. (2011, July 24). Yo violada. *El Faro*. Retrieved from http://www.salanegra.elfaro.net/es/201107/cronicas/4922/.

Valencia Caravantes, D. (2014, Aug. 17). La región de los que huyen. *El Faro*. Retrieved from http://www.salanegra.elfaro.net/es/201408/cronicas/15827/La-región-de-los-que-huyen.htm.

WOLA (Washington Office on Latin America). (2009). *DR-CAFTA and workers' rights: Moving from paper to practice*. Washington, DC: Author.

Wolf, S. (Coord.). (2013). *Diagnóstico del Instituto Nacional de Migración: Hacia un sistema de rendición de cuentas en pro de los derechos de las personas migrantes en México*. Mexico City: INSYDE.

Woodhouse, M. (2013, Jan. 1). Reluctant migration: The vicious cycle of debt, deportation and flawed policy that drives Central Americans over the border again and again. *Truthout*. Retrieved from http://truth-out.org/news/item/13596-reluctant-migration-the-vicious-cycle-of-debt-deportation-and-flawed-policy-that-drives-central-americans-over-the-border-again-and-again.

7

Immigration Detention in Greece and the UK

MARY BOSWORTH AND ANDRIANI FILI

Immigration control has always been a key site and means of nation building. As nation states grow unable to prevent unauthorized arrivals under conditions of mass mobility, immigration control has also become a new avenue for the expansion of penal power. Although climate change, conflict, and economic insecurity force more and more people from the global south to move in search of security and opportunity, northern states such as Britain and Greece are ever more determined to deny them entrance, securitizing the border, instituting strict visa regimes and building an ever greater number of custodial centers in which to hold them. Even those fleeing war or persecution are unwelcome, notwithstanding international protections for refugees.

In all, 165,000 people crossed the Mediterranean from Africa in 2014 compared to 60,000 in 2013. Estimates suggest that between July and October 2014, nearly half of the new arrivals were asylum seekers from Syria and Eritrea. Running alongside these arrivals, statistics tell us that, over the past six years, member states of the European Union have removed 1.3 million noncitizens from their territories and issued more than 3 million deportation orders (Eurostat, 2014). In both of these moments—of arrival and departure—member states are relying heavily on immigration detention centers.

In this chapter we explore conditions and experiences of detention in just two countries: the United Kingdom and Greece. Drawing on fieldwork in a number of detention sites in the two countries, we lay out the primary characteristics of each system and describe the challenges and experiences of staff and detainees in them (for more details see also Bosworth, 2012, 2014; Bosworth, Pickering, & Fili, 2015; Fili, 2013). We hope to contribute to the burgeoning academic field of study on detention, analyzing the immigration detention regimes in terms of their allegedly deterrent nature and their incongruous internal character. In so doing, we outline the need for more empirical analysis of life in immigration detention with a view to understanding the internal dynamics that condition how detention is experienced and managed in these two countries.

Greece and the UK in Fortress Europe

To understand the context within which migration management and detention policies have developed in the two countries, we need to create a framework for comparing them. Despite obvious differences inherent in their geographical location, in which Greece is an entry point and the UK a destination, the detention systems share some key main features, notably the range and variety of their populations and their reliance on arbitrary lengths of detention. Both seek to force immigrants out of the country and to deter prospective arrivals.

Greece is a main entry point for irregular migration to the European Union. Despite constructing a widely advertised 13.5 km fence across the land border with Turkey in the Evros region, which would allegedly stem the flow, Greece is currently under a similar migratory strain as it was before the fence went up, if not more so. The route, though, has shifted. According to UNHCR, in 2014 new arrivals through Greece's sea borders with Turkey increased by 223 percent, with around 8,000 people making the crossing in September 2014 alone.

In response to local and transnational politics, Greece has turned to detention as a key means of managing its border and its internal population of foreign nationals. Reflecting in part the scale of the issue, there is little official clarity as to how many people are actually detained. So it is also difficult to demarcate the detention "estate." According to the director of the Aliens Division of the Ministry of Public Order, there are nine dedicated detention facilities, most former military sites, with a total capacity of around 5,000 men, women, and children. Yet in reality, the resourceful Hellenic Police employ at least 18 more sites, ranging from border guard posts to police stations throughout the Greek territory (Global Detention Project, 2014). Since the economic crisis of 2008, funds have poured in from the European Union to build up Greece's capacity at the border, leading to a significant expansion of the detention system.

In Greece, detainees are most commonly new arrivals, caught at the border. As an entry point to Europe, Greece is particularly vulnerable to shifts in migration flows elsewhere. Consequently, its detained population currently includes an expanding sum of Syrian refugees fleeing the horrors of their protracted civil war. Police are required to arrest and hold all new arrivals for processing. This power extends to those claiming asylum, victims of torture and human trafficking, disabled persons, pregnant women, and minors, despite provisions in Greek law dictating that these categories are only to be detained as a measure of last resort. Most, should be siphoned to so-called reception centers for their case to be considered. However, because of the limited capacity of these centers and the well-documented obstacles to asylum requests, people often remain detained for a prolonged period. Men still make up the majority of those confined, but there is also a significant number of women.

In Greece, the maximum length of detention has been altered a number of times. From 3 months before 2009, it was increased that year to 6 months. By 2012 the government had lengthened the period again, to 18 months. Recently, the Greek Legal Council issued an advisory opinion (no. 44/2014), allowing the police to extend the length of detention beyond 18 months and prolonging detention indefinitely if they were considered to be noncompliant with their removal proceedings. The duration of detention is now subject to the discretion of higher-ranking police officers.

New dedicated detention centers, built as part of "Operation Xenios Zeus," are referred to as "closed hospitality centers" (Dalakoglou, 2013). Yet, as a number of legal rulings and NGO reports have made quite clear, many of the Greek facilities fail to meet basic standards of care. The dominant factors that define this form of confinement are fundamental: arbitrariness, sheer overcrowding, and poor conditions. For those who have often traveled great distances and already suffered severe privation, these conditions (those enduring them report) are a "living hell." Few of those who arrive in Greece wish to stay. Most hope merely to pass through, en route to greater economic opportunities, friends, and relatives in Northern Europe. Reflecting both its colonial past and the abiding influence of the English language in the contemporary world, Britain is a key destination for many. Yet because of its physical location and its immigration policies, it has become very difficult to access the UK legally. Whereas the Greek government tends to use detention as a method of managing new arrivals, immigration detention centers in Britain are primarily filled with foreigners who have been resident in the nation's territory. Some have lived in the UK for quite some time. Few are held at the point of entry. Unlike with Greece, basic descriptive statistics are readily available.

On any given day in the UK, around 3,000 men and women are held in one of eleven "immigration removal centers" (IRCs). They are joined by an additional 1,000 in prison and an unreported number in police cells, hospitals, and reporting centers. Just over 100 can be found in short-term holding facilities at major ports and airports in the UK and across the Channel on the north coast of France, while children may be held as part of family groups in the "pre-departure accommodation" institution of Cedars in West Sussex.

In the UK, detainees constitute a varied population, united primarily by their lack of British citizenship. Some are former prisoners, others have been working without a visa, and still others have broken the terms of their visa. Although, in principle, they should all have reached the end of their immigration case and be facing imminent removal or deportation, in practice many continue to appeal their asylum decisions, and seek other means of redress. Reflecting Britain's historical colonial role, most of those in detention are from the Commonwealth, drawn to Britain by family or cultural ties. In addition to these people, a significant number hail from current or recent war zones, and there are always some from the edges of Europe. Men make up around 90 percent of this population. Since 2010, when the UK pledged to stop detaining children, detainees should all be over 18. Nonetheless, a small number of children continued to be detained as part of family groups in another pre-departure accommodation, near Gatwick airport.

Unlike with the rest of Europe, there is no statutory upper limit in Britain on how long someone can be detained. Statistics indicate that the majority are held for less than three months, but all the centers house individuals who have been in the system for more than six months and some even for years. Such uncertainty in the duration of detention is difficult for many to bear. The following sections investigate what kind of external control policies, which touch on their differing interests in entry and receiving points, the two countries have implemented to control their borders and how these sets of policies have been challenged from the inside.

Coping with Uncertainty: Immigration Detention in Britain

The uncertain nature of immigration detention in the UK permeates all aspects of confinement, affecting daily routines, relationships, and people's interpretation of the aims and justifications of these sites. It is not just detainees who struggle to understand these places, but also staff, who at all levels reveal confusion and some level of concern about them. In their testimonies, we start to gather a sense of the challenges of daily life in these institutions, raising profound questions about the legitimacy of this form of state practice (Bosworth, 2013).

By definition, those who are in detention have been identified first of all as foreign nationals and second as without a right to remain. Whereas the Home Office views such matters as purely legal, for those subject to this form of confinement identification is highly affective, touching on a person's sense of self. IRCs, in other words, considered in official terms as sites of identification and administration, for detainees and staff feel like places where identity is forcibly renegotiated. For many, this experience is painful. Originally from Nigeria, but resident in the UK for 15 years, Hali complained that she no longer knew who she was, nor where she belonged: "I don't know who I am!" she wailed. "I'm just someone in detention. I don't feel myself. I don't know who I am anymore" (Nigeria, at Yarl's Wood). Confined and awaiting deportation, her years in the UK had been stripped away, leaving her unable to support her legal claim to remain and thus rendering it meaningless. Under these circumstances, her past and future were cast adrift, leaving her wondering who she was.

Most feel the stigma of the "detainee" label keenly, aware that if they are to avert deportation or removal, they must convince the Home Office that their identification is incorrect. They also worry about its impact on how they will be received in their country of birth, and so many do not tell their family and friends where they are—a decision that forces them to endure their anxieties alone. As a result, many women and men craft alternative subject positions, from which they might not only seek legal remedy (for instance in proving their grounds for asylum), but also desire understanding of their experience. Thus, detainees commonly create a hierarchy in which they emphasize their hardworking past, their familial ties, their law-abiding nature. Such claims to an equivalent form of citizenship, though usually ineffective in a court of law, act as powerful bulwark against their sense of rejection (Bosworth, 2012, 2014; Isin & Nielsen, 2008).

It is not just detainees who are unsure of how to present themselves; staff members too are often unclear about what a "detention custody officer" is, or should be. Many turn to detention work, after insecure employment in other sectors. "Last year was a bad year for me," Gordon recalled, "because I had a few jobs, and being over 50 it was rather difficult to get work" (Detention Custody Office, Campsfield House). A few saw custodial work as a stepping stone for more interesting opportunities.

> My main goal was to be a police officer. Obviously they're not recruiting and stuff like that at the moment, so I thought I'd come, come here as a DCO to gain experience and knowledge, that would help me out to become a police officer.
>
> —Rowan, DCO, Brook House

More commonly, these officers made sense of their job in relation to the prison. For some, it was the original frame of understanding.

> I went to the interview completely open-minded. I didn't know what level of care, what level of custody, what level of restriction was placed on detainees when they were in detention. Whether it was like the prisons I'd seen on telly . . . I really had no idea.
>
> —Roddy, detention custody manager or DCM, Brook House

For others, it would be an easier option. "Prison officers have said that we do a tougher job," Ashby boasted (DCO, Tinsley House), citing the complexity of the population and their relative lack of sanctions to control them. IRCs, unlike prisons, do not operate with a formal "adjudication process" in the UK. Detainees considered to be difficult or dangerous can be removed from the mainstream population and placed in segregation, but only for control purposes and not for punishment. Any decision to do so has to be ratified by the onsite Home Office contract manager and can be for only a brief period of time. Those who are unable to obey the rules of an IRC will be held in prison (Bosworth, 2014).

Not quite a prison guard, yet in uniform and carrying keys, officers, like detainees, search around for a vocabulary and a framework for understanding themselves. In making sense of their custodial role, they turn to those whom they guard, differentiating among them both practically and managerially, and also in an affective explanatory fashion according to predictable racialized and nationalized categories (Bosworth & Kellezi, 2014; Hall, 2010, 2012). Differences in detention are how people make sense of one another.

> Nationalities do tend to stick together. For instance Chinese and Jamaicans . . . you've also got religions as well though . . . Muslims, some people don't like Muslims in the room because they wash their feet in the sink, they do this. And so it's, they see that as unclean, so again there's an understanding, yes we're all grownups, we all need to get along, and people have got to live together. But if you were at home, you wouldn't want to necessarily have that. So again you take that into account, so you put two Muslims in a room together, ideally.
>
> —Ronny, DCO, Brook House

Most detainees struggle with the open-ended nature of their time in detention. Unsure whether or when they will be released or removed, they find it hard to act and fill their days. Some find solace in a timetable; others attempt to sleep away their days. "I don't think about outside," Karieme pronounced firmly. "I just fill time coming to class. English and computers" (Sudan, Campsfield House). Fearful of being returned to Sudan, he managed his uncertainty by trying not to think about it.

Staff frequently complained about the unclear nature of the duration of detention. Some criticized it for the unsettling effect on those in their care, others for the challenges it posed to maintaining order and security. On a pragmatic level, it was difficult to devise a clear timetable of events when nobody knows how long anyone will remain. All centers offer some activities as well as some paid work, but much of it is quite informal. Staff members often do their best with limited resources, yet for the most part, events and opportunities in detention are few and restricted in their range. Thus, even though in each center a core group take advantage of all that is on offer, the majority stay in their rooms watching television and talking to a small group of fellow nationals.

Time and identity are key ordering mechanisms for how we make sense of ourselves and others as well as how we navigate our daily life. In detention, where both issues are unclear, it becomes apparent that the purpose and nature of these places is also contested. Unsure about whom they were guarding, staff wondered what their job was actually about. For some, such questions raised other, more uncomfortable ones about the legitimacy of detention. "To be honest, I wouldn't want to be stuck, stuck in here," Amonn admitted (DCO, Tinsley House). His colleague Alisa agreed: "I don't think personally that anyone detained should have to live in wings [like in a prison] . . . because they've only broke the law of paperwork, haven't they, really"? (DCO, Tinsley House)

Some were more uncomfortable still. Although detention custody officers do not personally enforce removal, unless they have taken on extra work in their time off to do so, they are required to hand over individuals from detention to the overseas escort firm. Rebecca explained:

> We've got to go and use force on somebody, you're potentially forcing somebody into a situation where they're going to be taken back and tortured, killed, whatever. And I'm not suggesting that happens every time, but there have been occasions where you think "Is it right, what I'm doing?" Moral, you know?
>
> —DCM, Brook House

In any case, Arvil pointed out, in a fairly paternalistic fashion, immigration is really just an accident of birth.

> Well, I mean (pause) rules are rules but I forget about them, you know. If . . . . if you're born, if somebody's born in the wrong place at the wrong time, yeah, for the grace of God go I, you know what I'm saying. If I was born, if I was born in a shithole in Lagos, I'd wanna get out of it 'cos I've been there.
>
> —DCO, Tinsley House

To be sure, not all staff members are concerned about such matters (see, e.g., Hall, 2010), and there are powerful bureaucratic measures in place to preclude too many questions (Bosworth, 2014). The sheer turnover of the population makes it difficult for many to make the kinds of emotional attachments with detainees that generated such uncertainty. Nonetheless, and in stark contrast to the reductive political message that is often communicated about IRCs, the ambivalence of some staff and the critique of most detainees suggest that such institutions are by no means assured and could, if the political will were there, be imagined and run quite differently.

Bare Life? Detainees and Staff in Greek Detention Centers

The story is far less optimistic in Greece. Over the years, migration there has reached crisis proportions. Migration-related developments such as the Greek-Turkish border emergency, a collapsed asylum system, and a de facto ghettoization of certain areas of downtown Athens have been taking place in, and been exacerbated by, an acute economic crisis and a concomitant rise of far-right political racism (Triantafyllidou & Ambrosini, 2011). Human rights organizations routinely castigate Greece for its treatment of irregular migrants and asylum seekers in detention (CPT, 2012; Human Rights Watch, 2013; Amnesty International, 2010, 2012; Médecins Sans Frontières, 2014) at the same time as European Union member states blame Greek authorities for the excessive permeability of its borders and demand the enforcement of ever-tighter border control.

In response to such international pressures and criticisms, there have been significant improvements in the asylum procedure. Notwithstanding positive steps, Greek immigration policy has moved backward rather than forward, erasing good practices with disparaging, yet conspicuously stagnant, detention conditions and policies. For many years now, a snapshot of any detention center at a given time would show overcrowding so high that often detainees have to sleep in shifts. At the most extreme overcrowding conditions, men, women, and children are held together. Lack of ventilation, limited sanitation, and poor hygiene are but some of the serious deficiencies the Greek immigration detention system is facing. Furthermore, outdoor access and medical provision have been found to be a rare occurrence, while maltreatment by detention officers abounds (Amnesty International, 2010, 2012; Fili, 2013; Human Rights Watch, 2011; Médecins Sans Frontières, 2014; Pro Asyl, 2012).

The idea behind such conditions is straightforward: immigration is seen as a phenomenon that can be eradicated. The task is to deter. "We have to make their lives miserable, otherwise they will be under the impression that coming to Greece they will be free to do what they want," the head of the Hellenic Police advised his officers. In this view—unsubstantiated by any research evidence and willfully ignorant of the kinds of factors propelling people to move in the first place—faced with the prospect of a prolonged stay inside a Greek detention center under deplorable conditions, irregular migrants will decide to return to their home countries and possibly discourage new arrivals. The size of the migrant population will gradually shrink, its proponents believe, and Greece will have largely addressed irregular arrivals (Triantafyllidou et al., 2014). This simplistic view of deterrence places the safeguarding of Greece's borders over any consideration of human rights; the inevitable result is a capricious, unpredictable, and reactive system with significant collateral damage for individual lives.

Deterrence is not the only narrative circulating around detention in Greece. There too, racialized ideas are legion (Bosworth et al., 2014). According to Nikos Dendias, former minister of public protection, for example, "The migrant from the ex-Soviet Union that goes to Sweden has some kind of level. Greece gets migrants from Bangladesh, Afghanistan, who have a different culture; they belong to a different world. That's our misfortune." In this kind of political discourse, an additional argument slips in, about EU burden sharing. Such populist accounts both appease and enflame the native citizens, building consensus against "lower quality" immigrants. In the process, detention practices become "untouchable."

One cannot but note a sharp contrast between the amount of resources and political emphasis given to building detention strategies in Greece, which criminalize irregular entry and residence, and the lesser emphasis placed on how detention practices are actually implemented. Humanitarian NGOs, political parties, and media outlets on the left express their concern about what is going on behind iron doors; however, they cannot reach beyond their own circles, which do not have any political capital all the same. Though tolerance and consensus is carefully built on the outside, on the inside anger and desperation are growing.

The effects of inhumane treatment and the uncertainty over their future are not lost on immigrants and refugees detained throughout Greece. In remote places, behind wire and under constant surveillance, forms of resistance flourish. In some instances it is spontaneous, triggered by an incident of violence; in others it is organized in advance. Detainees often engage in hunger strikes. Others issue statements, with the support of human rights organizations, against current practices. In other places, detainees initiated a mutiny by setting mattresses on fire. "They treat us like animals here. We may be immigrants but we are humans with human rights, no?" a young man from Eritrea cried, reiterating most detainees' claims to humanity (Attica Aliens Police Directorate at Petrou Ralli).

There is no doubt that detention practices in Greece seek to and often succeed in producing a bare life. However, as Bailey (2009) highlights in his work on resistance in Australian camps, these claims to humanity should not be seen as just a cry for more dignity, but as a stubborn declaration: those within will not be reduced to bare life. Thus, detainees at the infamous Corinth pre-removal detention center, one of Greece's largest detention sites, commenced a hunger strike in protest against a ministerial order that effectively allows authorities to prolong their incarceration indefinitely: "With the systematic and open end detention the Greek government is massacring us. . . . Today on 9.6.2014 we people detained in the detention center of Corinth have started a hunger strike. We feel an immense pressure due to our unknown destinies."

Such aspects of detention rarely attract the public eye and when they do, are all too often dismissed as manipulative behavior. Detention officers in particular find such criticism difficult to stomach. Some go so far as to attribute poor conditions to the rebellious nature of immigrant detainees. "You know, they are smashing chairs now and afterwards they are going to complain about the lack of furniture," a detention officer commented cynically at the Amygdaleza closed hospitality center during an uprising of Pakistani detainees.

However, as in the UK, some are concerned about the legitimacy of the institution. In 2013 a local court in Igoumenitsa dismissed criminal charges against 15 migrants who had escaped from long-term detention in police cells. As the judge ruled, it was a reasonable act of escaping from humiliation and life-threatening conditions to freedom. The absolute state of necessity most detainees find themselves in is not lost on detention officers either. "Do you think we like it here?" Andreas at the airport detention facility demanded angrily. "The government puts all these people in here and we suffer too . . . we are not their servants here. They cannot go to the toilet whenever they want. They are too many, so we will take them only when we can." Severe overcrowding combined with major pay cuts in the armed forces have contributed to a growing level of dissatisfaction among officers, leading some to agree with human rights organizations that detention centers are much worse than prisons.

Conclusion: What Is to Be Done?

In both Greece and the UK, detention practices raise a series of profound normative questions. Indeed, these sites are regularly disputed by staff, detainees, and NGOs and national and international agencies, committed to the end, or at least significant reform, of such places. There is also a growing body of critical academic literature, to which this collection contributes. And yet, whether or not detention is seen as productive and necessary or unproductive and harmful, its position, in both Greece and the UK, seems hard to challenge (Bosworth, 2013). Rather, countries that can invest in detention will continue to do so, at least for the foreseeable future.

Under these circumstances, scholarly work may feel somewhat self-indulgent. Yet politics and reform must be based on understanding, and it is one of the privileges of academic life that research can unfold slowly, over time and across a number of sites, developing insights and testing ideas as it goes. Drawing on ethnographic research in immigration detention centers in two European member states, this chapter has contributed to the nascent body of applied research in this field. Setting out the uncertainties and pains of the two systems, we have sought both to unveil some aspects of life within and to move the discussion forward as to what can be done.

One of the most unsettling aspects of research in this field is the unwieldy nature of the problem. It exists at more than one site, both because it is inherent in the institutions and it reflects entrenched global inequalities. It is difficult to see how matters can improve in one site, for example in Greece, without the peaceful resolution of hostilities in sending countries. Likewise, both states reflect, contribute, and are simultaneously restrained by EU law and policy, and by the broader economic crisis. Although it is tempting to respond to such matters by giving up, an alternative view is to recognize them as multiple sites for action and understanding. Academic research in British removal centers or in the "hospitality centers" of Greece cannot solve the kinds of problems that have led to their creation in the first place. But by humanizing those within, and in particular by working with staff and detainees, we can at least open these hidden sites to a public gaze. In so doing, we remind ourselves always of our shared endeavor and intertwined responsibilities. These people have the right to live safely somewhere. If not here, then where?

References

Amnesty International. (2010). *Greece: Irregular migrants and asylum-seekers routinely detained in substandard conditions.* London: Author.

Amnesty International. (2012). *Greece: The end of the road for refugees, asylum-seekers and migrants.* London: Author.

Bailey, R. (2009). Up against the wall: Bare life and resistance in Australian immigration detention. *Law Critique, 20,* 113–132.

Bosworth, M. (2012). Subjectivity and identity in detention: Punishment and society in a Global Age. *Theoretical Criminology, 16*(2), 123–140.

Bosworth, M. (2013). Can immigration detention be legitimate? In K. Aas & M. Bosworth (Eds.), *Migration and punishment: Citizenship, crime control, and social exclusion.* Oxford: Oxford University Press.

Bosworth, M. (2014). *Inside immigration detention.* Oxford: Oxford University Press.

Bosworth, M., & Kellezi, B. (2014). Citizenship and belonging in a women's immigration detention center. In C. Phillips & C. Webster (Eds.), *New directions in race, ethnicity and crime.* Abingdon, UK: Routledge.

Bosworth, M., Pickering, S., & Fili, A. (2015). Women's immigration detention in Greece: Gender, control, and capacity. In M. J. Guia, V. Mitsilegas, and R. Khoulish (Eds.), *Immigration detention, risk and human rights.* (New York: Springer.

CPT. (2012). *Report to the government of Greece on the visit to Greece carried out by the European Committee for the Prevention of Torture and Inhuman or Degrading Treatment of Punishment (CPT) from 19 to 27 January 2011.* Strasbourg, France: Council of Europe.

Dalakoglou, D. (2013). From the bottom of the Aegean Sea to Golden Dawn: Security, xenophobia, and the politics of hate in Greece. *Studies in ethnicity and nationalism, 13*(3), 514–522.

Eurostat (2014). Third country nationals returned following an order to leave—annual data (rounded). Retrieved from http://appsso.eurostat.ec.europa.eu/nui/show.do?dataset=migr_eirtn&lang=en.

Fili, A. (2013). The maze of immigration detention in Greece: A case study of the Athens Airport Detention Facility. *Prison Service Journal, 205,* 34–38.

Global Detention Project (2014). Immigration detention in Greece. Geneva: Izabella Majcher and Michael Flynn.

Hall, A. (2010). These people could be anyone: Fear, contempt (and empathy) in a British immigration removal center. *Journal of Ethnic and Migration Studies, 36*(6), 881–898.

Hall, A. (2012). *Border watch: Cultures of immigration detention and control.* London: Pluto Press.

Human Rights Watch. (2011). *The EU's dirty hands: Frontex involvement in ill-treatment of migrant detainees in Greece.* New York: Author.

Human Rights Watch. (2013). *Turned away: Summary returns of unaccompanied migrant children and adult asylum seekers from Italy to Greece.* New York: Author.

Isin, E. F., & Nielsen, G. M. (Eds.). (2008). *Acts of citizenship.* London: Zed Books.

Médecins Sans Frontières (MSF). (2014). *Invisible suffering: Prolonged and systematic detention of migrants and asylum seekers in substandard conditions in Greece.* Athens: Author.

Pro Asyl. (2012). *Walls of shame: Accounts from the inside—the detention centers of Evros.* Frankfurt/Main: Author.

Triantafyllidou, A., & Ambrosini, M. (2011). Irregular immigration control in Italy and Greece: Strong fencing and weak gate-keeping serving the labor market. *European Journal of Migration and Law, 13,* 251–273.

Triantafyllidou, A., Angeli, D., & Dimitriadi, A. (2014). Detention as punishment: Can indefinite detention be Greece's main policy tool to manage its irregular migrant population? Midas Policy brief. Athens: ELIAMEP.

8

Detaining Asylum Seekers and Refugees in Indonesia

ANTJE MISSBACH

> Conditions in immigration detention centers resemble those in prisons. . . . But asylum seekers and refugees are victims of human rights violations . . . not criminals.
>
> —Komnas HAM, *2012a*

Over the last decade, Indonesia—the world's most populous archipelagic state, consisting of more than 17,000 islands—has become an important transit hub for asylum seekers en route to Australia. Resettlement in Indonesia is not an option for them. Not only is Indonesia not a signatory to the 1951 Refugee Convention and its 1967 Protocol, but, more significantly, it has no domestic legal framework for processing the protection claims of asylum seekers and refugees, which means that many are legally, socially, and economically stranded while they are in Indonesia (Missbach, in press). Nevertheless, political stability, porous borders, and relatively low living costs have made Indonesia an attractive place of transit. Moreover, as the country with the world's largest Muslim population, Indonesia holds some promise of Muslim solidarity in the eyes of asylum seekers who share the same beliefs. Although Indonesia has been rather lenient in controlling its borders and intercepting irregular travelers in the past, since 2009, in response to Australian political pressure, it has directed more attention to stalling the movement of asylum seekers and undocumented migrants by arresting and detaining them.

This chapter seeks not only to highlight what immigration detention means for the detainees kept in Indonesia, but also to point out the political implications that derive from transnationally implemented bordering policies and migration management schemes. Unwilling to accept responsibility for asylum seekers and refugees or dedicate substantial amounts of money to their care, the Indonesian government relies to a great extent on collaboration with the

UN High Commissioner for Refugees and the International Organization for Migration, despite the fact that Indonesia is neither a party to the Geneva Refugee Convention nor a member state of the IOM, in which it holds only observer status. The UNHCR and the IOM are the two international organizations primarily concerned with handling asylum seekers, refugees, and stateless persons in Indonesia and with managing their regular onward migration.

The majority of asylum seekers coming to Indonesia are young men, some of them under the age of 18, from Afghanistan, Iraq, Iran, Sri Lanka, and Somalia. In early 2014, more than 10,567 asylum seekers and refugees were registered with the UNHCR in Indonesia. According to the UNHCR, this number included 7,241 asylum seekers and 3,326 refugees. Asylum seekers of different nationalities choose their own modes of travel and entry points, depending on the exit options from their home country, the accessibility and availability of their travel documents, the visa restrictions on their arrival in Indonesia, and financial considerations.

The majority of asylum seekers travel through Malaysia and Thailand before taking a boat or flight to Indonesia. Those who enter Indonesia with a valid tourist or business visa and proper travel documents enjoy regular visitor status, at least for a short time. Only when they decide to stay longer than their visa permits or to leave Indonesia from somewhere other than an official port of embarkation does their presence become irregular. If they have valid documents, they have more time to register as asylum seekers or organize the next leg of their journey to Australia, more often than not in an unseaworthy fishing boat. Those who enter Indonesia without valid documents face arrest and detention from the minute they enter the archipelago, not least because surveillance operations and arrests by Indonesian law enforcement officers have been intermittently expanded. Most asylum seekers are not arrested when they arrive in Indonesia; they are arrested when they attempt to exit the archipelago (Missbach, 2014). Arrested asylum seekers without valid visas or documents usually face immigration detention. Whereas in the past asylum seekers would do anything to avoid arrest and detention in Indonesia, since late 2013 more and more asylum seekers have surrendered themselves to authorities rather than be captured. Ever since the Australian government implemented Operation Sovereign Borders in September 2013, which has made it nearly impossible for asylum seekers to reach Australia by boat, many of them have gotten stuck in Indonesia and run out of money. Out of despair, they sacrifice their freedom for food and hand themselves over to the Indonesian immigration authorities in order to be detained.

Originally, these immigration detention centers were called *karantina* (quarantine) and, under the old Indonesian Law on Immigration (Law 9/1992, para. 44), they served the sole purpose of temporarily housing foreigners who had been apprehended in Indonesia without valid residence permits or visas or who awaited their expulsion or deportation from Indonesia. Under the new Indonesian Law on Immigration (Law 6/2011, para. 85), those awaiting deportation can be detained for a maximum of 10 years. Even though illegal entry into and exit from Indonesia is not a criminal offense and under Law 6/2011 attracts a sentence of only one year in prison and/or a fine of up to Rp100 million (US$10,000), those arrested may face detention for much longer than one year. Placement in detention centers is supposedly "temporary," but in practice those asylum seekers, refugees, and undocumented migrants who are held in them are treated as criminals. Their incarceration is arbitrary, as they are often detained for an unspecified period of time, without judicial review or bail.

Although the new Law on Immigration does not mention asylum seekers and refugees, Article 86 rules that victims of human trafficking or people smuggling should be treated differently from general offenders against immigration law. Article 87 states that "victims of human trafficking and people smuggling who are in Indonesia should be placed in the immigration detention center or elsewhere specified." The UNHCR in Jakarta has long expressed its concern about the continued use of immigration detention facilities to hold asylum seekers, refugees, and stateless people, including children and others vulnerable to exploitation and abuse (UNHCR, 2014a). Given the limited capacity of the detention centers, most asylum seekers and refugees are allowed to reside in Indonesian communities. This creates a number of its own challenges but is definitely more desirable than detention for those apprehended. Many asylum seekers in Indonesia will, however, have experienced immigration detention at some point in their journey.

Australian Funding for Indonesia's Immigration Detention Regime

Indonesia has 13 immigration detention centers operating across the archipelago with a combined capacity of about 1,300 detainees. These centers are located in Medan, Pekanbaru, Batam, Jakarta, Semarang, Surabaya, Pontianak, Balikpapan, Manado, Makassar, Denpasar, Kupang, and Jayapura. Although immigration detention centers are under the responsibility of the Indonesian Ministry of Justice and Human Rights, a substantial amount of their funding derives from external sources. In particular, costs of refurbishing and extending the detention facilities have been covered by the IOM, which in return receives the main part of its funding from several Australian government agencies. For example, according to the budget estimate hearing of May 21–22, 2012, the Department of Immigration and Citizenship (DIAC) provided AU$2.1 million in order to refurbish immigration detention facilities in Batam, Balikpapan, and Semarang.

Previously, the IOM also covered the costs of renovating and extending the immigration detention centers in Kalideres (Jakarta) and Tanjung Pinang, amounting to more than US$6.5 million. On top of the costs for building, maintaining, and refurbishing these centers, Australian funding, channeled through the IOM, also covers the daily costs of accommodating detainees in immigration detention. Whether they are detained or outside of immigration detention centers, IOM provides them with basic accommodation and medical care. Even though the IOM does not have a mandate to assist asylum seekers and refugees, the Indonesian immigration authorities or the UNHCR refers asylum seekers and refugees to the care of the IOM (Taylor & Rafferty-Brown, 2010).

Endorsed by a tripartite Regional Cooperation Agreement signed in 2001 by the government of Australia, the government of Indonesia, and IOM, the IOM in Indonesia works in rather diverse fields, among them immigration and border management, labor migration, counter trafficking, and migrant care, which includes in particular programs tailored for asylum seekers and even refugees. The IOM, which generally refrains from transparency about its budget and funding, received AU$41.5 million from the Australian Department of Immigration and Border Protection between January 2013 and June 2014. Given that the accommodation of a single asylum seeker in an Australian immigration detention center costs AU$119,000 per person per year and that the costs of running detention centers in Australia for the 2012–13 fiscal year increased to more than AU$1 billion dollars (Merope, 2013), Australian government reliance on Indonesian immigration centers helps it save money. Without such funding incentives, the Indonesian government would be less inclined to incarcerate asylum seekers for the long run within its national territory and thereby prevent their movement into Australia. However, the human costs borne by those who are locked up in Indonesian immigration detention centers indefinitely and under harsh conditions are incalculable.

Similar to many countries in the European Union, in which the IOM has been of the utmost importance during the 1990s in creating stricter policies on asylum and migration, the IOM in Indonesia has also proved to be a leading stakeholder in shaping debates on how to control streams of migration in general and how to manage irregular migrants in particular. As a number of scholars have demonstrated in their research (Andrijasevic & Walters, 2010; Georgi, 2010; Georgi & Schatral, 2012), IOM's agenda for managing migration is driven first and foremost by conceptions of neoliberal governmentality that seek to ease the mobility of highly skilled, young, and healthy mobile populations into Western countries but obstruct the mobility of the unskilled, old, sick, and poor. Given the breadth of engagement in migration issues, a number of conflicting interests emerge, especially when it comes to protecting borders over protecting asylum seekers. Hence, it does not come as a surprise that IOM field staff also provide their clients with counseling, often simply a euphemism for convincing their clients to accept "voluntary" repatriation offers (Nethery, Rafferty-Brown, & Taylor, 2013; Missbach, 2015).

Detaining Asylum Seekers in Indonesia

In February 2014, 1,926 persons (1,327 asylum seekers and 599 refugees), of whom 326 were female and 364 were children (including 100 unaccompanied minors), were held in Indonesian immigration detention centers (UNHCR, 2014a). Despite UNHCR recommendations that families of arrested asylum seekers and refugees should be exempt from detention and housed in monitored community housing schemes, families with children, including unaccompanied minors, continue to be locked up in the centers. The inmates of immigration detention centers are generally segregated by gender. Single adult men, by far the largest cohort of transit migrants, are housed in separate detention blocks from women with children; fathers and older male children are frequently separated from the rest of their family (HRW, 2013). Unaccompanied minors were usually housed in the same blocks as adult men, and are thus exposed to the risk of abuse. In some centers, such as in Kupang, detention facilities have been extended with extra family rooms to accommodate detained families. Because they face the risk of physical and sexual assault from other inmates, families have to stay in small cells, often completely separate from other detainees, who mingle in the yard or in the common rooms.

Although conditions in detention centers have, overall, improved over the last decade, thanks to Australian funding channeled mainly through the IOM, several reports indicate that, in general, conditions in Indonesian detention centers remain poor by Western standards (ibid.; Taylor, 2009; Missbach & Sinanu, 2013). The list of deficiencies and defects in detention centers is long, ranging from overcrowding, low-quality accommodation, poor hygiene standards, lack of medical attention, and insufficient nutrition to corporal punishment, physical abuse, and torture.

This chapter highlights some of the most notable problems within Indonesian immigration detention. Data were collected mainly during 14 months of fieldwork in 2012 and 2013, when I had the chance to visit several detention centers and interview detention staff as well as formerly detained asylum seekers after their release. Because I had relatively good access to the detention centers in Kupang and Tanjung Pinang, I draw illustrations and examples from my experience and observation of those two centers, both of which are very strategically placed. Tanjung Pinang, the largest and most modern immigration detention center, with the capacity to house up to 600 people, is situated on the island of Bintan in the Riau Archipelago, the entry point for many asylum seekers coming to Indonesia from Malaysia. Kupang, located on Timor in eastern

Indonesia, is on one of the two main exit paths for asylum seekers trying to leave Indonesia by boat.

Everyday Hardship in Detention

A common problem in Indonesian immigration detention centers is that they are generally overcrowded, housing many more inmates than they have capacity for. For example, in February 2014, the immigration detention center in Kupang accommodated 134 people even though its capacity is supposedly 90 (Prasetyo, 2014). At times, the center has had to deal with up to 240 inmates. Frequent overcrowding causes many problems ("Indonesia perlu . . . ," 2012). Detaining too many people in confined spaces leads to unrest and frustration and has a negative impact on their overall mental health. Housing detainees in inappropriate conditions such as in cells where sleeping areas are flooded during the monsoon (HRW, 2013) has many other deleterious effects on their health. Widespread deficiencies in hygiene standards and the lack of clean water cause diseases such as gastroenteritis and dermatitis among detainees (Meliala & Perdana, 2011).

Detainees often complain about the bad quality and insufficient quantity of food; for example, detainees found insects, metal, and other items in their food (HRW, 2013). Maintenance and sustenance costs of immigration detention centers as well as staff expenses are covered by the Indonesian central government. Detention centers allocate Rp15,000 (US$1.50) per person per day for food (Kurnia, 2011), an amount that is often insufficient to provide adequate meals, especially in the outer islands, where food is generally more expensive than on Java. To improve nutrition in immigration detention, the IOM has been supplementing this amount by about Rp45,000 (US$4.50) per person per day for food, which means that, in this respect, detainees in immigration detention are better off than ordinary prisoners in Indonesian jails. However, the extra allowance is only extended to asylum seekers and refugees who are registered under UNHCR and not to migrants who are still undocumented or to other detainees, such as "illegal" fishermen, who are also held in immigration detention centers until their deportation. Although detainees are allowed to register with UNHCR while they are in detention, it may be several months until a UNHCR representative comes to the center to conduct the necessary interviews. Given the discrepancy in food provision and other services, those who do not receive the extra allowance often express their envy of those who do and occasional thefts occur (Komnas HAM, 2012b).

Although the total of Rp60,000 (US$6) could be considered sufficient by Indonesian standards to give detainees three decent meals a day, complaints about meals are widespread in detention centers. In a number of centers there are strong suspicions that some of the funds allocated for detainees registered under the

UNHCR are embezzled and misappropriated. Opportunities for abuse of food provision are rife. For example, the detention center in Kupang initially employed a chef to cook Middle Eastern dishes for the detainees, but when a new head of the center was appointed he outsourced provision of meals to a catering company owned by his wife and the quality of food declined. Corrupt officials also enrich themselves by claiming false costs for the inmates of detention centers, thereby overcharging the IOM for its services. According to IOM staff in Kupang, they receive bills from the detention center for drinking water that are so high they estimate every inmate must be drinking an average of 200 liters every day.

The unlimited flow of funds from the IOM has given rise to other forms of embezzlement; for example, exchange of inmates between some detention centers across the archipelago seems to be inexplicably frequent. Because of the regular overcrowding, a head of a detention center can request transfer of inmates to another, less-crowded detention center. However, that same head, after a group of detainees has been transferred, might then be seen to offer allegedly available spaces to other overcrowded detention centers. The IOM fully funds the travel of inmates and their escorts (prison guards or officers from the provincial immigration department), paying all airfares and providing a generous daily allowance. At times irregularities in their travel can be observed, such as the travel of security escorts a day before or after the detainees travel, or their travel on a different airplane.

Entrenchment of a culture of embezzlement, extortion, and self-enrichment among detention center staff causes many problems for the detainees. For example, at the beginning of their stay in detention detainees are given a set of clothes, consisting of a pair of trousers, t-shirts, socks, and a pair of shoes; and once a month the IOM provides them with shampoo, detergent, toothpaste, soap, toothbrush, sugar, and tea. According to former inmates, these services often arrived late and sometimes not until complaints had been made to the central IOM office in Jakarta. Detainees also complained that guards expected to be handed over a share of the goods furnished by the IOM. If detainees have not already lost their belongings to the police during their initial arrest, they are exposed to confiscation of their mobile phones, money, and other valuables in detention centers, which, according to former detainees, are rarely returned on release. To make phone calls and communicate with members of their family back home or in the country of destination, inmates would then have to pay bribes to guards in order to use their phones, or to pay visitors to smuggle in phones and phone cards. There was no general rule on whether detainees were allowed to have phones or laptops in their cells; it varied from center to center and was mostly at the discretion of the head of detention. Detainees who were deemed unlikely to escape or who rendered certain services to the security guards enjoyed special privileges. For example, some detainees in Kupang cleaned the offices and made tea for the guards and were allowed to watch TV with them during the afternoons.

Some detainees found temporary relief by giving in to the widespread culture of bribery. For example, although detention center inmates are not officially allowed to leave the premises, some, if they can afford to pay a small fee to the guards and are unlikely to abscond, can leave for an afternoon on their own. A detainee I met inside Kupang detention center admitted that he took advantage of center guards who wanted to earn extra income on the side. Whenever he needed to go to a shopping center in Kupang to buy new clothes, use the internet, or collect money his relatives had wired him, he had to pay for renting a car, invite the guards for a meal at Kentucky Fried Chicken or McDonald's, buy them a t-shirt, or give them a minimum of Rp50,000 (US$5) in cash. During interviews with other detainees, it became obvious that many guards expected tips from detainees for all sorts of favors to improve their daily supplies of such things as extra food or cigarettes. Those who could not afford to engage in bribery found life very difficult indeed. Detainees stated that guards threatened them not to mention the bribes to outsiders.

A special kind of bribery is the one-off payment, known as "exit fee" or "thank-you money," which detention center staff expect in exchange for faster processing of the papers of detainees about to be released or transferred, or even for processing their papers at all. The amount of the payment is not necessarily fixed but depends on the financial circumstances of individuals. Iranians, for example, are considered to be generally better off and always have to pay more than other detainees. The payment varies between US$100 and US$500.

Violence in Detention

While in immigration detention, many inmates experienced physical and psychological violence perpetrated by security guards and fellow inmates. Corporal punishment, such as kicking, punching, and slapping, has been reported widely (HRW, 2013). Bystanders, including children and minors, often observed their fellow inmates being beaten and abused.

The first death of an asylum seeker in custody to be made public was that of Taqi Nekoyee, a young man from Afghanistan. Taqi died on February 28, 2012, in the Pontianak immigration detention center at the hands of several security guards. Together with five fellow detainees, Taqi had escaped from the detention center but was later recaptured by the police (Missbach & Sinanu, 2013). A medical report made on their arrival in the detention center stated they were all in good health. During the night that followed, Taqi and the two other recaptured detainees were mistreated by a group of 10 guards (Komnas HAM, 2012b). Taqi was severely injured, and because the guards failed to get medical assistance in time, he died the next morning. Taqi's autopsy revealed massive wounds and cigarette burns, which indicated he had been severely beaten and tortured.

Another violent incident that resulted in eight fatalities and 15 severely injured people was a three-hour brawl between Muslim and Buddhist detainees in the Belawan immigration detention center near Medan in April 2013 (UNHCR, 2013b). The police investigation indicated that a group of Muslim Rohingya men attacked a group of Buddhist men in retaliation for alleged sexual harassment of Rohingya female refugees. The detention center was understaffed at the time, so the guards present that night did not intervene while the detainees attacked one another with metal and wood from broken chairs (Missbach & Sinanu, 2013). Tension and deep animosity had been building in the center between the Burmese Muslims and Buddhists, yet no precautions had been taken to prevent violence between them. Unaware of ethnic and religious tensions, the guards had detained the two groups in the same rooms and refrained from intervening, which might have dispensed the violence more quickly.

Forms of Protest and Solidarity

Despite the ethnic and religious tensions among detainees in immigration detention, especially among Afghani and Iranian inmates, on certain occasions detainees would put aside any animosity to show solidarity and join together in protesting the general conditions of their detention. Hunger strikes were a frequent form of resistance inside a number of detention centers and occurred for various reasons. For example, in late July 2011, 250 detainees in Tanjung Pinang held a hunger strike to urge the UNHCR to come to the detention center to start the refugee determination process for those who had not been interviewed and to speed up the decision-making process on applications already submitted (Kistyarini, 2011b). Another hunger strike took place in Tanjung Pinang detention center in May 2012, when more than 160 detainees, some of whom had been detained for almost two years, refused food in protest against their imprisonment and the long processing times at the UNHCR. Lacking any response from the UNHCR, they continued their hunger strike for more than two weeks, and some 40 people had to be treated in nearby hospitals. Hunger strikes were also launched for petty reasons, as in Kupang in February 2012, when the head of the detention center employed a new catering company whose food supplies did not meet the expectations of the detainees.

Other forms of protest among detainees are suicide attempts and self-harm. After a long period of detention and not knowing what the future holds for them, many detainees suffer from depression. According to staff at the detention centers in Kupang, Kalideres, and Tanjung Pinang, detainees in those establishments have attempted suicide by cutting their wrists or inflicting electric shocks, for example, but they have not succeeded. Proper psychological counseling was rare; most detainees relied instead on strong sedatives provided by the detention center's medical unit. In some detention centers, the IOM offered language classes to divert detainees and help them fill their time. In other centers, the Jesuit Refugee Service organized aerobics sessions to help detainees release their stress, but in some centers these were terminated because breakouts were attempted during sports and recreational activities (JRS, 2011; Komnas HAM, 2012b).

Escape and Re-Arrest

Given that immigration detention centers were generally understaffed, breakouts from centers were widespread and frequent, and sometimes involved fatalities (Missbach & Sinanu, 2013; Muhardiansyah, 2013; Komnas HAM, 2012a). Methods used in breakouts varied. Some escapees cut the iron bars of their windows; others used ropes or sheets and sarongs for abseiling; some even dug tunnels (Kistyarini, 2011a). Some detainees planned their escape well and arranged for cars to pick them up outside the detention facility (Missbach & Crouch, 2013), while others who lacked the financial means to organize outside support just hoped to get away on their own.

It differed from one breakout attempt to another whether the security guards were paid for silent complicity or whether they were taken by surprise and outnumbered. Some of the tunnels and holes in the wall, allegedly used in escapes, were too small for a person to fit through, which suggests that the guards had consented, at least tacitly, to the escape; the inadequate tunnels and holes, which had been intended as evidence of a clandestine escape strategy, raised suspicion that the guards may have willingly escorted them out of the detention center. To protect the guards from disciplinary action, the escapees had prepared the false evidence to excuse the guards from any claims of negligence they might face. However, payment of a bribe to detention guards was not necessarily a guarantee of permanently avoiding arrest and return to detention. When re-arrested, escapees were often beaten by the prison guards (HRW, 2013) and, occasionally, also by civilians involved in their recapture. Back in detention, detainees usually faced one to two weeks of solitary confinement.

Improving Regulation of the Centers

One of the main problems of immigration detention centers in Indonesia has been their general lack of regulation and the extent of the discretionary powers of center staff, especially the head of detention. For example, the decisions at the discretion of detention center heads include whether inmates can telephone their families or receive legal representatives or guests. In the course of implementing the National Action Plan for Human Rights, Indonesia has become more aware of the need to uphold the human rights of immigration detention center inmates. This awareness has led to development and delivery of training programs for center staff. In particular, UNHCR Indonesia has offered workshops and seminars to staff to enhance safety and protection of refugees and asylum seekers in detention (UNHCR, 2013a).

In 2011 the Ministry of Justice and Human Rights published a short guidebook on the human rights of the inmates of immigration detention centers. Nevertheless, the many instructions in the guidebook given to staff to ensure better protection for the detainees are still often ignored. For example, the guidebook specifically mentions that detainees are entitled to contact their national consulate or embassy and their family to inform them of their detention, and that they are allowed to receive or reject assistance from their national consulate. Furthermore, they are entitled to receive visits from family members, sponsors, legal counselors, spiritual leaders, doctors, and state representatives. However, lawyers and even members of the national Human Rights Commission (Komnas HAM) have repeatedly been refused entry to visit the inmates of detention centers.

Not only has there been no independent complaint mechanism for detainees to access; there has also been no system in place to check whether detention center staff adhere to the regulations outlined in the guidebook. Staff found responsible for human rights abuses against their wards have generally faced fairly lenient penalties, as in the case of the 10 guards who beat Taqi Nekoyee to death and were sentenced to only 10 months in prison before resuming employment with the local department of immigration (Missbach, in press).

Currently, the minimum political demand is to improve the performance of immigration detention staff by developing a binding standard operating procedure. Having clear, nationally applicable, standard operating procedures for immigration detention might help prevent the detention of asylum seekers and refugees, establish benchmarks for acceptable conditions of confinement, and give those detained access to an effective complaints procedure about the conduct of immigration staff.

From their investigations concerning the treatment of asylum seekers and refugees in immigration detention centers, members of the Indonesian Human Rights Commission have stated, "The placement of refugees and asylum seekers in prison-like detention centers breeds negative consequences, both for the mental health of refugees and asylum seekers as well as for respecting and upholding the rights of asylum seekers and refugees" (Komnas HAM, 2012b, p. 25). On the basis of such findings, Komnas HAM has made more far-reaching political demands, urging the Indonesian government to sign the 1951 Refugee Convention as well as the 1967 Protocol and to design a national strategy for the handling of asylum seekers. Although Indonesian Law 37/1999 on Foreign Relations mentions the right to apply for asylum in Indonesia, the procedures to apply for asylum have never been spelled out properly. Because of the political situation in Indonesia at the moment, it is highly unlikely the Indonesian government will sign the Refugee Convention and the Protocol or establish a domestic asylum framework. Not only is Indonesia unwilling to bear the costs that a proper refugee status determination process would require, but more importantly, the nation does not want to permanently host Australia's unwanted asylum seekers (Missbach, in press). Aware of the current political constellations and prospects, Komnas HAM and other human rights organizations have been demanding that the government establish alternative shelters for asylum seekers (Komnas HAM, 2012b). Possible alternatives include, for example, reception centers where, instead of being incarcerated, asylum seekers are provided with the basic necessities and remain free to leave.

Conclusion: The Transnational Dimension of Immigration Detention in Indonesia

Although the Indonesian government bears responsibility for the treatment of detainees in the immigration detention centers in the first place, Australia's interests and its push for regional burden sharing cannot be overlooked (Nethery et al., 2013; Nethery & Gordyn, 2014). For years successive Australian governments have exerted pressure on Indonesia to arrest and detain transiting asylum seekers, refugees, and undocumented migrants, and thereby to act as a final bulwark for Australia. Australia has generously funded Indonesian border protection and anti-people-smuggling initiatives by the Indonesian police (Missbach, 2014), and it has also funded expansion of the Indonesian immigration detention system (Nethery et al., 2013). Although Indonesia is free to improve the conditions of detainees kept inside immigration detention (and outside of them), it will be impossible to abolish the "greater evil"— forced immobilization of asylum seekers—without causing setbacks in the Indonesia-Australia relationship.

From this account of how immigration detention works in Indonesia and what conditions are like for detainees held in these facilities, it has become clear that protection of the human rights of asylum seekers often comes second compared to transnationally implemented migration schemes that seek to protect borders as such and thus the national interests of potential host societies. Indonesia is in this regard no exception, but rather the rule. Extraterritorialized forms of immigration detention are being established as means to create further disincentives for asylum seekers who seek to move freely so as to find protection on their own account, rather than relying on the extremely slow-operating UNHCR refugee status determination and resettlement schemes.

Australia has benefited greatly from the immobilization and warehousing of asylum seekers in Indonesia, which reduced the number of people reaching its shores. However, in Indonesia more and more critical voices are appearing, given that most Indonesian immigration detention centers are already overcrowded and resettlement of refugees from Indonesia has slowed again in 2014. Especially since Australia launched its Operation Sovereign Borders in September 2013, which has seen forced returns of several asylum-seeker boats to Indonesia and thus also led to a decrease in irregular departures of asylum seekers by boat, it has become clear that Indonesia has neither the capacity nor the willingness to host more asylum seekers for the long run. Given the many problems in regard to hosting asylum seekers in Indonesia that have emerged over the last decade—both inside and outside of immigration detention centers—more criticism can be expected in the near future. In particular, Indonesians are starting to reject the notion of being Australia's "dumping ground" for unwanted asylum seekers.

References

Andrijasevic, R., & Walters, W. (2010). The International Organization for Migration and the international government of borders. *Environment and Planning D. Society and Space 28*(6), 977–999.

Georgi, F. (2010). For the benefit of some: The International Organization for Migration and its global migration management. In M. Geiger & A. Pécoud (Eds.), *The politics of international migration management* (pp. 45–71). Basingstoke: Palgrave Macmillan.

Georgi, F., & Schatral, S. (2012). Towards a critical theory of migration control: the case of the International Organization for Migration (IOM). In M. Geiger & A. Pécoud (Eds.), *The new politics of international mobility: Migration management and its discontents* (pp. 193–222). Osnabrück: Institut für Migrationsforschung und Interkulturelle Studien.

Human Rights Watch (HRW). (2013). *Barely surviving: Detention, abuse and neglect of migrant children in Indonesia.* New York: Author.

Indonesia perlu ratifikasi Konvensi Tentang Pengungsi. (2012, Feb. 10). Retrieved from http://www.hukumonline.com/berita/baca/lt4f351aacc4a70/indonesia-perlu-ratifikasi-konvensi-tentang-pengungsi.

Jesuit Refugee Service (JRS). (2011, July 18). Indonesia: Finding ways to release stress in immigration detention. Retrieved from http://www.jrsap.org/news_detail?TN=NEWS-20110719010058.

Kistyarini. (2011a, June 28). Bikin tali handuk, 13 tahanan kabur. *Kompas.* Retrieved from: http://bola.kompas.com/read/2011/06/28/10172062/bikin.tali.handuk.13.tahanan.kabur

Kistyarini. (2011b, July 25). Imigran gelap demo tuntut status. *Kompas.*

Komisi Nasional Hak Asasi Manusia (Komnas HAM). (2012a, Feb. 10). Jangan kriminalisasi pencari suaka!, press statement. Retrieved from http://kajiankomnasham.wordpress.com/2012/02/14/pengungsi-pencari-suaka/.

Komisi Nasional Hak Asasi Manusia (Komnas HAM). (2012b, Nov. 11). *Penelitian tentang pengungsi (refugee) dan pencari suaka (asylum seeker) di Indonesia.* Jakarta: Author.

Kurnia, A. (2011). *Imigran ilegal: potret penanganan dan pencegahan dalam perspektif sistem manajemen nacional.* Jakarta: IOM.

Meliala, A., & Perdana, A. (2011). *Critical assessment on people smuggling in Indonesia and its various impacts, research report.* Jakarta: Department of Criminology, University of Indonesia, in collaboration with Jakarta Center for Law Enforcement Cooperation.

Merope, S. (2013, Apr. 15). The economic cost of our asylum seeker policy. Retrieved from http://rightnow.org.au/topics/asylum-seekers/the-economic-cost-of-our-asylum-seeker-policy/.

Missbach, A. (2014). Indonesia's treatment of transit migrants: Everyday life realities between human rights protection and criminalization. In J. Pietsch & M. Clark (Eds.), *Migration flows and regional integration: Comparisons between Europe, Southeast Asia and Australia.* Amsterdam: Amsterdam University Press.

Missbach, Antje (2015). *Trouble transit: Asylum seekers stuck in Indonesia.* Singapore: ISEAS.

Missbach, A., & Crouch, M. (2013). The criminalization of people smuggling: Legal insights from Indonesia. *Australian Journal of Asian Law, 14*(2) 1–19.

Missbach, A., & Sinanu, F. (2013). Life and death in detention. *Inside Indonesia,* 113. Retrieved from http://www.insideindonesia.org/current-edition/life-and-death-in-immigration-detention.

Muhardiansyah, Y. (2013, May 6). Imigrasi terus cari 25 imigran yang kabur dari Rudenim Belawan. Retrieved from http://www.merdeka.com/peristiwa/imigrasi-terus-cari-25-imigran-yang-kabur-dari-rudenim-belawan.html.

Nethery, A., & Gordyn, C. (2014). Australia-Indonesia cooperation on asylum-seekers: A case of incentivized policy transfer. *Australian Journal of International Affairs, 68,* 177–193.

Nethery, A., Rafferty-Brown, B., & Taylor, S. (2013). Exporting detention: Australian-funded immigration detention in Indonesia. *Journal of Refugee Studies, 26,* 88–109.

Prasetyo,W.B.(2014,Mar.26).RudenimKupangDisebutyangTerbaikdiIndonesia.Retrievedfrom http://www.beritasatu.com/nasional/173974-rudenim-kupang-disebut-yang-terbaik-di-indonesia.html.

Taylor, J. (2009). Behind Australian doors: Examining the conditions of detention of asylum seekers in Indonesia. Retrieved from http://www.safecom.org.au/pdfs/behind-australian-doors-examining-the-conditions.pdf

Taylor, S., & Rafferty-Brown, B. (2010). Difficult journeys: Accessing refugee protection in Indonesia. *Monash University Law Review, 36*(3), 138–161.

UN High Commissioner for Refugees (UNHCR). (2013a, Mar. 11). Safety and security training in Tanjung Pinang Detention Center. Retrieved from http://www.unhcr.or.id/en/safety-and-security-training-in-tanjung-pinang-detention-centre

UN High Commissioner for Refugees (UNHCR). (2013b, Apr. 5). UNHCR saddened by loss of life in Indonesia detention center incident. Retrieved from http://www.unhcr.org/515eae199.html.

UN High Commissioner for Refugees (UNHCR) (2014a, February). Fact sheet & statistical information. Jakarta, Indonesia: Author.

9

Detaining the Immigrant Other in Hong Kong

GORDON MATHEWS AND CHEE WAI-CHI

The "Immigrant Other" in Hong Kong

Hong Kong is unusual, in that the dominant "immigrant other" until recently has been from the same country and of the same ethnicity as most Hongkongers. Hong Kong returned to Mainland Chinese sovereignty in 1997, but the border between Hong Kong and Mainland China nonetheless has remained essentially a border between foreign countries, with immigration officials carefully checking entry permits. Mainlanders were widely derided in Hong Kong, in the 1970s and 1980s as unsophisticated bumpkins (Mathews, Ma, & Liu, 2008), and today as *nouveau riche* "locusts," buying up luxury goods and flats and making Hong Kong unaffordable for its own residents. This is despite the fact that most Hongkongers, or their parents or grandparents, came from Mainland China; and it is despite the fact that mainland visitors to Hong Kong today bring considerable economic benefits to the territory. Viewing Mainland Chinese as "the ethnic other" in Hong Kong is highly ironic, both because of the common ethnicity and nationality of Chinese and Hongkongers, and also because China will in a few short years have the world's largest economy; the stereotypical "scare story" in developed-world societies of developing-world hordes clamoring to enter does not quite fit Chinese coming to Hong Kong. Nonetheless, the ppp-adjusted per capita income of China is still only 25 percent that of Hong Kong, and some on the mainland do indeed come to Hong Kong to make a better living for themselves and their families and have indeed been jailed, whether for violating the terms of their visas or for other offenses (Law & Lee, 2006; Lee, 2007).

However, the number of mainlanders arrested in Hong Kong for immigration offenses has very significantly decreased in recent years, largely because of a progressive easing of immigration rules between Mainland China and Hong Kong and rising incomes and job availability on the mainland. Instead, the role of the "immigrant other" is increasingly being played by asylum seekers from South Asia and Africa, of whom there are now about 6,000 in Hong Kong. The first wave of asylum seekers to come to Hong Kong consisted of Vietnamese boat people in the 1980s and 1990s (McCalmon, 1994), an influx that apparently still influences the draconian Hong Kong government policy toward asylum seekers today (Choi, 2014). The current wave of South Asian and African asylum seekers began coming to Hong Kong in the wake of 9/11 and the tightening of visa restrictions in other developed countries. Asylum seekers can live freely in Hong Kong on a very minimal government stipend of HK$2,700 (about US$350) for rent assistance and food rations with no cash ever entering asylum seekers' own hands. Asylum seekers are forbidden to work, although many do so illegally. Because of a large backlog of cases, some asylum seekers in Hong Kong have stayed for six or eight or more years. For a brief period beginning March 2009, thanks to a High Court ruling, asylum seekers were allowed to work in Hong Kong, but that loophole was quickly closed ("Illegal immigrant . . . ," 2009). The Hong Kong government defends its refusal to allow asylum seekers to work by citing the stipend given to asylum seekers, claiming that this is enough to stave off destitution while avoiding "a magnet effect" of asylum seekers flocking to Hong Kong (Chan, 2013); but asylum seekers all say that this is insufficient, and that they have no choice but to work. Hong Kong asylum seekers long relied on the UNHCR to make their claims, with fewer than 10 percent of claimants accepted, to be relocated in Canada or the United States (Chen, 2013); since 2006, Hong Kong asylum seekers have also turned to the Convention Against Torture, with well short of 1 percent accepted (Justice Center Hong Kong, 2014). This represents a far lower rate of acceptance of asylum seekers than for other societies in the developed world (Chen, 2013). In late 2012, there was a protest of around 300 asylum seekers, organized by the NGO Vision First, proclaiming Hong Kong "a prison without walls" (Chiu, 2012).

A significant difference between Hong Kong and other developed-world societies dealing with the "immigrant other" is the fact that because of its relatively liberal immigration regime, many of the foreigners who would be turned away at the borders of other developed-world societies are admitted to Hong Kong on tourist permits. If visitors from Kenya, Indonesia, Colombia, Egypt, Tanzania, or India arrive at the airport in New York, Tokyo, or Sidney without a visa, they will probably never get past immigration counters and will be sent home on the next return flight. In Hong Kong, on the other hand, they will probably be granted at the immigration counter a 14-, 30-, or 90-day tourist permit to remain in the territory (Hong Kong Immigration Department, 2014a). This is not the case for all societies—Nigerians and Pakistanis, along with citizens from other countries, require visas to get into Hong Kong—but it is true for citizens of most societies across the globe. Most of these "foreign others" are indeed tourists, but others work illegally, and still others declare themselves to be asylum seekers.

The "immigrant others" who wind up in prison or in detention in Hong Kong include (1) those who overstay their tourist permits, or are otherwise illegally in Hong Kong; (2) those who have declared themselves as asylum seekers, who, if they have overstayed their visas, may spend anywhere from a week to nine months in detention; (3) those in Hong Kong on tourist permits or as asylum seekers who are caught working; and (4) those who have committed some other crime during their stay in Hong Kong. Our distinct impression is that most of the "foreign others" who wind up in jail fit category (2) or (3), with (3) often leading to a jail sentence of 15–18 months. Police can arrest a visa overstayer in Hong Kong simply by checking the person's passport, but they cannot arrest an illegal worker unless they can find clear evidence of such work—a waiter at a restaurant in Hong Kong's Chungking Mansions (Mathews, 2011), for example, can simply sit at a table on being warned that an undercover policeman is nearby and easily evade detection and prosecution.

Number of Immigrant Detainees

Hong Kong has a moderate imprisonment rate compared to most other Asian and Western countries but continues to have the highest proportion of female prisoners in the world (Lee, 2010, p. 78). According to Lee (2007), "at the heart of this prison crisis in Hong Kong is the routine use of imprisonment as a mechanism of ... migration control" (p. 847), and particularly the imprisonment of Mainland Chinese sex workers. However, these numbers have dropped substantially of late. As Lam writes (2014), "Between 2010 and 2013, the number of mainlanders overstaying their visas more than halved—from 3,381 to 1,567." An expert quoted in the article, John Bacon-Shone, stated of mainland sex workers in 2014, "There used to be large numbers of women who would come [to Hong Kong} to work as prostitutes ... and get arrested, but it's not attractive to come on an illegal basis anymore.... Frankly, they can get jobs of the mainland." Overall, the number of prisoners now in Hong Kong is 8,906, a record low number (in 2004, the number was 13,138), 72.6 percent of whom are from Hong Kong, and another 12.9 percent from the mainland, Taiwan, or Macau (ibid.). This means that 14.5 percent are foreigners, a significant proportion of whom are the asylum seekers discussed in this chapter arrested for working illegally or other offenses.

In 2013, 7,536 detainees were admitted to the Castle Peak Bay Immigration Center awaiting removal or deportation, but these are not included in the statistics cited above. Although this center is the site where those awaiting deportation are placed, the "immigrant other" is present in prisons throughout Hong Kong, including at least 12 immigration detention sites. Statistics released by the Hong Kong Immigration Department concerning investigation of offenses are in Table 9.1.

Table 9.1 **Hong Kong Immigration Department Statistics]**

	2012	*2013*
Forged travel documents detected	688	765
Mainland illegal immigrants apprehended and repatriated	1,336	976
Illegal workers prosecuted	2,394*	2,145**
Employers of illegal workers prosecuted	358	269
No. of prosecution instituted	6,790	5,532

* Includes 1,455 prosecuted for illegal employment and 939 prosecuted for sex work.
** Includes 1,344 prosecuted for illegal employment and 801 prosecuted for sex work.
Source: Hong Kong Immigration Department (2014b).

These statistics should be viewed in conjunction with these additional data: in 2012, the Immigration Department received 1,174 Convention Against Torture claims, and in 2012 it prosecuted 6,790 claimants (Lo, 2014). As Lo writes, "In the 1,809 torture claims received in . . . 2010, 606 claims were lodged from former foreign domestic helpers. . . . Furthermore . . . from November 14, 2009 to June 30, 2011, there were 244 torture claimants being arrested for illegally working." These data suggest to Lo that the Torture Claim system is being abused; but whether or not this is the case, it seems clear that torture claimants—asylum seekers—make up a significant proportion of those incarcerated in Hong Kong. This, increasingly, is becoming the face of the "immigrant other" in Hong Kong detention.

Experiences of Detention/Prison in Hong Kong

Mathews has taught asylum seekers in Hong Kong in a weekly class for the past nine years and written about asylum seekers in the context of Chungking Mansions (2011); Chee, over the past several years, has interviewed many female asylum seekers as well as Mainland Chinese right-of-abode seekers and detainees. To their surprise, Mathews and Chee found independently in their investigations for this chapter that many asylum seekers and other foreign detainees expressed a degree of appreciation for their time in detention or in prison. This was partly because, simply put, being locked up in Hong Kong is a stabler and less traumatizing experience than being locked up in South Asia, Africa, or Mainland China. Conditions, if not pleasant, are tolerable, and violence against inmates, whether from guards or from fellow prisoners, is rare. The authorities—the prison guards—can by and large be trusted not to abuse their power.

Most asylum seekers go to detention when they make their claim to be an asylum seeker. Detention centers are also for those who are waiting for deportation. By contrast, when an undocumented immigrant commits a crime apart from immigration status, he or she will be sent to prison. There is not much difference between these two, except that prison typically involves working for extremely minimal wages, while detention, more short-term, generally does not. Among the asylum seekers we have known, some—often those who are more articulate and more clearly able to explicate their situation—do not spend even a day in detention. If an asylum seeker is able to lodge a claim to be an asylum seeker before his or her visa has expired, then the asylum seeker has committed no offense and will not be jailed. However, very often it seems, from what asylum seekers say, that the police tell the enquiring asylum seeker to return to them once the visa has expired, guaranteeing that the person will be placed in detention.

But detention, as noted earlier, is not seen as a bad experience by most of the asylum seekers Mathews and Chee have spoken with. "If you compare detention in Hong Kong to that of some African prisons, it's like a five-star hotel," Jordan, an East African commented. It is uniformly agreed that inmates will not be arbitrarily beaten by guards: "If they hit you, it must be because you tried to hit them first," asylum seekers who come out of detention say. "The food is good," it is commonly said, with asylum seekers being given a choice as to whether they want *halal* food or not; "they give you time to exercise; you can take showers; you can get medical attention. There's a TV to watch."

This is true of prison as well. Ali, an asylum seeker from the Middle East, described his time in prison, which is where he wound up for using a fake passport (an imprisonable offense) to get into Hong Kong and then to try to fly to Europe:

> In prison in my country, you can get killed by prisoners. It's easy—maybe someone paid them to kill you. You can't imagine the cell I was in there. Have you seen dungeons in movies? Multiply that by 10 or 20 and then you can find out about prison in my country. I was tortured—it was horrible. . . . In Hong Kong, none of that would happen. It wasn't like prison for me, but like military—no, there was no violence in the cell. You wake up around six, then wash and go to breakfast. Then you do your work shift—I was in laundry. The work was hard, so I got paid more: HK$500 per month. . . . Prison—well, I wasted six months of my life—no one is going to give me back those six months. But the six months in a safe place was a gift—I tried to use it well. I exercised, wrote—did things I never did outside: my schedule was set. Now, I'm free—there's no schedule. So I can't use my time like I did then. . . .

Ali, although regretting his lost time, is almost nostalgic for his time in prison because it enabled him to live his life within a disciplined time structure in a way that he has never been able to do since. The asylum seekers as a whole whom Mathews interviewed were generally favorably impressed by detention and by prison in Hong Kong for two reasons. There was first the quality of life—the fact, for example, that food was generally quite edible, and TV and newspapers were available. In journeying from their home country to Hong Kong, asylum seekers were moving from the developing world to the developed world, and this was reflected in the nature of prison life. There was, second, the degree of order in jail in Hong Kong, with little to fear from the violence of fellow inmates or guards. This differs not just from the developing world but also from places such as the United States, where prisons are widely portrayed as being violent and dangerous. Several of the male asylum seekers I interviewed were astounded when I asked them about the possible danger of prison rape in Hong Kong detention: "How can there be rape? There are no women in there." They had never heard of male-on-male rape, and Hong Kong detention and prison would not be the place where they would be introduced to such a thing.

Chee, working entirely independently from Mathews, found a similarly positive attitude among her Mainland Chinese and African female informants (Chee and Mathews divided their interviewees by gender because the majority of asylum seekers are Muslim, and many practice strict gender segregation). Though all of the detainees described being held in a detention center as in some sense shameful, since most had never been detained before and found it to be profoundly jarring in a psychological sense, many of them talked about their detention experience as a period when they had peace of mind. Meitin, a Mainland Chinese, arrived from Fukien in 1999 to seek right of abode, and was on recognizance until renewal was rejected in 2002. One day in 2003, she was stopped by the police in the street for an ID check, was arrested, and was put in detention for two days before deportation. She recalled:

> I know it sounds weird, but I felt calm when I was arrested. I had peace of mind because I had not done anything wrong, and because I saw it as a chance for me to stop and rethink my future . . . about what I really wanted and what direction I should take further down the road.

Liza, from Uganda, was in detention for eight months, by her account not because she overstayed her visa but because her roommate had stolen her passport and used it to sell a stolen watch. She talked about her detention experience:

> Life was simple and regular in the detention center. We got up early at the same time every day and had breakfast. We had three meals a day at regular times. I did some simple job—making envelopes. We had time for exercise. We had our free time. We could read books and write letters. We also chatted with each other a lot.

It is ironic to have "free" time under detention, but it was the stability and regularity that provided such a sense of peacefulness. The detainees did not need to worry about food or safety or finding a place to sleep.

Related to this paradox of detention as peace of mind is another paradox: the detention experience has served to convince the detainees that the Hong Kong government is humane. Both Meitin and Liza mentioned that they were treated well under detention in Hong Kong. Meitin was detained in Hong Kong for two days before being deported to Shenzhen, a city in China near the border, where she was detained again. She compared her experiences under detention in Hong Kong and in China.

> That day when I was arrested in Hong Kong I was shopping in a market near my home. There were frequent police raids targeting black market labor. The police found me suspicious probably because I was wearing ragged clothing and looked gaunt. I looked really haggard. I had no income and didn't have money for clothing. They approached me and asked for my ID. I took out my recognizance papers. They said, "It's long expired." I told them honestly, "Yes, I am here to fight for the right of abode. I failed to get my recognizance renewed more than a year ago." One policewoman sympathized with me and said, "Let's not use handcuffs on her. She is not a criminal. Let her follow us." It was a kind of respect. I really appreciated that. At the detention room, there was a policewoman with me. She was pregnant. We talked with each other. There were a lot of mosquitoes. . . . She was so kind as to light mosquito repellent incense for me. She gave me a rice box but I was so down that I couldn't eat. Then, seeing that I didn't touch the food, she offered me a carton of fresh milk, "This is from me personally." Before she left, she said, "Now I am off duty. Tomorrow someone from the Immigration Department will pick you up. I hope when you return, you can apply for a formal document. Then you don't have to be like this. We are law enforcers and must repatriate any overstayers." I told her I understood it was their duty.

This stands in greats contrast with her experience of detention in Mainland China, where she felt much less respected:

> I was sent to the China border. It was during a critical time of SARS. People said I was from an infected area; I was locked up for seven days for quarantine. I was provided with meals, but had to sleep on the cement floor, with not even a blanket. You know, mainland China is not as humane as Hong Kong. . . . There are just too many people in China.

Patricia from Uganda was seriously ill when she was under detention and stayed in the hospital for two weeks. She said, "The Hong Kong government paid for the thousands of dollars of hospital fees; I was grateful for this." She was given medical care for free in Hong Kong while she was in detention; it would have been inaccessible in her home country.

Navigating Detention/Prison

Both Chee and Mathews did hear a variety of complaints about prison and detention. Hassan, from Ethiopia, told Mathews, "I had five months in detention. Detention was really hard. No matter how you are suffering, they don't care. The people who are there in the detention center, they look like losers. The guards view us as someone who's lazy!" Asylum seekers often come from middle-class backgrounds: if they were able to fly into Hong Kong, as many did, they clearly have resources. Because they are from such a background, imprisonment may be a particular source of shame. Beyond this, there were distinctly unpleasant aspects to jail. Mathews heard several times about how asylum seekers are strip-searched when they first arrive in jail, and this was a great affront particularly to Muslims, who maintain a high degree of bodily modesty. A number of prisons where asylum seekers are detained have in cells, which may contain 20–30 detainees in bunks, only an open toilet, which was extremely difficult for those used to privacy in their bodily functions. This varies from one detention facility to another. Some offer private toilet stalls, leading one of the asylum seekers Mathews spoke with to wait a week before having a bowel movement, when he knew he would be in a facility offering the privacy of a toilet stall.

Another matter concerned complaints to prison authorities. Two asylum seekers, Michel from Togo and Charles from Nigeria, spoke as follows:

> M: When they detain you, they ask for any complaints you may have. But if you make a complaint, they will find a way to keep you longer. So people are afraid to make any complaints if they have been treated badly. Yes, they ask you if you have any complaints. But people say that if you make a complaint, they will hold you.
>
> C: Not me! I complained a lot. I didn't want to be a silent victim. The big boss comes maybe twice a month. He's trying to get the right information from the right inmates, not from the officers. I voiced out my ideas to the big boss. I was supposed to be detained for a long time. But the officer told me, "We will bail you out if you have a guarantor. . . ."

As this dialogue shows, detainees may be well aware of the power structures within prisons and detention centers and may be savvy enough to play them to better their lot. Chee heard about a more difficult situation: a female asylum seeker from Africa was imprisoned for attacking the police. She complained that the Correctional Services Department officers used excessive violence on her. As she reported, the officers accused her of hiding food, which she said was a false accusation, and held her down. When she resisted, they used pepper spray on her face from a short distance and she was scalded. She did not follow the one cardinal rule of detention and prison in Hong Kong: do not resist. At the same time, one may ask if hiding food is a sufficiently heinous offense to lead to pepper spray.

Detainees in prison and in detention are well aware of the possibility of ethnic tension, as are the authorities. As Ismael, from Somalia, told Mathews:

> Yes, we are kept separate from mainlanders in detention. Some I was with were from Mongolia. The Vietnamese had their own cell—they don't mix with others because they are too violent, it is said. My roommates were Nepalese, Africans, some Arabs. . . . In the detention center, there are people who have just been released from prison too—I met a South African who had been in prison for ten years who had never seen a touch screen for a phone. He was caught smuggling drugs. . . .

As Ali, from the Middle East, described prison:

> Most prisoners were Hong Kong Chinese. No, most of them couldn't speak English well. They kept their distance—in prison, Chinese are on one side, and Pakistanis on the other side. . . . The authorities put everyone together, but for their own people, they wanted them to be separate.

Finally, no one wants to be in detention or prison for long; regardless of how stable that environment may seem, it still represents a loss of freedom. A court interpreter said:

> The average length of detention for the people I talk with is three months. But I've seen nine months. People get very tired of it—it's about freedom. You have to wake up at a certain time each day, go to sleep at a certain time—if you don't, there's a punishment. They can lock you up in solitary confinement.

Prison may seem, initially, to be relatively pleasant, but after weeks and months the asylum seekers we spoke with dreamed of being free, and were joyous on finally being released.

Discussion: Why Is Detention/Jail in Hong Kong Viewed Favorably?

The most remarkable finding of our research is, to repeat, that the people we talked to—a somewhat representative if small sampling of Hong Kong's "immigrant other"—found detention and prison to be, for the most part, a tolerable and even salutary experience. We did not expect this to be the case.

The most obvious explanation for this has already been noted. For someone coming from the developing world—Africa or South Asia—or from the Chinese mainland, prison or detention in a developed-world society such as Hong Kong may seem remarkably good, with its free edible meals, exercise yards, and television as well as a high degree of stability and order; it is probably much better in its conditions than prison in one's home society. This explanation no doubt has considerable truth, though it surprising that many of the asylum seekers are not from poverty-stricken backgrounds, but from the middle class of their home societies; this is why many of them were able to fly to Hong Kong to seek asylum, thousands of miles from home. If they were starving at home, then prison in Hong Kong might seem to be a great improvement; but most were not, and indeed some of the asylum seekers Mathews has spoken with come from a background of considerable wealth.

Another explanation is that prison and detention are seen in a good light exactly because the situation of illegal immigrants and asylum seekers in Hong Kong is so terrible. We earlier mentioned how Hong Kong at large has been labeled by asylum seeker protesters as "a prison without walls" (Chiu, 2012). One recent article (Branigan, 2014) describes the plight of a Hong Kong asylum seeker:

> Shortly after leaving prison, Mohammed went to the grocery store where he was last arrested, and stole another item. Then he waited quietly for the police to come. "It's no good outside. It's better in prison," he said, days after his latest release. "You have food, you can work; you have a room."

This portrayal definitely applies to asylum seekers who obey the law and do not work. The stipend they receive from the government is so minimal that prison may indeed seem to be an improvement over daily life outside of prison in Hong Kong, simply because HK$2,700 in rent and food subsidy is insufficient to live on in Hong Kong. But what portrayals such as this leave out is that most asylum seekers illegally work (Mathews, 2011), in junkyards or construction, carting goods, in restaurants and guesthouses in places like Chungking Mansions, earning, typically, between HK$3,000 and $5,000 per month—low wages, but in many cases, more money than they could make if they were working at home. Asylum seekers' illegal work contributes to Hong Kong's economy (Vecchio, 2013), and seems implicitly tolerated by the Hong Kong government, since police often don't seem to devote great effort to apprehending illegal workers, and in any case, illegal workers are very difficult to catch. (However, one who is caught may go to prison for 15 months or more, and the employer may be subject to punishment as well.) Because illegal work is readily available, Hong Kong really is not "a prison without walls" for most asylum seekers, and their lives, although certainly difficult, are typically not nearly as hellish as some NGOs and media reports claim. The idea that jail is an improvement over freedom in Hong Kong is an idea that is decisively rejected by most asylum seekers.

A third explanation for why detention or prison is viewed more or less favorably may simply be that it really is a more or less positive experience. Hong Kong's police and correctional services were, up to the early 1970s, seen as hopelessly corrupt; but following establishment of the Independent Commission Against Corruption in 1974, and with the raising of police salaries, corruption has all but vanished. Police and correctional services officers in Hong Kong are generally regarded as performing to a very high standard. In addition to this, NGOs and human right lawyers make every effort to inform asylum seekers, domestic helpers, and other vulnerable "immigrant others" in Hong Kong of their rights (Rice, 2014). Violations of rights indeed occur, and police do act badly on occasion, as a few asylum seekers have related to Mathews and Chee, and this is apparent in the recent police brutality against pro-democracy activists in Occupy Central ("Police launch probe . . . ," 2014). Hong Kong is changing and becoming more like Mainland China, a shift that may yet have a negative effect on the jailing of the "immigrant other." But this seems not to have happened yet, judging from the accounts of our interviewees. Though there is much to be ashamed of in Hong Kong's treatment of asylum seekers, conditions in Hong Kong prison and detention centers seem to be something about which Hongkongers can feel proud, for they seem, by and large, to be decent places.

References

Branigan, T. (2014, Mar. 6). Hong Kong's dirty secret: Thousands of asylum seekers left waiting in squalor. *The Guardian*. Retrieved from http://www.theguardian.com/world/2014/mar/06/hong-kong-asylum-seekers-waiting-in-squalor.

Chan, W. (2013, July 18). Hong Kong's shameful treatment of asylum seekers exposed. *CNN*. Retrieved from http://edition.cnn.com/2013/07/18/world/asia/hong-kong-refugees-exposed/.

Chen, T. (2013, July 16). Hong Kong changing the way it handles refugees. *Wall Street Journal*. Retrieved from http://www.wsj.com/articles/SB10001424127887324694904578601171702287356.

Chiu, J. (2012, Oct. 31). Protesters brand the city a prison without walls. *South China Morning Post*. Retrieved from http://www.unhcr.org/cgi-bin/texis/vtx/refdaily?pass=463ef21123&date=2012-10-31&cat=Asia/Pacific.

Choi, C. (2014, May 21). Controversy over Hong Kong's asylum seekers harks back to Vietnam. *South China Morning Post*. Retrieved from http://www.scmp.com/news/hong-kong/article/1516648/controversy-over-hong-kongs-asylum-seekers-harks-back-vietnam.

Hong Kong Immigration Department. (2014a). Visit Visa / Entry Permit Requirements for the Hong Kong Special Administrative Region http://www.immd.gov.hk/en/services/hk-visas/visit-transit/visit-visa-entry-permit.html.

Hong Kong Immigration Department. (2014b). Facts and statistics, investigation. Retrieved from http://www.immd.gov.hk/en/facts/investigation.html.

Illegal immigrant job loophole closed: Govt. (2009, Dec. 11). *China Daily* Hong Kong edition. Retrieved from http://www.chinadaily.com.cn/hkedition/2009-11/12/content_8954037.htm.

Justice Center Hong Kong. (2014). Meeting the bare minimum: Hong Kong's new screening process for protection. http://www.justicecentre.org.hk/framework/uploads/2014/03/USM-Briefing-Meeting-the-Bare-Minimum-HK-New-Screening-Process-for-Protection.pdf

Lam, L. (2014, Sep. 7). Number of prisoners in Hong Kong hits record low. *South China Morning Post.* Retrieved from http://www.scmp.com/news/hong-kong/article/1586883/prison-population-hits-record-low-theyre-spending-more-time-remand.

Law, K., & Lee, K. (2006). Citizenship, economy and social exclusion of Mainland Chinese immigrants in Hong Kong. *Journal of Contemporary Asia, 36*(2), 217–242.

Lee, M. (2007). Women's imprisonment as a mechanism of migration control in Hong Kong. *British Journal of Criminology, 47*(6), 847–860.

Lee, Maggy. 2010. *Trafficking and Global Crime Control.* Thousand Oaks, CA: Sage.

Lo, T. F. (2014, Mar. 26). Is torture claim being misused? Hong Kong law blog. Retrieved from http://hklawblog.com/2014/03/26/is-torture-claim-being-misused/.

Mathews, G. (2011). *Ghetto at the center of the world: Chungking Mansions, Hong Kong.* Chicago: University of Chicago Press.

Mathews, G., Kit-wai Ma, E., & Liu, T. (2008). *Hong Kong, China: Learning to belong to a nation.* Abingdon: Routledge.

McCalmon, B. (1994). Winding it up in Hong Kong: The increasing impatience with Vietnamese asylum seekers. *Georgetown Immigration Law Journal, 8*(2), 333–342.

Police launch probe after alleged beating of Civic Party's Ken Tsang caught on camera. (2014, Oct. 15). *South China Morning Post.* Retrieved from http://www.scmp.com/news/hong-kong/article/1616880/police-launch-probe-after-alleged-beating-civic-partys-ken-tsang?page=all.

Rice, J. (2014). Take your rights seriously: On educating yourself as to your legal rights. *Hong Kong Human Rights Monitor.* Retrieved from https://books.google.co.th/books/about/Take_Your_Rights_Seriously.html?id=hM-bGwAACAAJ&redir_esc=y.

Vecchio, F. (2013). The economy of seeking asylum in a global city. *International Migration.* Retrieved from http://onlinelibrary.wiley.com/doi/10.1111/imig.12126/full.

10

Transnational Migration and Control

Immigration Detention on the Edge of Europe

ĊETTA MAINWARING

The Republic of Malta currently detains for 18 months all migrants and refugees who enter the country without authorization, the longest time period allowed under European Union (EU) law. Situated on Europe's southern periphery in the Mediterranean Sea, the island state acceded into the union in 2004. Malta had experienced a significant increase in unauthorized migrant arrivals by boat in the previous years: in 2002, 1,686 migrants and refugees arrived on the island without authorization, a 30-fold increase from 57 in 2001. The increase was in line with the larger migration flows occurring across the Central Mediterranean at the time, which scholars argued were in part due to increased migration controls along the West African coast and around the Canary Islands (e.g., Lutterbeck, 2006).

In the early 21st century, Malta's membership in the EU, alongside the increase in unauthorized migrant arrivals and the country's new role on the EU's periphery as a migration gatekeeper, converged to catapult the issue of irregular immigration and immigration detention into the political and public spotlight. Since then, Malta's detention policy has regularly come under attack for its length and conditions by local and international advocacy organizations, including Human Rights Watch (2012), the Council of Europe (2005), and Amnesty International (2012). Such organizations have put forward various proposals for alternatives to detention, such as reporting or residency requirements (e.g., Edwards, 2011; European Commission, 2014; IOM & UNHCR, 2014; UNHCR, 2012). In 2013, the European Court of Human Rights (ECHR, 2013a, 2013b) also ruled against Malta on the subject of immigration detention, finding violations of the right to liberty, the right to an effective remedy, and the prohibition of inhuman and degrading treatment. The court concluded that Malta's immigration detention policy was a "defective national system hindering human-rights protection" (ECHR, 2013b), a position echoed by the Council of Europe (2011), which maintained the policy is "irreconcilable with the requirements of the European Convention of Human Rights (ECHR) and the case-law of the Strasbourg Court." Despite this criticism, immigration detention continues to enjoy bipartisan backing in Malta. This short chapter argues that the role of immigration detention in Malta is inextricably linked with the country's geopolitical position within the EU as well as the role of the military within immigration detention. Indeed, Maltese immigration detention is a transnational phenomenon in four ways: it is justified as a reaction to the transnational, clandestine mobility of migrants and refugees; it is shaped by the regional politics and policies of the EU; it is part of a broader transnational attempt by Malta and other member states to limit mobility in the Mediterranean region; and finally, resistance to the policy by advocacy organizations depends on transnational networks.

The chapter first examines how immigration flows and immigration detention developed in Malta, focusing in particular on changes prompted by accession into the EU in 2004. It then analyzes how the government has framed immigration flows and immigration detention. Finally, the chapter turns to transnational efforts to control immigration through detention and other practices as well as transnational challenges to such practices.

The Evolution of Immigration and Immigration Detention in Malta

The Maltese Immigration Act of 1970 first allowed the mandatory detention of foreigners who arrived on the island without state authorization or who were issued a removal order by the government. At this time, a foreigner could be detained indefinitely. The number of people subject to the policy was minimal, however, until the increase in unauthorized arrivals in 2002. The policy and political framework of immigration detention was also transformed at this time, because of impending EU membership and the increasing number of migrants and refugees in detention.

In 2002, as part of the pre-accession process, Malta decriminalized entry without leave into its territory. Despite this development, indefinite, mandatory immigration detention remained in place as an administrative offence. In 2005, the efforts of local and international advocacy organizations, notably those of the Council of Europe (2005), prevailed and the government limited detention to 18 months. Before 2005, the average length of detention was between 22 and 24 months (UN Human Rights Council 2010). The 18-month limit was later adopted into EU law as part of the Returns Directive (European Union, 2008). Moreover, an earlier EU directive on the minimum reception standards for asylum seekers stipulated that detainees must be released after 12 months if their asylum claim is still pending (European Union, 2003).

Consequently, today the Maltese government detains unauthorized immigrants for up to 18 months. Asylum seekers are released either when they are granted some form of protection or after 12 months if their claim has not been resolved. More than 90 percent of migrants arriving by boat in Malta apply for asylum (Human Rights Watch, 2012). Moreover, the vast majority are successful in their claim: for example, in 2013, 71 percent of applicants received international protection (refugee status or subsidiary protection), with a further 11 percent granted some form of complimentary protection (UNHCR, 2014). Migrants who do not apply for asylum or whose claims are unsuccessful are held in detention for the maximum 18-month period.

In 2013, the average length of detention in Malta was more than three times higher than in any other EU member state: migrants and refugees were held for an average of 180 days. Estonia had the second-longest detention period at 58 days. The average across all member states was 40 days, with the lowest averages seen in Sweden with 5 days and Finland with 11.8 (European Commission, 2014).

Vulnerable migrants and refugees, including children, the elderly, and people with mental or physical disabilities, are also detained on arrival. Although procedures exist for early release of vulnerable migrants through self-identification and identification by NGOs or government officials, these measures are not comprehensive enough to ensure that all vulnerable migrants are identified. Moreover, the process of attaining release can be lengthy even for those who are identified. For example, unaccompanied minors are detained during the age determination process, which can take weeks or months. Among children interviewed by Human Rights Watch (2012) who were detained between 2008 and 2012, the average length of detention was 3.4 months, and the most egregious case involved a child detained for 7 months before release.

Migrants and refugees arriving in Malta without authorization are predominantly adult males (66 percent in 2012 and 63 percent in 2013) from Sub-Saharan Africa. They typically travel to Malta by boat, having departed from Libyan shores. Many of those who arrived in Malta over the last decade spent many months or even years in Libya before making the journey across the Mediterranean and often claim that Italy was their intended destination. Indeed, most migrant boats do not arrive on the island but are rescued within Malta's search-and-rescue area in the Mediterranean when they encounter inclement weather or problems with their boats. Those on board may use their transnational networks in order to acquire the telephone numbers of other migrants or advocacy organizations in Malta and Italy, who they can call to alert the authorities of their presence at sea. Such transnational networks are the key to migrants' mobility: family members in other countries may finance the voyage across the Mediterranean, for example. Many of the male migrants and refugees who arrive in Malta have wives, children, and other family members who remain in refugee camps in Kenya or in other countries of transit and who hope to reunite in Europe.

The high rates of refugee protection in Malta, which peaked at 90 percent in 2012, reflect the nationalities of those who arrive without authorization and subsequently apply for asylum. Somalis and Eritreans make up the largest groups. For example, 50 percent of the 2,008 people who arrived by sea in 2013 were Somali and 23 percent were Eritrean (UNHCR, 2014). Similarly, between 2002 and 2011 the highest numbers of asylum applications were Somalis (4,471), Eritreans (1,810), Nigerians (883), and Ivorian (641) and Sudanese (620) migrants. Despite this, the vast majority of successful asylum applicants in Malta receive subsidiary forms of protection that deny them access to family reunification and freedom of movement within the EU. For example, in 2012, although 60 percent of asylum applicants were Somali, only 2 percent were awarded full refugee status (NSO, 2013).

There are currently two operational detention centers in Malta, both located within military barracks: B Block in Safi Barracks and Hermes Block in Lyster Barracks. A third center, the Warehouse facility in Safi Barracks, was closed for refurbishment at the beginning of 2014. The number of people detained in these barracks fluctuates in response to the number of arrivals on the island. During 2013, 1,900 people were detained (JRS & aditus, 2014). The cost of operating these detention facilities is high: in 2008, the government spent more than €8.2 million, an increase from €6.8 million in 2005 (Parliamentary Question, 2009).

International and local advocacy organizations continue to criticize the conditions inside detention, including inadequate hygiene and sanitation provisions, lack of privacy for detainees, the dearth of female detention staff, and general inadequacy of shelter. Although these organizations note that conditions have improved over the last few years, poor conditions persist. For example, detainees have limited privacy, with very little space between beds and nowhere to store personal possessions; the centers have inadequate heating and ventilation and thus expose detainees to extreme heat and cold; and detainees at Lyster Barracks have outdoor access for only an hour and a half every day. Furthermore, the government provides no recreational or educational activities in the centers. Overcrowding, which regularly occurs during periods of high arrivals, exacerbates the minimal standards found in detention facilities (Human Rights Watch, 2012; JRS & aditus, 2014; ECHR, 2013a).

Organizations have also highlighted the adverse effects of detention on the long-term mental and physical health of detainees (McLoughlin & Warin, 2008; Steel et al., 2006). In extreme cases, migrant deaths have occurred at the hands of detention staff. For example, in 2012 Mamadou Kamara, a 32-year-old asylum seeker from Mali, died after being beaten by detention staff; and in 2011 a Nigerian man, Christian Ifeanyi Nwokaye, died while in custody after also being beaten by detention staff (JRS & aditus, 2014).

Immigration detention is run by Detention Services, which falls under the Ministry for Home Affairs and National Security. The Armed Forces of Malta

(AFM) play a significant role in Maltese immigration detention and immigration controls generally. Not only are immigration detention facilities located on AFM bases, but the vast majority of detention staff members are also current or former military and police personnel: in May 2013, Detention Services employed 188 people, of which 22 percent were current military officials, while the remainder were former police or military personnel (Parliamentary Question, 2013). The longstanding head of Detention Services is also a lieutenant colonel in the AFM.

The violent conditions of detention result in detainee protests and riots every few years. The most recent, in February 2014, occurred during a fact-finding mission by Maltese parliamentarians and resulted in five detainees being hospitalized (Ministry for Home Affairs and National Security, 2014; cf. D. DeBono, 2013). Nineteen asylum seekers escaped from detention the following month. Advocacy organizations argue that the length and conditions of detention encourage protest and escape attempts.

Immediate detention of migrants and refugees on arrival in Malta depicts them as dangerous and unwanted. The emphasis on security is reinforced by the role of the armed forces in detention and practices such as routine use of handcuffs on detainees when outside detention. Detention also isolates migrants and refugees: they are hidden from the wider Maltese community, surrounded by tall fences and barbed wire. The media have limited access, and family and friends are denied visitation rights. This marginalization persists after release. The detention policy has been associated with the rise in racism in Malta (Mainwaring, 2012a; cf. Schuster, 2003). Moreover, a survey carried out by *Malta Today*, a local newspaper, reported that only 28 percent of respondents had spoken with a migrant for longer than five minutes (J. Debono, 2013).

Framing Immigration Detention

Despite the financial, social, and human costs associated with detention, the policy enjoys strong bipartisan backing in Malta. It has been politically useful in reinforcing the image of a small island overwhelmed by irregular immigration flows in order to attract more support from the European Union. EU policies, such as the Schengen Agreement (1995), have underlined the need to control migration at the external border, ostensibly in response to relaxed internal controls. The EU's Dublin Convention (1997) also placed responsibility for asylum applications on the first country of arrival, often one of the member states along the external border (Mainwaring, 2012b). Faced with these new responsibilities as a small EU member state along the external border, Malta has portrayed irregular immigration as a crisis and immigration detention as a necessary response (Mainwaring, 2012a, 2014). Thus, Malta's immigration detention policy is intimately linked with membership in the European Union and the regional policies and politics of asylum and immigration.

In this context of a constructed immigration crisis, the Maltese government has defended its widely criticized immigration policy on the basis of the number of migrants arriving in relation to the size of the Maltese population. Securitized discourse based on "control" and "order" juxtaposed against vulnerable borders is at the heart of this justification (cf. Mainwaring, 2012a). For example, in 2014 the Minister for Home Affairs and National Security responded to a proposal put forward by the International Organization for Migration (IOM) and the UN High Commissioner for Refugees (UNHCR) to limit detention of unaccompanied minors and refugee children by saying, "[W]e feel that the public security and the health issues are paramount and [we] will have to strike a balance between the interest of the irregular immigrants themselves and certain national interests" (IAFR, 2014). Indeed, some officials go so far as to defend the detention policy as necessary "in order to protect migrants" (interview with government official, 2009).

With some exceptions, the Maltese judiciary has echoed political rhetoric. In a case brought again the Commissioner of Police in 2009, the Constitutional Court (2014) ruled:

> Detention can be considered, in the particular circumstances of our country, as a necessary measure required for the stability of the country so as to, as much as possible, avoid a deluge of "irregular" people running around Malta, and this without having established the prima facie interest and disposition of the person. (p. 13)

In concert with these justifications for detention based on law and order and control, government officials have also defended the policy as a deterrent measure. Despite a lack of evidence to support the claim, government officials believe immigration detention to act as a "powerful deterrent" (interviews with governmental officials, 2008–09; cf. Edwards, 2011). A senior official in the Ministry of Foreign Affairs (interview, 2009) explained the ministry's position on immigration detention: "[I]t is good to persuade [illegal migrants] that they have to go back home. . . . It's good that they contact their relatives and say, listen, don't come to Malta because it's terrible here" (cf. Mainwaring, 2012a; Council of Europe, 2005).

A recent UNHCR report highlights the lack of empirical evidence to support the claim that detention is an effective deterrent (Edwards, 2011). Indeed, interviews with migrants and refugees in Malta (2008–2010) reveal that the vast majority have no knowledge of the immigration detention policy before arriving on the island, a finding echoed by other advocacy organizations (Human Rights Watch, 2012). International law also prevents states from employing immigration detention as a deterrent, especially with regard to asylum seekers, as it does not allow cases to be examined individually and can amount to collective punishment (Edwards, 2011). Detention is permitted only in exceptional cases if it is reasonable and proportional, it is necessary to verify identity, and alternatives to detention prove to be inadequate. In light of this, the legal scholar Guy Goodwin-Gill (2003, p. 225) concludes, "The use of detention for the purposes of deterrence is . . . impermissible."

Nevertheless, detention remains in place as a perceived deterrent in Malta. Moreover, it is used to encourage migrants and refugees to participate in the assisted voluntary repatriation (ARV) scheme established in partnership with the IOM in 2007. The scheme offers migrants and refugees up to €2,500 to return to their country of origin. Although AVR has had limited success—in 2012, for example, only 39 people participated, while the government forcibly removed 266 others (EMN, 2013)—government officials explicitly link the punitive nature of detention with their ability to recruit migrants and refugees to the AVR scheme. An official within the Ministry of Foreign Affairs (interview, January 2009; cf. Mainwaring, 2012a) explained:

> If they are in detention they're not enjoying it for sure. In detention they can't dream, but once they are in open centers they can dream of escaping Malta. . . . I think detention is tough on the individual and conditions could be improved, but for us it's a blessing that people get disgusted and want to leave. (p. 691)

In line with this logic, AVR recruitment shifted from open centers to detention centers since the scheme's implementation in Malta. Despite a poor AVR participation rate and an absence of other evidence, officials continue to believe that detention encourages participation and thus see little incentive to improve conditions in detention or to review the detention policy more generally.

The defense of immigration detention as a deterrent and security measure is intimately linked with Malta's membership and geopolitical position in the EU. The EU's emphasis on controlling immigration along the external border in order to "secure" the union and compensate for relaxed internal controls encourages member states along the external border to adopt securitized rhetoric and practices of control. In this context, Maltese governmental officials exploit the tension within the humanitarian-security nexus seen across the EU, where, for instance, securitized control practices are juxtaposed against pronouncements of Europe as an area of protection for asylum seekers and refugees (cf. Andersson, 2014). Officials are thus quick to discredit EU criticism of Malta's detention policy, pointing to the responsibility the EU simultaneously places on the country to control migration and secure the external border (interviews with government officials, 2008–2011).

Transnational Control and Resistance

Malta's detention policy lacks effectiveness in realizing the policy outcome goal of deterrence; migrants and refugees continue to arrive on the island. Nevertheless, the Maltese government benefits from its detention policy reinforcing the spectacle of control over its sovereign borders (cf. De Genova, 2013). Other actors also contribute to and benefit from this spectacle, which is embedded in a transnational enforcement effort. For example, the contribution of the Armed Forces of Malta serves to militarize immigration controls and reinforce the spectacle of enforcement and the related portrayal of migrants as a security concern.

Since 2002, when Malta experienced the initial increase in irregular immigration, the remit of the AFM has expanded to include various facets of immigration control. These new roles have reinforced the AFM's legitimacy and power in a country that enshrined neutrality in its constitution in 1987. The AFM has responsibility for boats in distress in the island's large search-and-rescue area, which spans more than 250,000 square kilometers of the Central Mediterranean, almost 800 times the size of the island (316 square kilometers). In parallel with the larger flows of irregular migration across this stretch of sea, the maritime squadron's responsibilities and profile have increased. As already mentioned, the AFM is also inextricably linked to management of detention centers on the island, providing space and personnel.

The AFM's prominent role in detention and other immigration controls results in monetary benefits for the organization. EU funds from the Solidarity and Management of Migration Flows Program have been used to purchase new military hardware, to expand the Maritime Squadron's fleet, and to refurbish detention centers. Their new role has also extended across territorial borders as they are now involved in the political endeavor to contain migration flows in North Africa—a longstanding goal of Italy and Malta—through externalization of migration controls. For example, in 2008 Italy signed a Treaty on Friendship with Libya's leader, Muammar Gaddafi, which informally allowed Italy to return migrants and refugees from the high seas to Libya. Training and other measures also created incentives for Libya to exert greater control over its borders by preventing the departure of migrants and refugees from its northern Mediterranean border. The European Court of Human Rights (2012) subsequently ruled that the much-criticized "push back" practice was contrary to various human rights provision, including the principle of non-refoulement.

The ruling has arguably strengthened efforts by Malta, Italy, and the wider European Union to create incentives for Libya to control its borders. In 2012, the AFM sent 46 officers and other enlisted men to train Libyan officials in border control practices (Anon., 2012). Since then, Maltese officers have joined the EU Border Assistance Mission in Libya (Sansone, 2014). The transnational control effort has also involved provision of training by the AFM, in collaboration with the U.S. Coast Guard, in search-and-rescue coordination and planning to personnel from countries such as Albania, Cameroon, Equatorial Guinea, and Kenya.

States' transnational attempts to control and contain particular forms of mobility are countered in part by migrant and advocacy organizations. These organizations point to how control measures are ineffective and cause more harm in encouraging migrants and refugees to take longer and more dangerous routes into Europe. In terms of immigration detention, local and international organizations were significant in limiting the previously indefinite detention policy. Local organizations and the Council of Europe exerted pressure on the Maltese government by, for example, publishing reports that exposed the inhumane conditions and length of detention (see Council of Europe, 2005). Since then, organizations have maintained pressure on the government to reconsider the policy through exposing persistent substandard conditions (e.g., Human Rights Watch, 2012; Médecins sans Frontières, 2009).

Such organizations have transnational networks across Europe, and beyond, that bolster these attempts to improve conditions inside detention centers in Malta. They contribute to projects and reports that map detention practices around the world and provide comparative information. Others document best practices and the availability of alternatives to detention in place in Europe and beyond. Some also operate inside detention. In Malta, the UNHCR and Jesuit Refugee Services (JRS) have a permanent presence in detention and provide significant support and services to detainees. Their work in detention gives them access and expertise that other organizations, journalists, and researchers do not have. Firsthand experience and relationships with migrants and refugees within and outside detention give these organizations a wealth of knowledge that often forms the basis of reports on immigration detention.

Moreover, advocacy organizations have been crucial in bringing cases against the government before national and regional courts. For example, the head of JRS Malta and the head of a local human rights organization, aditus, defended former detainees against the Maltese government in cases at the European Court of Human Rights (2013a, 2013b). In both cases, the court ruled that immigration detention violated multiple human rights. These efforts require organizations to maintain transnational networks with migrants and other organizations across Europe and North Africa.

Conclusion

Although the evolution of immigration detention in Malta must be understood within developments at the EU level, these regional policies and politics have in contrast been plagued by national logics. The limited success in achieving a

Common European Asylum Policy is one example: member states have been reluctant to establish higher standards of reception and protection for asylum seekers and refugees at the regional level, while finding more common ground on control measures. On the one hand, radically divergent reception conditions and levels of recognition reveal the lack of harmonization across member states. On the other hand, the decision to enshrine 18 months as the limit on immigration detention in EU legislation indicates emphasis on control and use of the lowest common denominator in protection measures.

Malta's particular geopolitical position within the European Union has also offered little incentive to review the emphasis on deterrence through policies such as immigration detention. Stephen Castles (2004) has argued that such migration controls fail in part because they follow a national logic, while the factors that drive migration follow a transnational or global logic. National deterrent measures, such as immigration detention, are unlikely to be effective in the face of such global dynamics as increasing inequality between the first and third worlds, the effects of globalization that create the cultural capital and technical means needed for migration, and the structural dependence of some countries on emigration and of others on immigrant labor (ibid.). In light of this, states have increasingly responded with transnational attempts to control migration beyond their borders through externalization measures (e.g., Hyndman & Mountz, 2008).

In Malta, this has taken the form of support for Italy's previous "push back" policy and the more recent training of Libyan border officials, alongside the enduring, unfounded belief in immigration detention as deterrent. Despite transnational resistance by advocacy organizations and the readily available alternatives to detention that are in place in 24 EU member states (European Commission, 2014), government officials continue to support the mandatory, 18-month detention policy. Maintaining the policy comes at exorbitant social and human costs for migrants, refugees, and Maltese society. Indeed, the detention regime in Malta continues to detain children, the elderly, and the mentally and psychically disabled. A recent Human Rights Watch (2012, p. 2) report concludes that immigration detention in Malta "operates in an automated, indiscriminate and blanket manner in violation of international law."

References

Amnesty International. (2012). *Punishment without a crime: Detention of migrants and asylum-seekers in Cyprus*. London: Author.

Andersson, R. (2014, Oct. 30). Mare Nostrum and migrant deaths: The humanitarian paradox at Europe's frontiers. *OpenDemocracy*. Retrieved from https://www.opendemocracy.net/5050/ruben-andersson/mare-nostrum-and-migrant-deaths-humanitarian-paradox-at-europe%E2%80%99s-frontiers-0.

Anon. (2012, Aug. 27). AFM detachment in Tripoli to train Libyan forces. *Times of Malta*. Retrieved from http://www.timesofmalta.com/articles/view/20120827/local/afm-detachment-in-tripoli-to-train-libyan-forces.434561.

Castles, S. (2004). The factors that make and unmake migration policies. *International Migration Review, 38*(3), 852–884.

Constitutional Court. (2014, Apr. 29). *Essa Maneh et. v. Commissioner of Police*. Appeal Number 53/2008/1, Civil Court, First Hall, Malta. Retrieved from http://www.refworld.org/cgi-bin/texis/vtx/rwmain/opendocpdf.pdf?reldoc=y&docid=51a86d424.

Council of Europe (2005, Sep. 10). Report to the Maltese government on the visit to Malta carried out by the European Committee for the Prevention of Torture and Inhuman or Degrading Treatment or Punishment from 15 to 21 June, 2005. CPT/Inf (2007) 37, Strasbourg.

Council of Europe (2011, June 9). *Report by Thomas Hammarberg, commissioner for human rights of the Council of Europe, following his visit to Malta from 23–25 March 2011*. CommDH (2011) 17, Strasbourg.

DeBono, D. (2013). Less than human: The detention of irregular immigrants in Malta. *Race & Class, 55*(2), 60–81.

Debono, J. (2013, Aug. 12). *MaltaToday* survey: The Great Siege syndrome—one in five thinks Malta is being invaded. *MaltaToday*. Retrieved from http://www.maltatoday.com.mt/news/data_and_surveys/29039/maltatoday-survey-the-great-siege-syndrome-one-in-five-thinks-malta-is-being-invaded-20130812#.VHECt4ewH-I.

De Genova, N. (2013). Spectacles of migrant illegality: The scene of exclusion, the obscene of inclusion. *Ethnic and Racial Studies, 36*(7), 1180–1198.

Edwards, A. (2011). Back to basics: The right to liberty and security of person and alternatives to detention of refugees, asylum-seekers, stateless persons and other migrants. Geneva: UNHCR.

European Commission (2014). The use of detention and alternatives to detention in the context of immigration policies. Synthesis report for the EMN Focused Study 2014.

European Court of Human Rights. (2012, Feb. 23). *Hirsi Jamaa and Others v. Italy*, Application no. 27765/09, Strasbourg.

European Court of Human Rights. (2013a, July 23). *Aden Ahmed v. Malta*, Application no. 55352/12, Strasbourg.

European Court of Human Rights. (2013b, July 23). *Suso Musa vs Malta*, Application no. 42337/12, Strasbourg.

European Migration Network (EMN). (2013). *Annual policy report 2012 on migration and asylum policy in Malta*. European Commission. Retrieved from http://ec.europa.eu/dgs/home-affairs/what-we-do/networks/european_migration_network/reports/docs/annual-policy/2012/18._malta_national_report_final_may2013_en.pdf.

European Union (2003, Feb. 2). Council Directive (EC) 2003/9/EC of 27 January 2003 laying down minimum standards for the reception of asylum seekers. *Official Journal of the European Union, L31*.

European Union (2008, Dec. 24). Directive 2008/115/Ec of the European Parliament and of the Council of 16 December 2008 on common standards and procedures in member states for returning illegally staying third-country nationals. *Official Journal of the European Union, L347*.

Goodwin-Gill, G. (2003). Article 31 of the 1951 Convention Relating to the Status of Refugees: Non-Penalization, Detention, and Protection. In E. Feller, V. Türk, & F. Nicholson (Eds.), *Refugee protection in international law: UNHCR's global consultations on international protection* (pp. 185–252). Cambridge: Cambridge University Press.

Human Rights Watch (2012, July). *Boat ride to detention: Adult and child migrants in Malta*. New York, NY: Human Rights Watch.

Hyndman, J., & Mountz, A. (2008). Another brick in the wall? Neo-refoulement and the externalization of asylum by Australia and Europe. *Government and Opposition 43*(2), 249–269.

International Association for Refugees (IAFR). (2014, Oct. 14). Alternatives to detention in Malta. Press release. Retrieved from http://iafr.org/news-2/253-iom-unhcr-report-launch-alternatives-to-detention-in-malta.

International Organization for Migration (IOM) & UN High Commissioner for Refugees (UNHCR) (2014). *Unaccompanied migrant and refugee children: Alternatives to detention in Malta.* Summary report. IOM-UNHCR Joint Technical Mission, Malta, Apr. 27–May 1, 2014. Retrieved from http://reliefweb.int/sites/reliefweb.int/files/resources/Unaccompanied-Migrant-and-Refugee-Children-Alternatives-to-Detention-in-Malta.pdf.

Jesuit Refugee Services (JRS) & aditus (2014, May). Country report: Malta, asylum information database. Retrieved from http://www.asylumineurope.org/reports/country/malta.

Lutterbeck, D. (2006). Policing migration in the Mediterranean. *Mediterranean Politics, 11*(1), 59–82.

Mainwaring, C. (2012a). Constructing a crisis: The role of immigration detention in Malta. *Population, Space and Place, 18*(6), 687–700.

Mainwaring, C. (2012b). Resisting distalization? Malta and Cyprus' influence on EU migration and asylum policies. *Refugee Studies Quarterly, 31*(4), 38–66.

Mainwaring, C. (2014). Small states and nonmaterial power: Creating crises and shaping migration policies in Malta, Cyprus, and the European Union. *Journal of Immigrant and Refugee Studies, 12*(2), 103–122.

McLoughlin, P., & Warin, M. (2008). Corrosive places, inhuman spaces: Mental health in Australian immigration detention. *Health & Place, 14*(2), 254–264.

Médecins Sans Frontières (2009). *Not criminals: Médecins Sans Frontières exposes conditions for undocumented migrants and asylum seekers in Maltese detention centers.* Berlin, Germany.

Ministry for Home Affairs and National Security. (2014, Mar. 13). Disturbance at Lyster Detention Center, Tuesday 25th February 2014: Final report of inquiry. Malta: Ministry of Home Affairs and National Security.

National Statistics Office (NSO). (2013, June 9). World Refugee Day: 2013. News Release, Malta.

Parliamentary Question (2009, Mar. 11). Detention centers—spiża totali. Legislature XI: no. 6969.

Parliamentary Question (2013, May 29). Detention services. Legislature XII, no. 2214.

Sansone, K. (2014, Apr. 19). Army officers in Libya to train coastguard. *Times of Malta.* Retreived from: http://www.timesofmalta.com/articles/view/20140419/local/army-officers-in-libya-to-train-coastguard.515544

Schuster, L. (2003). Common sense or racism? The treatment of asylum-seekers in Europe. *Patterns of Prejudice, 37*(3), 233–256.

Steel, Zachary, et al. (2006). Impact of immigration detention and temporary protection on the mental health of refugees. *British Journal of Psychiatry, 188*(1), 58–64.

UN High Commissioner for Refugees (UNHCR). (2012). *Detention guidelines: Guidelines on the applicable criteria and standards relating to the detention of asylum-seekers and alternatives to detention.* Geneva: Author.

UN High Commissioner for Refugees (UNHCR). (2014). *Malta asylum trend 2013.* Geneva: Author.

UN Human Rights Council. (2010, Jan. 18). *Report of the Working Group on Arbitrary Detention: Mission to Malta, 19 to 23 January 2009.* Report A/HRC/13/30/Add.2. Retrieved from http://www2.ohchr.org/english/bodies/hrcouncil/docs/13session/A.HRC.13.30.Add2.pdf.

11

Trapped to the Local

The Effects of Immigration Detention in France

STEFAN LE COURANT AND CAROLINA KOBELINSKY

The immigration detention apparatus and the possibility of being deported became part of French Law in 1980. The scandal of the discovery of a confinement site in Arenc (Marseille) for foreigners awaiting deportation in 1975 was the beginning of a wave of protests that put pressure on the Interior Ministry to legislate on the matter (Fischer & Makaremi, 2012). Since then, every reform concerning immigration laws increased the length of the detention period, as has become the general trend in the EU countries. In the political discourse, this rise is said to improve the efficacy of removal orders. The maximal length has gone from 7 days in 1983 to 10 in 1993, 12 in 1998, 32 in 2003, and 45 in 2011. Throughout this process, the meaning of immigration confinement changed: it was an exceptional practice that became the general rule. From 2003 until 2012, a period in which a right-wing government was in power, the Interior Ministry publicly announced the target number for deportations for each year. Deploying figures in political discourses was a way of illustrating the dynamism of the government—its "results culture" (*culture des résultats*).

Between 2004 and 2011 the expected figure of deportations rose from 15,000 to 28,000 and eventually to 30,000. The final increase was described as a "consequence" of the Arab Spring. In 2012, during the presidential campaign, the number of deportations became a central issue as the right-wing party promised to remove 40,000 foreigners during that year if President Sarkozy was reelected. When the socialist party took over, the numbers game stopped. The figures for deportations fell because of a reform that changed the financial incentive policy to leave France, which was implemented by the previous government and which counted these "voluntary" returns as removals. Police practices, however, have not changed. Despite the decriminalization of unauthorized stay—a policy implemented to parallel EU legislation—the number of unauthorized migrants arrested remained stable (ONDRP, 2013).

On September 9, 2008, Amadou Traoré, who had no legal status in France, was arrested as he exited the subway station on his way to a construction site where he worked five days a week. He was held in custody for a day, after which he was sent to a detention facility, where he remained for two days before finally going to court. The liberty and custody judge (*juge des libertés et de la retention*) decided to extend the detention period; Traoré was then transferred to another detention center. However, he was released as the administration was not able to complete his deportation procedure within 32 days, the maximum length of detention at the time.

Like Traoré, thousands of unauthorized migrants are detained in France so that the authorities can arrange for their deportation but are then released because of certain technicalities in the arrest procedure or because the administration is not able to obtain a travel document (*laissez-passer consulaire*). In 2008, the same year Traoré was detained for the first time, 35,592 foreigners were sent to a detention facility and 14,411 of them were deported (CC, 2009; CICI, 2009). The discrepancy in these figures is not very different from discrepancies in other years. In the public debate, these statistics were generally seen either as a reflection of this policy's total failure or as an assertion of its partial success.

The ethnographic examination we develop in these pages goes beyond this binary analysis. Instead we explore the role played by the removal apparatus in the daily life of undocumented migrants who have experienced at least one episode of detention and who remain in France. We argue that although in most cases confinement does not lead to expulsion, the state's power has far-reaching effects on the lives of these "non-deportable deported" beings, as is the case of unauthorized migrants who were actually deported (Lecadet, 2011). Immigration detention and border politics weaken migrants' possibilities of having an ordinary life, always wiping the slate clean, confining them to the local and perpetuating the present. French contemporary politics have (re)created the border by other means than actual and concrete deportation. We contend that this policy confines people to the local, inhibiting unauthorized migrants' transnational aspirations and practices, thus reinforcing the state's capacity to create and impose its power within national borders.

The chapter draws on data collected between 2006 and 2013 among undocumented migrants who remained in France after at least one detention period. The first encounter with most of our interlocutors took place in a detention facility in the Parisian suburbs where Stefan Le Courant provided pro bono legal assistance as a volunteer for an NGO from 2006 and 2009 (Le Courant, 2013). We then participated in the daily activities of many migrants after being released: from appointments with NGOs or private lawyers to visits to the Préfecture, and even more ordinary activities such as going to work, to the hospital, to the market, inter alia.

Three clarifications are necessary before concluding this introduction. The first deals with the language applied in these pages to the individuals targeted by immigration detention. We prefer the terms *unauthorized* and *undocumented* to *illegal* when describing foreigners without any official immigration status in France. It seems to us that the word *unauthorized* stresses, as does the French term *étranger en situation irrégulière,* the nonconformity to bureaucratic standards while "undocumented" emphasizes the absence of documents considered as "powerful" material artefacts (Riles, 2006). The second remark concerns the choice of masculine pronouns when describing the actions of a singular unauthorized migrant. As men are the main target of immigration detention policy—because of the migrant's stereotype as being a single (young) man—most of the undocumented migrants who are arrested and deported are men, and most of our interlocutors are men as well. The data on women's experiences show that although different strategies are used for legalization and stay in France, the effects of immigration detention are very similar for both genders. Finally, we have an ethical responsibility toward our interlocutors. All the names of unauthorized migrants that appear in these pages have been changed in order to preserve their anonymity and the sensitive information provided.

Forced to Wipe the Slate Clean

Before becoming a reality, detention and confinement were a daily threat for undocumented migrants. All our interlocutors agree that once in detention this threat becomes palpable and real. During confinement they become aware of the fragility of their situation in France. If they are not deported they remain in a state of "deportability" (De Genova, 2002) once released. This potentiality of deportation shadows undocumented migrants, contributing to the perception of a temporality at the margins, a temporality that is uncertain and cyclical.

Just after being released, Amadou Traoré and the men we met had two clear projects in mind: regularizing their status in France or returning home. Most of our interlocutors affirm that if the legalization attempts do not work, they will go back to their home country. However, this idea is soon abandoned. Only a very small portion of undocumented migrants decide to go back home, and if they do it is with the unique objective of finding a "legal" way to return to France. "If I do not get papers in six months, I leave. I cannot stay like this, without work, doing nothing," said Oumar Diakité, who lost his job after being arrested. Legalization becomes all the more urgent as he seeks to rid himself of this feeling of deportability reinforced by the confinement period. In 2008, after being released from a detention center, Tidiane Diallo announced he would go back to Mali if he was not legalized within six months. In a conversation one afternoon a year later, he declared: "If I still have nothing in 2011, I'll go back. I am wasting my life here. I need a wife and children. It's not easy here." Precise deadlines are constantly set and revised. Going back home appears simply as a possibility to escape from deportability, but the time spent in France would be useless if Oumar Diakité or Tidiane Diallo had to return as they left, that is, "without a land, without a house, with nothing." Legalization is then the first and most important goal, but the attempts are full of obstacles: every time an undocumented migrant goes to a Préfecture the deportation order issued comes up again and the legal ways to find a solution become very difficult if not impossible. As such, confinement produces illegality (Darley, 2009). In the best-case scenario, the civil servant at the Préfecture suggests that the person come back again once it expires (i.e., after a year); in the worst-case scenario, the foreigner is arrested at the desk and sent back to a detention center.

In order to get legal status, the unauthorized migrant needs to have recourse to the law. If he does not master legal tools, his agency is severely reduced and he has to depend on experts—lawyers, NGOs. In addition to all this, he is forced to deal with a temporal difference between the urgency to put a term to his situation and bureaucratic and legal times, which can be very lengthy. For instance, the removal orders can last a year and, in theory, prevent the start of a legalization procedure. Although it is a case-by-case decision, the usual way of redressing legal status is to apply for a residence permit after spending at least 10 years in the country. Today, legalization through work is privileged to the detriment of legalization through family. Familial ties are increasingly suspected of being false, and current policies promote what is supposed to be "useful" to the national economy. In exceptional cases, undocumented migrants receive legal permits for "humanitarian" reasons (e.g., life-threatening illness). This practice justifies the securitization and hardline policies against (the majority of) migrants who do not elicit compassion (Fassin, 2012; Ticktin, 2011). Still, these possibilities are full of obstacles and make legalization very hypothetical. Soon after being released, undocumented migrants find themselves in a state of latency; their legalization project seems impossible and the whole trajectory is reoriented by the experience of detention. Everyday life conditions are jeopardized immediately after a detention period.

Most of the time, unauthorized migrants have to look for a new job, as was the case for Oumar Diakité, since "discovery" of his illegal status by the employer—who ignored or pretended to ignore it—often leads to dismissal of the employee. On their release, migrants also have to move. At times this comes as the result of being evicted by a landlord because they themselves are afraid of police harassment at their place of residence. A detention period then breaks the migrant's trajectory. "How many arrests, how many detention centers and how many jobs lost because of papers . . . how many times I have lost my flats because of that . . . ," remembered Moussa Kanouté some days after getting a three-month residence permit. Looking back on eight years of living undocumented, he remembers many arrests, too many confinement periods, and all the times he was forced to wipe the slate clean; as many interlocutors put it, it was a "*retour à zéro*." These are only some of the very concrete effects of detention on the material life conditions of unauthorized migrants.

Treated as a Criminal

Another effect of containment is to be found in the transformation of the self-image of the unauthorized migrant. Use of handcuffs by the police is usually seen as one of the most striking events in the detention experience. "I have never had handcuffs. It's humiliating for us. I did not steal anything," recalled an outraged Béatrice Tamba, arrested at the bank when she had an appointment to open an account. Confinement crystallizes a bureaucratic situation that is considered to be felony by the law. "I am not a thief" is a sentence frequently heard inside detention facilities. At the same time, conversely, the illegality of the stay is also compared to an infraction: "In my head I used to tell myself that one day I would be arrested, when you steal, one day you are caught." During the procedure, the use of coercion tools affects undocumented migrants' self-representation. As Dario Achadoo put it:

> It is not only the handcuffs; it is also the uniforms, the blue lights. For someone so simple, who did nothing. And the police escorts that take you to court, the police van, the small cell, as you're handcuffed at the back. It is horrible, humiliating. There were six policemen, as if I were a terrorist.
>
> —interviewed Jan. 25, 2010

As is the case for many other interlocutors, the way Achadoo was treated does not correspond to his self-representation. Although their presence in France is *illegal*, undocumented migrants envisage their stay as legitimate both because they perceive their behavior (as workers, as parents, as tax payers, etc.) as irreprehensible and because their infraction of the immigration law seems minimal (Coutin, 2006 [2000]). Use of coercive tools is symbolically charged and contributes to the image of the undocumented migrant as a "criminal." The testimonies of the detention experience stressing the physical feeling of mortification, given by both deported migrants—from Europe (Lecadet, 2011), the United States, and Canada (Peutz, 2006, 2010)—and undocumented migrants who remain in France, translate the experience of a body stranger (exterior) to the self. The treatment to which an immigrant is subjected is not what would be expected for a worker who pays his taxes, or for a father who sends money to his children. Something blurs the self-image of the foreigner, who has to face the implications of his status. He often immediately tries to distance himself from the image of a criminal, declaring, "I did nothing," "I did not steal," or "I did not kill anyone." During an interview, Vololona Ravaomanely questioned the means deployed by the state in order to send him back to Madagascar:

> I don't know why they attacked like this, this is what I cannot . . . the others were released after two days, five days . . . but why me? I don't know [later he adds:] It is true that France has already given me a lot, but I also

> gave, even if it's not much compared to what I received, in my work, in all I have done. But what is it? Is it because I have been operated on, because France paid for my surgery, is it that? Is that what gets into their criteria?
>
> —interviewed Jan. 9, 2009

Trying to explain the reasons for his confinement for thirty-two days, Ravaomanely ends by imagining that he was being punished for the medical treatment he received, which was paid by French Social Security. His self-representation is transformed by the experience of detention. This experience, as Foucault (1975) showed for prison, transforms the individual who committed an infraction—the lack of legal status—into a delinquent person. Immigration detention is then experienced as a punishment for having committed a fault. Ravaomanely understood his confinement through the prison model: the greater the perceived fault, the longer the duration of confinement. He believed that he remained in a detention center for a longer period than the other detainees because he had benefited from the health care system. He internalized the public discourse that imagines the migrant as a profiteer and sees detention as a response.

The degradation of self-image is stronger when undocumented migrants accept they have to turn to illegal practices to live an ordinary life. Many of our interlocutors purchase forged residence permits or use somebody else's ID in order to get a job. The impossibility of modifying one's legal status comes together with the emergence of a field of "illegalist practices" (ibid., p. 285). Positioned outside the law, many of their ordinary activities must be clandestine. Oftentimes our interlocutors explained that they "had no [other] choice;" as Ibrahim Keita put it: "We do not commit an offense. The only offence is the fake papers but we don't have a choice." The field of illegality that surrounds the undocumented migrants, as Coutin (2006 [2000]) puts it when speaking of unauthorized Salvadorans in the United States, renders illicit commonplace actions such as working, traveling, and driving.

Forever "Young"

Detention makes visible the precariousness of undocumented migrants' situation in France and is illustrated in confinement at the margins—of legality. On the one hand, detention breaks migrants' trajectories, forcing them to rebuild their ordinary life. The expression *"retour à zero,"* which could be translated as making a fresh start or wiping the slate clean, reflects a cyclic temporality wherein after every detention it is necessary to start over: look for a new job, a new place to stay, contact a lawyer, etc. On the other hand, the bureaucratic situation produces a temporal shift: the undocumented migrants are at once separated from social time in France and the progress of time in their home country. Abdoulaye Sacko was thirty years old when he returned for the first time to Mali. He knew he was "young" in the village while his peers were not young anymore. His youth is measured socially and not biologically. He was not married. The nine years he spent in France appeared as a temporal bracket, adjourning his passage into adulthood.

On January 2008, Masséré Diaby was released after two weeks in a detention facility, but the judge delivered a removal order valid for three years. During this period, he tried to legalize his status through an undocumented migrants' strike movement in April 2008, one that helped many migrants reverse their status. But it did not work for Diaby because of the removal order. On April 12, 2011, having spent almost 10 years in France, he went to the Préfecture to apply for legalization. The civil servant at the desk examined the pile of documents and affirmed that the first evidence of presence in France was dated November 2001. He was therefore told to return to the Préfecture seven months later. Once out of the building, Diaby looked disappointed. He explained "there will be a day . . . is that what French say? A day will come and all the suffering of Masséré Diaby will be over and I'll be happy."

Bureaucracy implies waiting: to wait a year before the removal order expires, to wait 10 years in order to start a legalization procedure, to wait for an answer for an asylum application. . . . Waiting is, as Bourdieu (1997) put it, a way of experiencing the effects of power. It is a source of anxiety and distress; it is also painful in that it reinforces the impression of being confined in a timeless present (Kobelinsky, 2010). Plunged into this perpetual present, their movement is considerably slowed, accentuating the disparities with those who, benefiting from globalization, have seen their displacements accelerated (Bauman, 1998).

In 2009, Diaby's younger brother was granted legal status following a workers' strike in his company. Since then, the brother has gone back to the village, gotten married, and had his first baby. He also bought land in Bamako, where he is building a house. Masséré Diaby explained that "generally among the Soninke" a younger brother has to wait until the elders get married before he himself can marry. If they were in Mali that would happen, but "when it comes to papers, it's every man and his luck." Patience is needed when dealing with the state (Auyero, 2011), it is not enough. Chance is also required. How could he otherwise explain that his younger brother, who arrived in France two years after him, has already gotten the papers? Bureaucracy does not only put individuals lacking legal status on hold, it also interferes in family relations, disturbing customary rules on the order of precedence. In comparison with his brother, Masséré Diaby "has not done anything." He tried to find a wife in France, but the first time the uncle of the bride refused the marriage: "How can an undocumented be in charge a family?" The second attempt also ended in failure. This time it was the bride who disappeared after receiving his gifts just before the wedding. Masséré Diaby was discouraged: "Anyway, I am late. There is no need to run now. I wait for the papers and then I'll look for a wife in Mali."

Diaby's situation summarizes the imbricated temporalities of undocumented migrants' experiences: the cyclical time imposed after detention, the waiting imposed by the bureaucracy when trying to legalize one's status, and the social time in the home country. These three dimensions give them the impression of having reached a deadlock; they are "locked" in time and, as we'll see, in space.

On January 11, 2011, we visited Amidou Sy in a room at a collective shelter for migrant workers. After some time discussing his "file" (i.e., application for legalizing his status), he explained that he was in a hurry as he had to prepare the evening meal for all the men from his village in Mauritania who live in the shelter—about 50 people. Only "the old ones" are exempted from this activity; the others have to cook once a month.

> One day we will be old and we will rest. It is tiring to cook such big cooking pot. We want youngsters to come, all the guys from my generation want the youngsters to come but nowadays there are not so many coming because of visa issues, money. . . .

Restrictive European politics obstructs a migratory system that has been in place for decades for people coming from different villages in West Africa. Before the restrictions, an informal organization of substitution was standard. The last-arriving migrant was expected to finance an incoming migrant's trip to France. The payment not only secured the arrival of a fellow villager but also meant that the financing migrant was no longer considered a "youngster." Since renewals are no longer easily achievable, the hierarchy is fixed. Migrants who arrive last are considered the "young ones" for as long as new members of the village do not arrive. "I lost my life here," "I wasted my life," "I lost my time," "I am late" are sentiments often expressed in detention facilities. Undocumented migrants systematically compare their situation with what would have happened if they had stayed at home. Particularly for young men affected by border politics, the temporal markers such as marriage and children become a way to calculate this delay. Migration politics increase the disconnection between chronological and social time, both in France and in the home country. This is particularly the case for migrants coming from Western Africa, for whom age is an important determiner of social position. However, the perception of time wasted is shared by other migrants as well.

Deportability is an everyday feeling, and the uncertainty of this threat does not allow much thought and action outside of trying to escape this status. Our interlocutors often repeat the phrase, "I have too many things in my head." The actual waiting time imposed by bureaucratic procedures is doubled in the subjective perception where time is fixed, suspended, and contingent on the hope of legalization. The body of the undocumented migrant becomes the only marker of time passing. The timeless present of anguish transforms the impossible social aging into an accelerated physical aging; compared to the pictures on their passports, many of our interlocutors seem much older than the number of years passed.

Transnational Aspirations, Local Confinement

Despite their legal status in France, many undocumented migrants try to depict themselves as transnational beings (Boehm, 2012). Without traveling—as they do not have "papers"—they are, through a variety of practices, at once both here and there (Chu, 2010). Souleymane Bâ sent money to his brother in Mali for organizing the wedding at the city hall of the village. His brother pretended to be Souleymane Bâ before the authorities, and this is how he got married and changed his status without (physically) leaving France. Moussa Kanouté and many other interlocutors coming from the region of Kayes, in Mali, participate in small NGOs, created during the 1980s, that promote development of their home villages. They regularly send money and closely follow the progress of specific projects as a way of preparing for the future.

These transnational practices help unauthorized migrants cope with the uncertainty of their present. It also helps in anticipating the future. But the risks of undocumented migrants' everyday life frequently thwart these ambitions. After an arrest or the loss of a job, sending money home becomes more difficult if not impossible. Phone calls, which allow them to participate in life back home (i.e., to follow the progress of a house under construction or participate in family decisions), are dreaded because they come with requests that cannot be satisfied. Contact with the family is then reduced to a minimum and building projects are suspended because of lack of means, for example. A house can therefore remain without a roof for months or years. Without a job, undocumented migrants withdraw into themselves in the private space. Unable to maintain this double presence, they are again confined in the space and time of their fragile local existence. The present politic of immigration detention hinders every form of transnational circulation (people's movements, money transfers, communication, etc.).

Conclusion

In this chapter we addressed immigration detention in France by examining its consequences on unauthorized migrants' lives after a period of confinement. The encounter with the police, coercion, and containment undermine the self-representation of these individuals and produce a disruption in their trajectories. They try to get rid of the threat of deportation, which is reaffirmed during detention; they spend a lot of money on lawyers, *marabouts* (Islamic specialists using esoteric powers), or any expert who might somehow help.

Their material life is destabilized, and their temporality is shaken. The urgency of regularizing their legal status collides with the waiting time imposed by the French bureaucracy; the experience of an endless present in France is emphasized when they are faced with inability to follow the social time of their village, where they remain young despite their biological age. Undocumented migrants try to be both here (in France) and there (in their village). Moussa Kanouté, Amadou Traoré, Béatrice Tamba, and all our interlocutors partake in transnational practices but are indeed confined to national borders. The irony is that immigration detention prevents people's movement through identification techniques and rules that have themselves created the *illegality* of these migrants. This politic does not remove most of the *illegals,* but it confines them inside French territory in a temporality at the margins. Because of the threat of deportation, undocumented migrants experience these national borders in their daily life, thus reaffirming the state sovereignty (De Genova & Peutz, 2010).

The perceptions of our interlocutors examined here do not seem very different from what thousands of undocumented migrants who were effectively removed from French territory have experienced. The humiliation and degradation caused by their treatment, its effects on their self-image, the impression of being confined in time, and the certainty of being contained in space (the duration of the entry ban issued generally lasts between two and five years from the removal date, as stipulated by the EU "Return Directive") are all effects of immigration detention and border politics shared by deported and deportable-nondeported migrants. For all of them, transnationalism is an aspiration and an everyday ordeal. The immigration detention apparatus justifies its existence in that it is supposed to remove the undocumented migrants already living in France and deter those who want to enter. The figures show that the first objective is only partially achieved, and the deaths at the EU borders dramatically remind us deterrence is not achieved either. However, the main effect of immigration detention is to confine people to a locality, either in their home country, for the minority of them who were removed, or within French territory for the majority.

References

Auyero, J. (2011). Patients of the state: An ethnographic account of poor people's waiting. *Latin American Research Review, 46*(1), 5–29.

Bauman, Z. (1998). *Globalization: The human consequences.* New York: Columbia University Press.

Boehm, D. A. (2012). *Intimate migrations: Gender, family, and illegality among transnationale Mexicans.* New York: New York University Press.

Bourdieu, P. (1997). *Méditations pascaliennes.* Paris: Le Seuil.

Cour des Comptes. (2009). *La gestion des centres et des locaux de rétention administrative (exercices 2006 à 2008)* [*The Management of Detention Facilities (between 2006 and 2008)*]. Paris : Cour des comptes.

Chu, J. Y. (2010). *Cosmologies of credit: Transnational mobility and the politics of destination in China.* Durham, NC: Duke University Press.

Comité Interministériel de Contrôle de l'Immigration. (2009). *Les orientations de la politique de l'immigration. Cinquième rapport établi en application de l'article L. 111-10 du CESEDA [The orientations of immigration politics. Fifth report established in accordance with the article 111-10 of CESEDA].* Paris : Secrétariat général du Comité interministériel de contrôle de l'immigration.

Coutin, S. B. (2006 [2000]). *Legalizing moves: Salvadorian immigrants' struggle for U.S. residency.* Ann Arbor: University of Michigan Press.

Darley, J. M. (2009). Morality in the law: the psychological foundations of citizens' desires to punish transgressions. *Annual Review of Law and Social Science, 5*, 1-23.

De Genova, N. (2002). Migrant "illegality" and deportability in everyday life. *Annual Review of Anthropology, 31*, 419–447.

De Genova, N., & Peutz, N. (Eds.). (2010). *The deportation regime: Sovereignty, space, and the freedom of movement.* Durham, NC, & London: Duke University Press.

Fassin, D. (2012). *Humanitarian reason: A moral history of the present.* Berkeley: University of California Press.

Fischer, N., & Makaremi, C. (2012). "L'horreur de la République": Les enjeux moraux de l'enfermement des étrangers. In D. Fassin & J.-S. Eideliman (Eds.), *Economies morales contemporaines* (pp. 217–241). Paris: La Découverte.

Foucault, M. (Ed.). (1975). *I, Pierre Rivi_re, Having Slaughtered My Mother, My Sister, and My Brother--: A Case of Parricide in the 19th Century.* Lincoln, NE, USA, University of Nebraska Press.

Kobelinsky, C. (2010). *L'accueil des demandeurs d'asile. Une ethnographie de l'attente.* Paris: Editions du Cygne.

Le Courant, S. (2013). What can we learn from a "liar" and a "madman"? Serendipity and double commitment during fieldwork. *Social Anthropology/Anthropologie Sociale, 21*(2), 186–198.

Lecadet, C. (2011). *Le front mouvant des expulsés. Lieux et enjeux des regroupements et des mobilisations collectives des migrants expulsés au Mali.* Paris: EHESS.

ONDRP. (2013). *Fiche thématique n°9: "Zoom sur les infractions aux conditions générales d'entrée et de séjour des étrangers en 2012 et au premier semestre 2013 enregistrées par les services de la police nationale", La criminalité en France.* Paris: Observatoire national de la réponse pénale.

Peutz, N. (2006). Embarking on an anthropology of removal. *Current Anthropology, 47*(2), 217–241.

Peutz, N. (2010). "Criminal aliens" deportees in Somaliland: An ethnography of removal. In N. De Genova & N. Peutz (Eds.), *The deportation regime. Sovereignty, space, and freedom of movement* (pp. 371–409). Durham, NC, & London: Duke University Press.

Riles, A. (Ed.). (2006). *Documents: Artefacts of modern knowledge.* Ann Arbor: University of Michigan Press.

Ticktin, M. (2011). *Casualties of care: Immigration and the politics of humanitarianism in France.* Berkeley: University of California Press.

12

Harm and Accountability in Transnational Detention Environments

The Case of Australia's Extraterritorial Processing of Asylum Seekers

TANIA PENOVIC AND AZADEH DASTYARI

In February 2014, the remote immigration detention facility operated by Australia on Manus Island in Papua New Guinea (PNG) became the site of extreme violence. Protests and rioting led to two days of mayhem and brutality during which more than 60 detainees sustained serious injuries, including bullet wounds, broken bones, and machete wounds to the head and neck. One man had his throat slit and another lost an eye. A twenty-three-year-old Iranian asylum seeker, Reza Barati, died from severe brain injuries sustained in an attack by a number of personnel working at the center during which he was punched, kicked, beaten with a nail-embedded wood plank and struck repeatedly in the head with a large rock.

The facility in which these events took place has assumed a key role in Australia's policy toward asylum seekers. Those who arrive in Australia by boat are now transferred to PNG or to the detention facility in the small Pacific island nation of Nauru. Adoption of extraterritorial detention and processing of asylum seekers, first in 2001 (until 2007) and again in 2012, was not an anomaly in Australia's approach to those who seek protection as refugees. It fits within a long-standing policy approach of reducing the desirability of Australia as a destination country for asylum seekers.

This chapter examines Australia's extraterritorial processing regime. After considering the foundations on which the policy and practice are built, we provide a brief history of offshore processing by Australia. The ramifications of offshore processing are then considered, including the fiscal cost, the harm done to international and domestic relations within the Asia-Pacific region, and the human cost, including the mental harm suffered by those detained offshore. The question of who is accountable for harms suffered in these offshore detention facilities is complicated by their transnational and privatized operation. The concluding section of this chapter examines the problem of accountability in such an environment.

The Foundations of Offshore Processing

Geographic characteristics such as distance and the absence of land borders have enabled Australia to exert a high level of control over its borders (Schloenhardt, 2000). While migration receives little attention in the public discourse, the arrival of asylum seekers by boat has, like the threat of criminal activity, excited anxieties in the public imagination. From as early as the mid-1970s, Australia's response to those who seek its protection as refugees has been one of deterrence (Schloenhardt, 2000). Media reporting and parliamentary debates concerning a wave of Indochinese boat arrivals that commenced in the late 1980s reveal growing fears of impending catastrophe in the form of inundation by boat arrivals (Watson, 2009). Such catastrophe was to be averted by a regime of immigration detention.

Introduced in 1992, the regime has operated since 1994 to require detention of all noncitizens in Australia without a valid visa (unlawful noncitizens) until their status is determined. The usual practice has been to detain those who arrive without a valid visa, most of whom arrive by boat. They are detained in prison-like detention facilities, many of which are isolated from Australia's urban centers, until their refugee status has been finally determined. United Nations (UN) bodies find the regime to be inconsistent with Australia's human rights obligations, and a significant body of medical research has charted the deleterious impact of indeterminate closed detention on mental health.

Immigration detention has perpetuated the view that spontaneous boat arrivals are transgressive, even criminal in their conduct. After visiting Australia's detention facilities, the UN Working Group on Arbitrary Detention considered that immigration detention itself creates a presumption that every unlawful noncitizen presents a danger to the community (UN Working Group on Arbitrary Detention, 2002). Detention insinuates criminal guilt, construing the detainee as "somehow suspect, potentially criminal, or associated with criminality" (Rygiel, 2012, p. 219). The transgression with which these detainees are associated is that of bypassing the legitimate process for gaining protection, namely waiting for resettlement while living in camps and settlements in developing countries after being recognized as refugees. Although the possibility of resettlement remains low, those who are resettled are widely perceived as genuine refugees, while spontaneous arrivals converge with criminals in the political and public discourse. Since 1996, the quotas for refugees resettled from overseas and those who arrived spontaneously have been consolidated. With every refugee who arrives spontaneously effecting a commensurate reduction in resettlement places granted, the "queue jumper" label gained a foothold in the Australian vernacular and popular imagination.

By the late 1990s, the language of deviancy permeated media representations of asylum seekers. They were frequently depicted as a threat to the integrity of the nation state, as the "racialized deviant" or a threat to the security or health of the nation, "corrupting and contaminating the fabric of society" (Pickering 2001, p. 173). In response, the administration of Australian law and policy concerning asylum seekers has converged with aspects of criminal law (for an examination of "crimmigration" in the United States, see Stumpf, 2006). The perceived threat presented by the "immigrant other" created a sense of moral panic that rationalized introduction of extreme measures in a process elsewhere described as the securitization of mobility (Buzan, Waever, & De Wilde, 1998). With reference to comparable developments in the United States, Pope and Garrett observe that immigration policy has become a "security policy to protect the citizen from the invasion of the non-citizen" (2012, p. 175).

A Short History of Offshore Processing

Phase 1: The Pacific Solution

The number of asylum seekers attempting to reach Australia by boat once again increased between 1999 and 2001. In August 2001, after almost a decade of immigration detention, came the widely reported efforts taken by the captain of the Norwegian-registered MV *Tampa,* to enter Australian territorial waters and discharge 433 asylum seekers rescued at sea onto the Australian territory of Christmas Island. A sense of calamity was engendered by political press releases and media reporting that framed the attempted landing as an unwanted incursion into Australia's sovereignty by putative refugees seeking to coerce the government into acceding to their demands to enter Australia. The threat of the *Tampa*'s disembarkation (with its implication that the government may not have control over Australia's borders) was averted through adoption of extraordinary measures on the part of the Australian government, then led by Prime Minister John Howard from the center-right Liberal Party, in coalition with the National Party. These measures included deployment of military (Special Air Services) personnel to take control of the vessel and forcible transfer of the rescuees to Nauru for processing. This marked the commencement of a policy broadly known as the "Pacific Solution." The policy included interception and diversion of boats at sea (under arrangements dubbed "Operation Relex") and extraterritorial detention and processing of asylum seekers. Any noncitizen intercepted at sea or arriving in certain parts of Australia, without a valid visa to enter Australian territory, became vulnerable to transfer to Australia's economically struggling former protectorates of Nauru and PNG for processing and detention.

The Pacific Solution was built on the foundations of immigration detention, replicating and expanding its objectives and methodology. Like immigration detention, it aimed to deter asylum seekers from seeking protection, to distance them from Australian society and exclude them from the protections afforded under Australian law. The exclusion and isolation experienced by detainees in Australia's remote detention facilities is exacerbated by offshore processing, which barred detainees from Australia itself. Asylum seekers detained in Australia were granted protection in Australia if recognized as refugees, but the position for those processed in Nauru and PNG was said to be different. The Pacific Solution sought to divest Australia of the burdens of both processing and protection. To explicitly fulfill its deterrence aim, refugees processed in Nauru and PNG were to be resettled in countries other than Australia. Some 39 percent of them were resettled in the United States, Canada, New Zealand, Sweden, and elsewhere. But resettlement places were not easily secured, with most countries regarding them as Australia's responsibility. The remaining 1,153 refugees were ultimately resettled in Australia.

Because of a drop in the number of boat arrivals, the number of asylum seekers transferred to PNG decreased over time, and by May 2005 there were no detainees in the PNG facility. However, detention in Nauru continued until December 2007, when Australia's newly elected center-left Labor government ended what it dismissed as the "cynical, costly and ultimately unsuccessful exercise" (Evans, 2008) of the Pacific Solution.

Phase 2: Offshore Processing Refashioned as "Humanitarian" Policy

While in government, the Labor Party's opposition to extraterritorial processing proved to be short-lived. In 2010 there was a sharp rise in irregular boat arrivals, which the Liberal-National coalition (in opposition) attributed to the government's softening of asylum seeker policy, particularly suspension of the Pacific Solution. Julia Gillard assumed office from Kevin Rudd in June 2010 after an internal leadership contest within the Labor Party, and Australia once again looked to its Asia-Pacific neighbors for a solution.

The Gillard government's plans to establish a regional processing center in the newest nation in the Asia-Pacific, East Timor, were rejected by the East Timorese government. Australia then looked to Malaysia, concluding a cooperative transfer arrangement in July 2011, which would see 800 boat arrivals transferred by Australia to Malaysia in exchange for resettlement of 4,000 refugees currently living in Malaysia over a four-year period. The arrangement was struck down by the High Court of Australia because the requirements of Australia's Migration Act of

1958 were not met under the existing arrangement. Malaysia had neither enacted domestic laws nor undertaken international treaty obligations that recognize refugee status. After attempting unsuccessfully to pass legislation to defeat the judgment's effect, the government convened an expert panel to advise on policy options available to prevent asylum seekers from undertaking dangerous boat journeys to Australia. The panel recommended greater engagement by Australia with its Asia-Pacific neighbors with a view to establishing a "comprehensive regional cooperation framework" subject to the "short-term circuit break" of processing in PNG and Nauru (Australian Government, 2012).

Following the expert panel's recommendation, the Gillard government announced resumption of processing in PNG and Nauru in August 2012. Transfers of asylum seekers to Nauru commenced in September 2012 and to PNG in November 2012. Although children were (and still are) detained alongside adults in Nauru, children were removed in June 2013 from the PNG facility, which has since accommodated single adult males. The "short-term circuit break" envisaged by the expert panel became fashioned as the new solution to the problem of asylum seekers arriving by boat, and the longer-term goal of a regional cooperation framework faded into insignificance.

Labor's offshore processing regime was in substance an iteration of the Pacific Solution, but its introduction saw a marked shift in political rhetoric. Following the tragic drowning of asylum seekers attempting to arrive in Australia by boat, offshore processing was refashioned as a humanitarian policy necessary to prevent deaths at sea. Unlike the discourse of invasion and queue jumping that preceded introduction of the Pacific Solution, asylum seekers emerged as the subjects of parliamentarians' rhetorical concern, the desperate victims of the "people smugglers" who facilitated their transit. Though it was imperative that deaths at sea be prevented, the parliamentary debates failed to comprehend why asylum seekers submit themselves to perilous boat journeys, including the absence of settlement pathways in the region. Humanitarianism became the rationale for the same harsh measures that had operated under the Pacific Solution. Such use of the humanitarian pretext is a manifestation the tendency for industrialized states to respond to refugee flows in ways that see "humanitarian considerations morph with state interests" (Kneebone, 2010, p. 239), diverging from their original meaning and becoming a basis for asserting sovereignty or border control measures (ibid.). The re-introduction of offshore processing by the Gillard government in 2012 exemplifies the pursuit of state interests cloaked in the mantle of humanitarianism.

Like the Pacific Solution, offshore processing under Labor proceeded on the basis that refugees would be resettled in countries other than Australia. In July 2013, the government announced that refugees who successfully entered Australia by boat would no longer have the opportunity to be resettled in Australia. Under a new arrangement signed with PNG, all asylum seekers arriving by boat after July 2013 would be transferred to PNG, where they would be detained in expanded facilities on Manus Island, undergo refugee status determinations by PNG officials under PNG law, and ultimately be resettled in PNG if found to be refugees. Where refugees processed at Nauru would be settled remained unclear.

Phase 3: Operation Sovereign Borders

Labor's resumption of extraterritorial processing was supported by the Liberal-National coalition, which regained government in September 2013 after running a campaign in which future Prime Minister Tony Abbott repeatedly declared that "we will stop the boats." Eleven days after the election, the new government established "Operation Sovereign Borders," a "military-led response" to address refugee boat arrivals, which were characterized as a "national emergency on our borders" (Liberal Party of Australia, 2013). Like the Pacific Solution's naval interdiction program known as Operation Relex, boats would once again be intercepted at sea and diverted to Indonesia. Limited information would be publicly available about attempted boat arrivals, and extraterritorial processing would continue. The government committed to increasing capacity in the Nauru and PNG detention facilities to ensure that no asylum seekers arriving in Australia irregularly by boat are processed or resettled in Australia.

As November 30, 2014, there were 996 detainees at Nauru and 1,044 at Manus Island, which has operated at double its planned operational capacity since October 2013. The Abbott government has maintained that refugees processed at Manus Island will be resettled in PNG despite concerns about the viability of resettlement, sustainable integration (Senate Committee, 2014 [4.77]), safety, and employability. Viable resettlement in Nauru is unrealistic in light of its small population (approximately 10,000 people) and socioeconomic conditions. The economy is reliant on aid money from Australia, the unemployment rate is around 90 percent, and the rule of law is in a precarious state following the dismissal of senior judicial officers in June 2014. Nauruan parliamentarian Mathew Batsuahas expressed his reservations about the viability of resettlement, saying "[w]e're a small country, we have many issues ourselves. We're struggling with infrastructure issues, health issues, education issues, so to take on extra people doesn't make sense for us" (Cornall, 2014). An unascertained number of refugees were resettled in Nauru during 2014. They are reported to be isolated, suicidal, destitute, living in fear of violent attacks by Nauruan nationals, and unable to access basic necessities such as food and water (Doherty, 2014). In September 2014, an agreement was concluded, with respect to refugees processed in Nauru, between Australia and another nation facing significant socioeconomic challenges. The agreement facilitated resettlement in Cambodia of refugees processed in Nauru, provided they consent to the resettlement and are transported voluntarily.

Arrangements for management of the offshore detention facilities have always been complex and remain so. Asylum seekers processed in Nauru and PNG under the Pacific Solution were held in the custody of the International Organization for Migration. The Nauru center is now managed by Transfield Services, an Australian company engaged primarily in construction, resource extraction, and asset management. Transfield Services assumed management of the PNG center in March 2014 and subcontracted security services to Wilson Security. Medical and counseling services at PNG are provided by International Health and Medical Service. The PNG center was previously managed by the multinational security company G4S pursuant to a contract signed in February 2013. Additional services, such as cleaning and maintenance, have been provided by a number of contractors.

The Price Paid for Australia's Offshore Processing Regime

The success of extraterritorial detention and processing as a deterrence measure is contested (Crock & Ghezelbash, 2010). Nevertheless, significantly fewer asylum seekers entered Australian territory in the period 2001–2007, under the Pacific Solution, than before its adoption or after its abandonment (Phillips & Spinks, 2010). Although this may have been attributable to other factors such as changing circumstances in refugee producing countries, there is a correlation in Australian public consciousness between extraterritorial processing and the ability of the Australian government to stop asylum seekers from coming to Australia by boat. It is for this reason that Australia resumed offshore processing and detention in 2012 (McCann, 2014) and why it is supported by Australia's major political parties and unlikely to be abandoned in the near future. Yet extraterritorial detention and processing is costly and unsustainable. The price paid for Australia's maintenance of the policy is examined next.

Fiscal Cost

Offshore processing is significantly more expensive than alternative modes of accommodating asylum seekers awaiting determination of their claims for protection. For 2014–15, budget expenditure for the operation of the PNG and Nauru centers exceeds $1.2 billion, with expenses for Nauru amounting to $582.4 million and expenses for PNG of $629.46 million (Official Committee Hansard, 2014). Although it cost in excess of $400,000 per annum to keep an asylum seeker in PNG or Nauru during 2013, it cost $239,000 per person for onshore detention and less than $100,000 to hold an asylum seeker under "community detention arrangements" pursuant to which the person could live in a specified place in the community subject to supervision and reporting requirements.

The costs of allowing an asylum seeker to reside in the community under a "bridging visa" pending status determination is $40,000, one-tenth of the cost of offshore detention (National Commission of Audit, 2014, [10.14]).

Standard Bearing in the Asia-Pacific

Australia is situated in a region in which few neighboring countries have ratified the Refugee Convention and other core human rights treaties and many nations have no domestic laws recognizing the status of refugees. Both Nauru and PNG are parties to the UN Refugee Convention but both have limited capacity, expertise, and infrastructure with respect to refugee status determination and protection. Nauru has signed up to some, and PNG to almost all, of the core UN human rights instruments, but their compliance with these treaties' standards remains a matter of great concern.

With its commitment to the rule of law, democratic traditions, and prosperity, Australia is uniquely positioned to lead by example. Yet countries such as Thailand and Indonesia shoulder a disproportionate burden of the region's refugees. In seeking to delegate its refugee processing obligations to other nations, Australia has demonstrated a preference for self-serving bilateral arrangements over regional cooperation. Australia has failed to honor its treaty obligations and undermined the integrity of the international system. Other nations with greater domestic challenges have been given little incentive to improve their treatment of asylum seekers. In eschewing the mantle of standard bearer in the region, Australia frustrates realization of durable solutions for refugees in the Asia-Pacific.

International and Domestic Relations

Offshore processing has had an adverse impact on Australia's image and reputation within the Asia-Pacific region by fueling the perception that it subordinates regional concerns to its own domestic political objectives (Senate Foreign Affairs, Defense and Trade Committee, 2003). The processing of asylum seekers in PNG has been characterized as "an expression of Australian neo-colonialist attitudes, and indicative of the bullying behavior for which [Australia] holds a reputation in the Pacific Islands region" (Stead, 2014).

Hosting of offshore processing facilities on Australia's behalf has also fed domestic resentment, starkly illustrated by rising tensions on Manus Island. The Australian and PNG governments engaged in poor communication (Senate Report, 2014, [3.47]) with local residents about the detention facility's planning and operation. Local residents were excluded from its construction and provision of services. There was a sense that resources were being spent on the center while

PNG nationals' access to government funding was minimal, and that detainees were living in superior conditions (Cornall, 2014). Infrastructure was seen to be exploited while the local economy appeared to receive no corresponding benefit. One landowner observed that Australia operated a "boomerang system" in which it contacted its "own companies and when the money comes in it bounce[s] back to Australia" (Senate Report, 2014, [1.59]). Tensions were further fueled by the dumping of large amounts of disposable waste from the detention center in the local environment (ibid., [3.53]). PNG nationals' anger "towards the operation of the center, its staff and asylum seekers" became a catalyst for the rioting of February 2014 (ibid., [3.48]). Local animosity toward the detainees was furthermore seen to be a major cause of the high level of violence that ensued and the severity of the resulting injuries (Cornall, 2014).

Human Cost

Although Australia's offshore processing arrangements come at exorbitant expense to the taxpayer, the greatest cost is borne by the asylum seekers held in offshore detention. In both Nauru and PNG, they are detained for an indeterminate period in crowded and harsh physical conditions, with limited access to health care and essential services. A major source of tension and distress is the status determination process, characterized by long delays and an absence of timelines or clear and consistent information. In November 2013, Amnesty International concluded that "[t]he combined effect of the conditions of detention on Manus Island, the open-ended nature of that detention, and the uncertainty about their fates to which detainees are subjected amounts to cruel, inhuman and degrading treatment or punishment" with the conditions in some sections of the facility violating the prohibition on torture and other ill treatment (2013, p. 1).

High rates of depression and self-harm have been reported in both facilities. In Nauru, detention of children alongside adults has seen children witness numerous acts of self-harm such as lip sewing, and engage in such conduct themselves. Allegations were raised by the Australian Broadcasting Corporation on October 3, 2014, of sexual abuse of women and children in the Nauru center (Wilson, 2014). At the Manus Island facility, the former head of occupational health and safety, Rod St. George, described suicide attempts and self-harm as an "almost daily occurrence," with some detainees being sexually abused and raped by others with full knowledge of the staff and no protection offered (Davis, 2013). Further concerns have been raised about hygiene, infection control, and access to medical services. In October 2014, 24-year-old Iranian asylum seeker Hamid Kehazaei died from a heart attack after contracting a rare infection that remained untreated for several days.

The isolation, indeterminate duration of detention, uncertainty, and absence of information about status determination and resettlement has seen rising tensions culminate in protests which on occasion become violent. Rioting at Nauru in July 2013 led to substantial property damage. Witness accounts of the February 2014 riots at Manus Island speak of warlike scenes, with an extraordinary level of brutality and savagery directed at the detainees, largely by local guards engaged by G4S, staff employed by other contractors, and PNG police. A bipartisan Australian Senate inquiry concluded that the rioting could have been prevented if detainees had been given a "clear pathway for the processing of their asylum claims" (Senate Committee, 2014 [8.5]). Although the committee identified a number of contributing factors, including tensions between detainees and PNG locals, harsh and inhumane conditions, and poor fencing and security infrastructure, it considered the main cause of the violence to be delay and uncertainty about status determination and resettlement arrangements. The committee considered that if these had been addressed, protest activity would have been unlikely to escalate to the level where violence ensued, with devastating consequences.

Control and Accountability

In offshore detention, Australia's human rights obligations are routinely breached. These include the right to humane treatment in detention, the right not to be subjected to cruel and inhuman treatment, the right not to be arbitrarily detained, the right to security, the right to health, and the right to life. States are bound to comply with their treaty obligations to respect, protect, and fulfill realization of human rights wherever they exercise jurisdiction, which may extend to other countries in circumstances where they are exercising effective control. The detention facilities at Nauru and PNG were established pursuant to agreements with Australia. They are funded by Australia and operated by service providers pursuant to agreements with the Australian government. Australian officials transfer detainees to the offshore facilities and make decisions about their day-to-day operation. Australia would appear to exercise effective control over these transnational facilities.

But even if Australia does not exercise effective control, it has joint responsibility with the host countries for breaches of human rights. Australia cannot absolve itself of international obligations by offloading asylum seekers to other nations. It furthermore cannot absolve itself of responsibility for the conduct of private contractors. This conduct is attributed to the state in circumstances where they are acting on the authority or direction of a state, even where the state's authority has been exceeded (International Law Commission, 2001). The host states and Australia also owe a general law duty of care to the detainees, which cannot be delegated to private actors.

But in these transnational facilities, accountability for harm is readily obscured. Verkuil has argued persuasively that when governments delegate their sovereign powers to outsiders, the capacity to govern is undermined (2007). The ability to exercise ministerial control is severely curtailed by the binary distancing effect of offshoring and outsourcing, which function as a shield through which responsibility can be too readily deflected and a mantle in which the government has been able to cloak itself and distance itself from a regime of its own design.

The Australian government has maintained the view that responsibility for the offshore facilities lies with the host states, characterizing its own role as one of assistance, mentoring, and training, with "influence but only in a supportive sense" (Senate Report, 2014, [1.56-1.60]). The government's reluctance to assume responsibility is further reflected by its refusal to allow the Australian Human Rights Commission access to the offshore facilities; the commission has powers to inquire into complaints of human rights violations. Control and accountability are seen to rest with the host state in an exercise of its sovereign jurisdiction, resulting in an accountability vacuum. A stark manifestation of this vacuum is the response to the PNG riots of February 2014. Australian government inquiries investigated the circumstances and causes of the rioting and made recommendations addressing the harms and how their recurrence may be prevented (Cornall, 2014; Senate Report, 2014), but neither the Australian nor the PNG government has taken responsibility for the human rights violations that occurred. No remedy has been provided for the harms caused and the criminal investigation into the death of Reza Barati has moved slowly, with charges laid against two former workers but no prospect of a conviction in the foreseeable future.

The horror of the February riots may be seen as another manifestation of the government's deterrence objective. Liz Thompson, a former staff member who was present during the riots, described the Manus Island facility in these terms:

> It's not designed as a processing facility. It's designed as an experiment in the active creation of horror to secure . . . deterrence. That's why . . . Reza Barati's death is not a crisis for the [Australian government]. It's actually an opportunity—it's an opportunity to extend that logic one step further to say, "This happens." But deterrence continues, Operation Sovereign Borders continues.
>
> (Davis, 2014)

Conclusion

The exorbitant price of Australia's deterrence-based policy of extraterritorial processing is most starkly exacted in human terms. Asylum seekers who have traveled to Australia by boat are relegated to transnational detention environments marked by hopelessness, despair, and preventable mental illness. In pursuing self-serving, bilateral strategies that seek to divest it of the burdens of processing and protection under the Refugee Convention, Australia continues to destroy lives, breach its human rights obligations, undermine international and domestic relations, and frustrate realization of durable solutions for refugees in the Asia-Pacific region.

References

Amnesty International. (2013). This is breaking people: Human rights violations at Australia's asylum seeker processing center on Manus Island, Papua New Guinea. Broadway, NSW, Australia: Author.

Australian Government. (2012). Report of the Expert Panel on Asylum Seekers.

Australian Government. (2014). National Commission of Audit, Appendix to the Report of the National Commission of Audit—Volume 2 [10.14] Illegal Maritime Arrival Costs.

Buzan, B., Waever, O., & De Wilde, J. (1998). *Security: A new framework for analysis.* Boulder, CO: Lynne Rienner.

Commonwealth of Australia. (2003). *A Pacific engaged: Australia's relations with PNG and the island states of the southwest Pacific.* Senate Foreign Affairs, Defense and Trade Committee.

Commonwealth of Australia. (2014a). *Estimates.* Official Committee Hansard, Senate Legal and Constitutional Affairs Committee.

Commonwealth of Australia. (2014b). *Incident at Manus Island Detention Center,* Senate Legal and Constitutional Affairs References Committee.

Cornall, R. (2014, May 23). *Review into the events of 16–18 February 2014 at the Manus Regional Processing Center.* Australian Broadcasting Corporation.

Crock, M., & Ghezelbash, D. (2010). Do loose lips bring ships—the role of policy, politics and human rights in managing unauthorized boat arrivals. *Griffith Law Review, 19,* 238.

Davis, M. (2013, July 23). *Manus whistleblower.* SBS Dateline. Retrieved from http://www.sbs.com.au/news/dateline/story/manus-whistleblower.

Davis, M. (2014, Feb. 25). *Manus insider.* SBS Dateline. Retrieved from http://www.sbs.com.au/news/dateline/story/manus-insider.

Doherty, B. (2015, Aug. 25). Resettled refugees say they are desperate and living like animals in the jungle on Nauru. *Sydney Morning Herald.* Retrieved from http://www.smh.com.au/federal-politics/political-news/resettled-refugees-say-they-are-desperate-and-living-like-animals-in-the-jungle-on-nauru-20140824-107sov.html.

Evans, Senator Chris, minister for immigration and citizenship. (2008). Last refugees leave Nauru. (Media release.)

International Law Commission. (2001). *Articles on responsibility of states for internationally wrongful acts, with commentaries.*

Kneebone, S. (2010). Refugees and displaced persons: The refugee definition and humanitarian protection. In S. Joseph & A. McBeth (Eds.), *Research handbook on international human rights law* (pp. 215–240). Northampton, MA: Edward Elgar.

Liberal Party of Australia. (2013, Aug. 26). Operation Sovereign Borders. Retrieved from http://www.liberal.org.au/latest-news/2013/07/26/operation-sovereign-borders.

McCann, D. (2014). How boat people brought down Rudd and Gillard. *Quadrant, 58*(7/8), 12.

Morrison, S. (2014, Jan. 14). Secrecy with a purpose in asylum policy. Retrieved from http://www.abc.net.au/7.30/content/2013/s3925614.htm.

Phillips, J., & Spinks, H. (2010). *Boat arrivals in Australia since 1976.* Sydney: Australian Parliamentary Library.

Pickering, S. (2001) Common sense and original deviancy: News discourses and asylum seekers in Australia. *Journal of Refugee Studies, 14*(2), 169–186.

Pope, P. J., & Garrett, T. M. (2012). America's Homo sacer: Examining UD deportation hearings and the criminalization of illegal immigration. *Administration and Society, 45*(2), 167–186.

Rygiel, K. (2012). Governing mobility and rights to movement post 9/11: Managing irregular and refugee migration through detention. *Review of Constitutional Studies, 16*(2), 211–241.

Schloenhardt, A. (2000). Australia and the boat-people: 25 years of unauthorized arrivals. *UNSWLJ*, 23, 33.

Stead, V. (2014, Feb. 20). PNG solution turns to nightmare on Manus Island. *The Age.*

Stumpf, J. (2006). The crimmigration crisis: Immigrants, crimes and sovereign power. *American University Law Review, 56*(2), 367–419.

UN Working Group on Arbitrary Detention. (2002). *Visit to Australia.* UN Doc E/CN.4/2003/8/Add.2.

Verkuil, P. R. (2007). *Outsourcing sovereignty: Why privatization of government functions threatens democracy and what we can do about it.* Cambridge: Cambridge University Press.

Watson, S. D. (2009). *The securitization of humanitarian migration: Digging moats and sinking boats.* Abingdon: Routledge.

Wilson, M. (2014, Oct. 3). Iranian asylum seeker on Nauru describes conditions there as God's own hell. Australian Broadcasting Corporation. Retrieved from http://www.abc.net.au/news/2014-10-03/asylum-seeker-on-nauru-describes-conditions-as-gods-own-hell/5787300.

13

From "Guesthouses" to Removal Centers

Europeanization of Immigrant Detention in Turkey

NURCAN OZGUR BAKLACIOGLU

Immigrant detention in the 20th century was intended to deter, through securitization procedures, the influx of "unwanted" immigrants and asylum seekers apprehended during illegal border passages or irregular stays in Turkey and other countries. As we move into the 21st century, this policy is being replaced by a transnational migration management approach aimed at fast and low-cost removal of such immigrants. By "Europeanizing" its immigrant detention policy, Turkey is following this global shift. After 2010, immigrant detention centers in Turkey were transformed from foreigner "guesthouses" to removal centers for accelerated deportation of irregular immigrants and asylum seekers. Although long-term detention in guesthouses was initially considered to be an "effective punishment" and a preemptive measure in fighting unwanted immigration, their insufficient capacity, inhumane and degrading conditions, human rights abuses (as charged by the European Court of Human Rights or ECHR decisions), and financial burden have challenged the guesthouse system. Detention is no longer approached as a deterrent but as an investigation, registration, and categorization procedure for rapid deportation and removal of unwanted immigrants and refugees.

With 77,000 temporary asylum seekers, 1.5 million Syrian prima facie refugees, and 24,800 detected passages to the European Union, in 2013 Turkey ranked as the second major transit country of the Eastern Mediterranean. Apart from its border surveillance system and 12-kilometer fence along the Greek-Turkish border, the Turkish-Bulgarian-Greek border triangle remains a central passageway for the trans-European migration (Frontex, 2014). In 2014, the Turkish airports of Antalya and Istanbul became the main transit gates for Syrian, Afghani, Iraqi, and African refugees hoping at crossing into EU territory via the borders with Bosnia, Serbia, and Kosovo. As a strategic passageway to EU territory, Turkey's rapid integration into the trans-European migration management system is seen as a way of forestalling these irregular passages into the European Union. Turkey's integration in this system is taking place in two ways:

1. Through implementation of the EU-Turkey readmission agreement that currently works via push-backs of apprehended migrants and asylum seekers between the Greek-Bulgarian and Turkish borders (TBMM, 2014a, pp. 12–14)
2. Through the Europeanization of legal and institutional infrastructure of Turkey's asylum and migration system and Europeanization of its integrated border management system (IBMS)

In the 2006 EU Implementation Directive, Turkey joined the transnational migration management sector through application of the EU legal framework and institutional reconstruction. This top-down implementation process followed significant legal and institutional changes; however, it has faced tough local challenges and undergone local political mutation.

Europeanization of the Legal Framework of Immigrant Detention in Turkey

Immigrant detention in Turkey has a history dating from the 1967 protocol introducing geographical limitations on refugees fleeing persecution from countries that were not members of the Council of Europe. After this protocol, the majority of asylum seekers and refugees in Turkey did not have access to international protection and underwent discrimination on the basis of their country of origin. Before the 1980s, detention usually ended up with imprisonment of foreigners (often Soviet Bloc citizens) under suspicion of dissidence, political agency, or violation of Article 4 of the Passport Law (Law No. 5682 of 1950) or Article 23 of the Law on Sojourn and Movement of Aliens (Law No. 5687 of 1950). Detention was based on the Ministry of the Interior's administrative ruling for investigation, deportation, or administrative supervision procedures. After the inflow of Iranian, Afghani, and later Iraqi refugees, the Ministry of the Interior took additional measures for fighting the growing pressure of these "unwelcome" refugees and (1) introduced two security-based immigration acts (the 1983 Foreigners Guesthouse Directive and the 1994 Asylum Regulation) and (2) established additional foreigner guesthouses. According to these acts, immigrants, asylum seekers, and refugees used to undergo long-term detention (up to three years) for basic administrative purposes such as illegal entry or overstay in the country or failure to comply with requirements of the "temporary asylum" system. Without any judicial review, immigrants could be prosecuted, criminally charged, imprisoned, or administratively detained up to six months, or up to two years for those who left their designated place of residence without permission (Article 25–26, Law No. 5687; Helsinki Citizens' Assembly, 2007). Refugees and immigrants under detention were denied access to asylum procedures, legal attorneys, and refugee rights defenders.

In 2009 the European Court of Human Rights (ECHR) ruled that these documents do not provide a legal basis for immigrant detention; thus the ongoing practice of administrative detention is in violation of Articles 3 and 5 of the ECHR (*Abdolkhani & Karimnia* v. *Turkey*, 2010). The ECHR also stated that detention for more than 18 months (*Ahmadpour* v. *Turkey*, Appl. 12717/08) and repeated detention with subsequent deportation resulted in violation of rights to liberty and protection from ill treatment and degrading treatment (*Ghorbanov & Others* v. *Turkey*, 2013). Following the ECHR judgments and the critiques of the European Committee for Prevention of Torture (ECPT), Turkey released its first Law (No. 6458) on Foreigners and International Protection in 2013. Framed by the EU conditionalities on immigration, asylum, reception, detention, and removal, the law raised criminal prosecution and prison sentences for illegal entry and stay in the country and brought significant changes in regard to legal conditions and the basis of detention and removal.

The law ordered administrative detention for "those who may abscond or disappear, who violate rules for entry into and exit from Turkey, who use fraudulent or unfounded documents, who do not leave Turkey in the granted period, who constitute threat to public order and security or public health" (Article 57/2). It increased the duration of detention to six months plus an additional six months (Article 57/3). It also limited administrative detention of asylum seekers to a maximum of 30 days of exceptional procedure based on performance related to verification of identity documents; assessment of asylum application; and prevention of irregular entries, violation of national "temporary asylum" procedures, exceeding 10-day limit for status renewal or legalization, illegal employment, abandonment of "satellite city," and serious danger to public order, security, or health (Article 68). The law provided for access to a "legal representative, lawyer, notary" and UN High Commissioner for Refugees (UNHCR) officers (Article 68/8) as well as UNHCR's access to applicants to international protection at the border gates (Article 92/3).

Some of these legal changes found reflection in the detention practices. Nevertheless, significant human rights violations are continuing. The geographical limitation and the priority of public order and security keep their priority. In an era of engendering migration, the new law lacks gender-based approaches and leaves wide space for administrative interpretation. Any subjective interpretation of a "reasonable period" for application for international protection provides grounds for criminal proceeding for illegal entry/presence or preremoval administrative detention (Article 65). The law adopted controversial provisions from the EU legislation as well. Asylum seekers continue to face accelerated procedures

(Article 79) and fast-track rejections of asylum applications at Kumkapi removal center (Human Rights Council, 2013). Detainees considered irregular immigrants are being invited to leave the country within 30 days without any early notification. Because of geographical limitations, many of these immigrants are prima facie refugees. Foreigners considered potential threats to public security/order are usually detained and deported (Af Orgutunden, 2014).

Approached as a threat to public order, security, and health, immigration continues to be subject to the authority of the domestic security sector. Indeed, Turkey`s National Program 2013–2015 places "illegal migration" among terrorist, financial, and organized crimes (including drug trafficking) as challenges to the effective security system based on strengthening of preventive and protective security forces and IBMS (T.C., 2013). Mandated to establish, manage, and inspect detention facilities and deportation practices, the newly established Directorate General for Migration Management or DGMM (UNHCR, 2014) adopted this hegemonic discourse and is transforming it into the civil branch of Ministry of Interior. According to the human rights lawyers, the DGMM staff remains inert because it lacks a relevant human rights–based approach and clear legal guidance (TOHAV, 2014). Thus MoI's traditional securitizing approach keeps its prevalence in the Europeanization of the legal and also institutional framework on immigration and asylum in Turkey. Indeed, the April 2014 Directive on Establishment, Management, Privatization, and Control of Reception, Detention and Removal Centers (Kabul, 2014) leaves apprehension and investigation of immigrants to "law-enforcement units" (i.e., MoI).

Europeanization of Institutional Infrastructure: From Guesthouses to Removal Centers and Satellite Cities

The EU's priority on trans-European migration management through cooperation and Europeanization of asylum and migration systems in the close neighborhood has merged with Turkey's hegemonic discourse on combating "illegal" immigration through IBMS and the accelerated removal system, on the basis of readmission agreements with neighboring countries of origin and Africa (TBMM, 2012). As prioritized in the EU Implementation Plan for Turkey, Law 6458 authorizes DGMM and MoI to sign readmission agreements and cooperate with international organizations, institutions of related countries, and nongovernmental organizations to assist deportation procedures (Article 60/4).

Under the requirements of the 2005 EU Action Plan for Asylum and Migration in Turkey and the signing of the Turkey-EU readmission agreement (T.C.,

2013), Turkey became part of the transnational migration management network (Amnesty International, 2014a). Under the 2007 Twinning projects on "Support to Turkey's Capacity in Combating Illegal Migration and Establishment of Removal Centers for Illegal Migrants" and "Establishment of a Reception, Screening and Accommodation System (Centers) for asylum seekers and refugees" as well as the 2010 "Establishment of Reception and Removal Centers—Phase II" project, the EU provided funding for construction of removal centers in Istanbul, Izmir, Ankara (Ayas), Gaziantep, Van, and Erzurum (Global Detention Project, 2014, pp. 6–7). Through this funding, many detention centers were reconstructed as removal centers.

From Guesthouses to Removal Centers

Before 2010, the Ministry of the Interior's Department of Foreigners, Borders, and Asylum as well as the Provincial Security Directorate Department of Foreigners used to issue accelerated deportation. The police stations were not sufficient for immigrant detention (Helsinki Citizens' Assembly, 2012). There was a broad assortment of sites for immigrant detention, among them police stations, airport detention rooms, ad hoc sites such as sport halls, foreigner guesthouses, and so on. There were numerous instances of ill treatment, overcrowding, inadequate food and hygiene, lack of access to health care and recreation, and censorship of correspondence in these sites. Foreign nationals held in the airport transit zone did not have access to legal representatives and asylum (ECPT, 2011; UNCAT, 2012). Under pressure from ECHR judgments, the doubled financial cost of the growing number of immigrants under detention, and the EU conditionalities, Turkey transformed these guesthouses into removal centers (Adana, 2009). Indeed, the Circular of the EU-Turkey Readmission Agreement had foreseen the fight against irregular migration through construction and capacity building of additional removal centers, development of EU funded infrastructure for processing the EU immigrant returns, and signing of readmission agreements with countries in the southeastern neighborhood (Kabul, 2014).

Defined as "centers for control and accommodation of foreigners under administrative detention" (April 2014 regulation) and "places for accommodation and health services to illegal immigrants until their deportation" (TBMM, 2012), these centers have a pivotal role in chain deportations from the EU territory to Turkey and onward. According to official data during 1999–2009, Turkey apprehended more than 750,000 irregular immigrants (TBMM, 2010). It processed 47,510 irregular immigrants in 2012 and 21,332 immigrants between January 1 and August 2, 2013. During 2012 Turkey deported 21,059 immigrants, and between January and August 2013 it deported 16,060 (European Commission, 2013). Both detention and deportation are approached as a significant financial burden on the MoI budget in Turkey. According to the government, between 1999 and 2008 Turkey spent $16.5 million for food, shelter, health, and transportation of irregular migrants (Frontex, 2014). Because of this financial cost, instead of building additional removal centers, authorities prefer short preremoval detentions combined with accelerated deportation or obligatory leave of the country within 30 days.

Compared with the number of apprehended immigrants, Turkey has removal centers in 35 cities with total capacity of 2,945 immigrants (TBMM, 2012). The most crowded removal centers are situated in cities along the western and Mediterranean borders, notably Edirne, Kirklareli-Gaziosmanpasa, Tekirdag, Istanbul-Kumkapi, Bursa, Canakkale-Ayvacik, Canakkale-Kucukkuyu, Izmir, Aydin, and Mugla. Hatay, Adana, Van and Agri host the major southeastern removal centers in the country. The majority of these removal centers are ad hoc places situated usually in the local MoI buildings, public school sport facilities, or civil ad hoc sites used during cross-border deportation of immigrants, as in the case of a deported Syrian student. This student claims that during his illegal deportation he was detained in Hatay, in the building of an Islamic group that later transferred him to another Islamic paramilitary group at the Syrian side of the border, who detained him in an underground detention facility (A.M.'s Advocate, 2014) This case shows that detention in Turkey is not limited to public places for detention that are usually available for monitoring; rather, detention can take place in private spaces controlled by certain ideological or religious groups. Interestingly, the 2013 law provides for noncustodial measures, such as residence at a designated address. Article 57/4 postulates that "foreigners whose administrative detention is ended may be subject to obligations such as living in a designated address and reporting to authorities in the form and periods requested."

There are no available clarifying clauses for the conditions and executors of detention or clauses for protection from human rights violations in such sites of detention. Any subjective reading and implementation of this article may lead to inhumane and degrading forms of noncustodial detention without any judicial decision, as in the case of the Syrian student. This legal clause is widely applied under the satellite cities system as a noncustodial alternative for surveillance of temporary asylum seekers in Turkey (Articles 57/4, 71/1). This noncustodial alternative to detention is obviously less expensive than removal or detention centers. It does not bring any financial burden on the MoI's budget; it does not require or accommodate any human rights monitoring or any eventual rulings by ECHR. For all these advantages, this system seems prioritized by the MoI authorities. Within three or four years, the number of satellite cities increased to 47. Nevertheless, this satellite city system contains significant sources of structural discrimination and violence against asylum seekers and refugees forced to live in the satellite cities.

The Satellite Cities: Noncustodial Alternatives for Low-Cost Detention of Asylum Seekers and Refugees

Refugees and asylum seekers who cannot be deported to their country of origin are usually assigned to one of the 37 satellite cities in Anatolia. Asylum seekers and refugees do not have a say in the selection of the satellite city. The distribution is based on the capacity of the cities and does not take under consideration gender or kinship-based criteria. The refugees and asylum seekers cannot leave the city without permission; they solve their accommodation problem on their own and have to pay for their residence permit. They are not given a right to employment and thus are usually exploited in the local black market.

Depending on low-cost unhealthy accommodation, social exploitation, and moral surveillance by local religious humanitarian aid agencies, refugees and asylum seekers are imprisoned within constant ethnic-, gender-, or religion-based discrimination as well as public control and surveillance by humanitarian agents and providers of basic everyday needs. For financial or administrative reasons, they have poor access to medical care, adequate food, hygienic accommodation conditions, and interpreters. Moral control and surveillance at the satellite cities has a discriminative impact on women and lesbian, gay, bisexual, and transgender (LGBT; KAOS-GL, 2012) asylum seekers, who are expected to obey local religious norms. They also face discrimination in distribution of humanitarian aid at the faith associations. Without safe accommodation and legal protection, women become targets of sexual exploitation and violence.

Entrapped within the administrative panopticon of the satellite cities, refugees and asylum seekers spend two to four years under cultural and structural violence, often leading to criminalization and social marginalization. Asylum seekers and refugees are perceived as a social burden and security threat to the public order, budget, and security (Ozgur Baklacıoğlu, 2011a).

Construction and Defeat of "Criminal" Immigrants and Temporary Asylum Seekers

Criminalization and social marginalization followed by expanding xenophobia constitute preemptive political mechanisms for fighting migration in Turkey today. Through these mechanisms, irregular immigration and asylum are reconstructed as a threat to public security, order, and welfare; thus these issues are appropriated as a domestic security affair of the growing domestic security sector (i.e., MoI and gendarmerie). Criminalization and social marginalization take place through discursive, legal, administrative, and psychological performances and practices under detention. Detention itself leads to direct and open securitization of the immigration-asylum nexus and is a violation of rights to freedom, self-reliance, and social safety. Considering that most detained immigrants are prima facie refugees, many refugees are a priori refused access to the right to asylum and are registered and processed under the category of "illegal immigrants." This status-based discrimination leads to prolonged detention, fiscal or administrative fines, or deportation according to ethnic or religious background. Indeed, Afghani, Syrian, Iraqi, and Iranian immigrants and refugees face differing legal and administrative procedures. Whereas Syrians are given special legal status of temporary asylum protection that foresees access to health and residence permit services and exemption from detention and deportation, Afghani, Iraqi, and some African refugees are often approached as irregular immigrants; thus they face extended detention or push-back deportation (Oktay Durukan, Helsinki Citizens' Assembly, interviewed Oct. 2014).

Indeed, since the beginning of the century many immigrants and asylum seekers have been subject to illegal push-back and collective detention at border zones with Bulgaria and Greece. As in the case of 300 African refugees dumped into push-back across the border between Turkey and Greece in mid-July 2001, detention at the border has led to death or miscarriage due to detention conditions, rape, sexual harassment, ill treatment, violation of property rights through confiscation of property and money, and violation of passports and travel documents (Human Rights Association Committee, 2001).

Criminalization through violation of right to asylum under detention is another practice taking place through forced signing of false statements of economic immigration as a precaution against future asylum claims (Afghani refugees, interviewed in Athens, June 2009). Until 2011 the detained refugees and immigrants were refused access to their procedural rights, judicial assistance, and legal services. They faced lack of information on asylum, deportation, and reasons for and rights under detention as well as police indifference to asylum applications. Although the 2013 law allows legal counsel and a right to appeal detention, practical problems related to access to legal aid, interpretation services, and information about the reasons and duration of detention are continuing. Even though the detainees are given informational brochures written in several languages (TBMM, 2014b), illiteracy or expensive legal services dissuade detainees from using legal services, and free legal services are in short supply (Global Detention Project, 2014). For example, only 168 of 22,664 apprehended immigrants in 2011 and 169 of 17,448 apprehended immigrants in 2012 applied for asylum in the Edirne detention center (TBMM, 2014b). After introduction of the new law, allegations of wide use of accelerated procedures and fast rejection of asylum applications increased (Human Rights Council, 2013).

Lack of legal decisions and clear prescribed rules setting out the criteria and process of detention constituted the main source of unlawful treatment and violence toward the detained immigrants in the former guesthouses. In the case of Abdolkhani and Karimnia, the detained asylum seekers spent three months in an overcrowded police station basement, without judicial review of length of detention or any explanation of the reasons for detention. The new law allows certain monitoring and rule mechanisms and order, yet punishment through imprisonment in the detention centers itself leads to feelings of hopelessness and depression among the detainees; thus it continues to work as a psychological deterrence measure against forthcoming arrivals to the country. The 2014 parliamentary human rights report paid attention to imprisonment, punishment, discrimination, and poor food services in the detention centers (TBMM, 2014a).

The 2013 law provides the right to judicial review. However, reviews of detention decisions usually prolong extensively the period of detention. In March 2013 a judgment by the ECHR concluded that "the Turkish legal system did not provide the applicant with a remedy whereby he could obtain a speedy judicial review of the lawfulness of his detention, within the meaning of Article 4 and 5 of the Convention" (*Athary* v. *Turkey*, 2013, Application no. 50372/09). There is no legal framework on monitoring detention facilities; thus communication with the detention police, monitoring, and receiving regular and thorough information about situation is difficult.

Significant, however, are the insufficiently monitored spaces of immigrant detention or "problematic passengers rooms" at Turkish airports. The immigrants and asylum seekers detained in these spaces lack access to lawyers or monitoring by human rights organizations. Important border crossing points with six million passengers traveling to the European Union each year, the airports in Istanbul and Antalya are reported as spaces of arbitrary denial of access to asylum and risk of imminent refoulement to unsafe countries of origin (Helsinki Citizens' Assembly, 2012). In nine cases of airport detention, the ECHR issued interim measures suspending deportation (Global Detention Project, 2014).

An important aspect of contemporary immigrant detention policies is the migration–social burden nexus. The severe detention conditions not only represent a form of punishment but also serve as a tool for social marginalization and deterrence through legal and administrative practices and performance. Since 2006 national and international human rights observers have repeatedly criticized the penal conditions at Turkish detention facilities (Helsinki Citizens' Assembly, 2007; Human Rights Watch, 2008; CHR, 2009; ECPT, 2011). The ECHR has issued rulings in several cases of violation of the safeguarding principles on immigrant detention. In *Abdolkhani & Karimnia* v. *Turkey* the court addressed violation of the principles for conditions of detention. The ECHR's rulings on *Z.N.S.* v. *Turkey, Kurkaev* v. *Turkey, Charahili* v. *Turkey,* and *Tahrani* v. *Turkey* confirmed that conditions at the detention facilities amounted to an exercise in violence, thus violating Article 3 of the ECHR. In 2009 the ECPT reported instances of collective beatings of male foreign nationals and physical ill treatment at the Edirne-Tunça, Agri, and Kirklareli detention centers (ECPT, 2011). Human rights reports released allegations of police mistreatment as well as verbal and physical abuse (Human Rights Association, 2001).

Detention conditions have amounted to inhumane treatment owing to the lack of adequate medical treatment for sicknesses caused by overcrowded detention conditions and insufficient food and clean water (ibid.). The poor health, nutrition, and living conditions in the detention centers cause disease and health problems, malnutrition, and social discrimination among detainees. There are some visible improvements in the general conditions at the renewed removal centers, yet there are still no preemptive medical checkups, facilities for persons with special needs, or adequate health services (*Asalya* v. *Turkey*, Case No.43875/09,15.04.2014), (Global Detention Project, 2014). The lack of social protection mechanisms for unaccompanied women and children, LGBT members, and immigrants with diverse religious or ethnic background exacerbates gender-based and ethnic/religious discrimination during administrative procedures and relations among detainees. Unaccompanied mothers and women, HIV groups, and LGBTI members are exposed to physical, social, and psychological violence and sexual discrimination (Human Rights Association, 2001).

The law provides protection only to victims of sexual harassment and violence and "victims of human trafficking benefitting from victim support processes." This protection is limited to protection from expulsion (Article 55/1) and provision of centers and shelters for victims of human trafficking (Article 108/1). No preemptive mechanisms for avoiding and minimizing sexual harassment and violence exist. Reports uncovered cases of prosecution, detention, and punishment of victims of human trafficking (UNHCR, 2012). In most of the cases, immigrants and refugees with HIV or sex workers are subjected to accelerated deportation (U.S. Department of State, 2012).

Indifference, lack of translation services, and absence of concern among employed staff facilitates discrimination, corruption, local conflict, and violence among detainees of different social backgrounds or ethnic/religious groups. Official reports emphasize availability of spaces for exercising religious identity under detention, such as the prayer rooms in the Kırklareli Gazi Osman Paşa Deportation and Removal Center. Nevertheless, safe spaces for detainees vulnerable to religious discrimination are still not provided. Moreover, adults and minors, convicted criminals and noncriminals are often housed in the same areas.

The law provides for separate accommodation for families and unaccompanied children and access to education (Article 59/1). It advises fast-track temporary asylum procedure for unaccompanied minors under 16 years of age, and shelter by the State Child Protection Agency (Topcuoğlu, 2012). Nevertheless, the lack of adequate family rooms forces unaccompanied minors to live alongside adults, or separated from the parent of the opposite sex. There are no psychosocial services provided (European Commission, 2013; TBMM, 2014b). Boys over the age of 12 apprehended with their mothers are usually placed in orphanages (Human Rights Council, 2013).

The severe security measures and fences around the detention centers as well as the use of fire fence doors makes these places resemble prisons for criminals. Common overcrowding results in inadequate bedding, poor ventilation, and dirty, smoke- and insect-infested rooms (TIHK, 2014). The search for sanitary and personal cleaning supplies results in marketization of basic human essentials at the removal centers. Detainees have to pay exaggerated prices for buying basic everyday supplies. Similarly, the high cost of treatment, medication, and communication leads to creation of an internal black market and financial exploitation of detainees (Helsinki Citizens' Assembly, 2007).

Recently, because of scarce capacity, procedures under detention have typically been accelerated to a maximum of 10 days' stay at the center followed by deportation or letter of leave. According to a parliamentary report, Afghani, Azeri, Iranian, Iraqi, , Moldavian, Pakistani, and Uzbek detainees generally face deportation for reasons such as carrying disease, illegal entrance, illegal stay, or employment. Many detainees overstaying three months are being released to leave the country within 30 days (TBMM, 2012). This procedure ends up in further criminalization of detainees who do not leave the country within this time limit. They continue to live in Turkey undocumented or with fraudulent documents and no access to human security or basic human rights. As such, the contemporary detention system ends up in accelerated deportation or illegalization of refugees and asylum seekers in Turkey.

Conclusion

The recent legal and institutional changes in its migration management system have transformed Turkey into an "open air" detention space for 77,000 asylum seekers and refugees (UNHCR, 2014), thousands of irregular immigrants, and more than 1,627,000 Syrian temporary "guest" refugees (TBMM, 2014a). Through the Europeanization of its asylum and migration system, Turkey has required significant legal provisions regarding its reception, detention, settlement, and deportation conditions. However, geographical limitations limit the implementation of these measures. The accelerated procedure under detention continues to produce more and more irregular immigrants and refugees, while removal and deportation became everyday practice in dealing with growing numbers of apprehended refugees and migrants. The majority of the detainees who are released with instructions to leave the country within 30 days continue to live in Turkey without papers.

Entrapped in legal limbo, many immigrants and asylum seekers undergo sexual and social exploitation and discrimination during their stay, border passage, or work. Many live without documentation and lack freedom of movement, the right to employment, and basic social rights. Although the removal centers have emerged as trans-European bases of accelerated removal, the satellite cities provide spaces for low-cost public surveillance and accommodation of asylum seekers. Alongside having relative freedom of movement within the borders of the satellite cities, the asylum seekers live under the constant surveillance and moral gaze of local "hospitality," often resulting in religious, ethnic, or gender discrimination. So far, the satellite city system has led to humanitarian marketization and public control of "temporary" asylum seekers and refugees in Turkey.

The Readmission Agreement between Turkey and the EU initiated accelerated procedures and facilitated transnational marketization of the migration management system on the basis of administrative detention for chain removal of "dangerous" immigrants and asylum seekers. Through this EU-initiated system (Directive 2008/115/EC), Turkey became a destination country for pushed-back refugees and immigrants from Greece, Bulgaria, and other EU countries (Amnesty International, 2014a). Intensification of illegal push-backs across Turkish, Greek, and Bulgarian borders resulted in forced encampment of apprehended Syrian refugees in southeastern Turkey (TBMM, 2014b). In this way, forced encampment became an alternative way of detaining Syrian refugees who had illegally crossed the northwestern borders or threatened the public order through begging or homelessness (Amnesty International, 2014b).

According to the parliamentary human rights commission, the solution for existing border security and migration management problems stems from the development of IBMS, institutional finalization of DGMM, and signing of readmission agreements with the country of origin in the near southeast (TBMM, 2012).

Many human rights NGOs point to a potential positive role for the DGMM. However, border detentions are still under the control of the MoI and gendarmerie. These institutions lack any integrated data exchange system and civilian monitoring. Severe conditions of predetention followed by accelerated procedures are susceptible to further violations of basic human rights. The immigrants are usually apprehended in poor physical condition and ill health as a result of arduous travel and direct push-back by the Greek or Bulgarian border forces (TBMM, 2014b). The new high-technology borders have not ended illegal passages but opened the way to human rights violations at the EU borders.

According to parliamentary reports, development of IBMS will increase cross-border exchange of information and promote introduction of important border security technologies such as border camera systems and a "face-recognition network," a system intended to prevent reentry into partner countries of the EU-IBMS (i.e., Bulgaria, Turkey, Greece, Hungary, Croatia, etc.). MoI's introduction of this system will lead to final accelerated deportations and build up unavoidable digital borders ahead of immigrants and asylum seekers who try to reenter Turkey, Bulgaria, or Greece. Completed by readmission agreements with neighboring countries at the southeastern borders (TBMM, 2014a), this trans-European migration management system will facilitate removal of irregular immigrants in the Mediterranean region.

References

Abdolkhani & Karimnia v. *Turkey*. (2010). No. 1, application no. 30471/08, retrieved from http://hudoc.echr. coe.int/sites/eng/pages/search.aspx?i=001-94127 ECHR.

Adana Milletvekili Hulusi Güvel ve 19 milletvekilinin, mülteci ve kaçak göçmenler sorununun araştırılarak alınması gereken önlemlerin belirlenmesi amacıyla Meclis araştırması açılmasına ilişkin önergesi. (2009). 23. Dönem, 4.Yasama Yılı 29. Birleşim,10. Aralık.

Af Orgutunden Acil Eylem: Kobaneli Sinirdisi Edilemez. (2014, Ekim 20). *Bianet Haber*. Retrieved from www.bianet.org.

Ahmadpour v. *Turkey*, Appl. 12717/08. (2010) Retrieved from http://www.refworld.org/pdfid/4c179ffa2.pdf

Amnesty International. (2014a). *The human cost of fortress Europe: Human rights violations against migrants and refugees at Europe's borders*. Index: EUR 05/001/.

Amnesty International. (2014b). *Struggling to survive: Refugees from Syria in Turkey*. Index: EUR 44/017/2014.

A.M.'s Advocate, personal interview, Istanbul, Taksim: October 18, 2014 "Bekir Bozadag: Turkiye Cezaevlerinde en cok Iranlilar Var" (2014) Interview

Athary v. *Turkey*, no. 50372/09 Article 5. (2013). Retrieved from http://hudoc.echr.coe.int/eng?i=001-115170#{"itemid":["001-115170"]}.

Commissioner for Human Rights of the Council of Europe, CHR. (2009) Executive Summary. Retrieved from http://madde14.org/english/index.php?title=CoE_CHR_-_Human_rights_of_asylum_seekers_and_refugees_Turkey

Directive 2008/115/EC of the European Parliament and of the Council. (2008, Dec. 16). On common standards and procedures in Member States for returning illegally staying third-country nationals. *Official Journal of the European Union*, L 348/98.

European Commission. (2013). *Turkey 2013 progress report*. Retrieved from http://ec.europa.eu/enlargement/pdf/key_documents/2013/package/brochures/turkey_2013.pdf.

European Committee for the Prevention of Torture and Inhuman or Degrading Treatment or Punishment (ECPT). (2011, Mar. 31). *Report to the Turkish government on the visit to Turkey carried out by the ECPT, 4–17 June 2009*. Council of Europe.

Frontex. *Annual risk analysis report*. (2014). Warsaw: Author.

Ghorbanov & Others v. *Turkey*. (2013, December). ECHR Decision no. 28127/09.

Global Detention Project. (2014). *Turkey detention profile*, pp. 6–7. Retrieved from http://www.globaldetentionproject.org/countries/europe/turkey/introduction.html.

Helsinki Citizens' Assembly. (2007). *Unwelcome guests: The detention of refugees in Turkey's foreigners' guesthouses*. Istanbul: Author.

Helsinki Citizens' Assembly. (2012, Nov. 16). *Briefing note on Syrian refugees in Turkey*. Retrieved from www.hyd.org.tr.

Human Rights Association Committee on Migration, Forced Displacement and Refugees. (2001, July 27). *Preliminary report on African immigrants and refugees in Turkey*. Istanbul: Author.

Human Rights Council (HRC). (2013). *Report by the Special Rapporteur on the Human Rights of Migrants, François Crépeau, mission to Turkey 25–29 June, 2012*, A/HRC/23/46/Add.2. Apr. 17, 2013. Retrieved from www.ohchr.org.

Human Rights Watch. (2008) Retrieved from https://www.hrw.org/legacy/wr2k8/pdfs/wr2k8_web.pdf

Kabul ve Barinma Merkezleri ile Geri Gönderme Merkezlerinin Kurulması Yönetimi, İşletilmesi, İşlettirilmesi ve Denetimi Hakkında Yönetmelik. (2014, Nisan 22). *Resmî Gazete*. Sayı: 28980.

KAOS-GL. (2012). *Sığınmacı ve Mülteci Lezbiyen, Gey, Biseksüel, Trans Bireyler Raporu*, Onderoglu, E. (2014, Ekim 9). Suructa Gozaltindaki 160 kisi Aclik Grevinde. *Bianet*. Retrieved from bianet.org.

Özgür, N. B. (2011a). Asylum policy and practices in Turkey: Constructing the refugee other. In U. Tekin, and B. Push (Eds.), *Migration und Turkei: Bewegungen am Rande der Europaischen Union*. Köln: Institut d'Orient İstanbuler Texte und Studien, Köln Universitet.

Özgür, N. B. (2011b). İltica Alanında Dolaylı Sınırdışı Pratiği Olarak Entegrasyon Politikası. *İltica, Uluslararası Göç ve Vatansızlık*. Ankara: UNHCR.

TBMM. (2010). *Genel Kurul Tutanağı*, 23. Dönem 4. Yasama Yılı 45. Birleşim 07. Ocak.

TBMM. (2012). *Insan Haklari Inceleme Komisyonu Raporu, Edirne, İstanbul ve Kırklareli İllerinde Bulunan Geri Gönderme Merkezleri Hakkında İnceleme Raporu*, 24. Dönem 3. Yasama Yılı.

TBMM. (2014a). *Edirne İli Yasadışı Göç İnceleme Raporu*, 24. Dönem 5. Yasama Yılı.

TBMM. (2014b). *Insan Haklarini Inceleme Komisyonu Ülkemize Sığınan Suriye ve Irak Vatnadaşlarının Barındıkları Çadırkentler Hakkında Inceleme Raporu*, 24. Dönem, 5. Yasama Yılı.

T.C. Orta Vadeli Program. (2013). Page 30. Retrieved from http://www.goc.gov.tr/icerik6/orta-vadeli-programlar_327_344_667_icerik.

TOHAV. (2014, October). *Personal interview with lawyers dealing with immigrant deportation cases*. Istanbul: Author.

Topcuoğlu, A. (2012). *Türkiye'de Göçmen Çocukların Profili, Sosyal Politika, ve Sosyal Hizmet Önerileri*, Uluslararası Göç Örgütü. *Türkiye Cumhuriyeti ile Avrupa Birliği Arasında İzinsiz İkamet Eden Kişilerin Geri Kabulüne İlişkin Anlaşma*, 16 Aralık 2013.

Türkiye İnsan Hakları Kurumu (TIHK). (2014). *İstanbul Geri Gönderme Merkezi Raporu*, 6 Kasım.

UN Commission Against Torture (UNCAT). (2012). *Concluding observations Greece*. UN Doc. CAT/C/GRC/CO5-6 paras. 14 and 20. New York: Author.

UNHCR. (2012). UNHCR releases new guidelines on detention of asylum-seekers. Retrieved from http://www.unhcr.org/505c461f9.html

UNHCR. (2014). *Global report, 2013: Turkey*. Retrieved from http://www.unhcr.org/5461e60c52.html.

U.S. Department of State. (2012). *Trafficking in persons report*. Washington, DC: Author.

14

Deportation as a Way of Life for Young Afghan Men

SHAHRAM KHOSRAVI

Clocks

When I arrived at the Märsta detention center in the early afternoon of a December day in 2014, a few people had gathered in the parking lot to protest the deportation of 15 Afghan migrants later that day. The streets around the detention center were crammed with police officers patrolling in their vehicles or on foot. Märsta detention center, 40 kilometers north of Stockholm and close to Arlanda international airport, is the biggest detention center in Sweden, with capacity for approximately 100 people. From the outside, it appears to be an ordinary building in an industrial area. However, its prisonlike interior is characterized by alarms, locks, security routines, visible presence of the police, and restricted movement for the detainees. The building is divided into a transit section on the ground floor and a detention center on the first floor. The detention area is divided into thirds, with a special section for women. There are several visiting rooms and a relatively generous visiting policy. Detainees have access to gym, a television room, and a few computers in each section.

I was there to interview Ruben, the head of the detention center. It was not my first visit; I had been there several times in 2008 to interview the staff and the detainees (Khosravi, 2009). The striking difference was the presence of uniformed police officers in some parts of the center. Ruben explained to me later that collaboration with the police has improved drastically in recent years. There is a police station close to the center, and officers visit it every day to meet detainees.

After the interview we went for a walk through different parts of the detention center. I did not see many changes since my last visit but in the main hall what caught my eye were five clocks on the wall showing time zones in other countries, other continents, to which many of the detainees would be deported. The clocks showed deportees time as if their time was not the same as the Swedish time.

The clocks make the same statement in terms of temporal disbelonging of the inmates, as the walls of the detention centers do in terms of spatial dis-belonging. The clocks, showing the several time zones, symbolize the geographical stretching out of relations between home country and host country, between deporting and receiving countries. They disclose the synchronizing operation of the removal between spaces and temporalities, a sort of time-space compression realized not through high-speed technologies but through the bodies of the deportees. In a room next to the hall where the clocks hang, I met some of the young Afghan men who were waiting to be removed from Swedish soil that day. They, like the majority of young Afghan men who have been deported to Kabul, will start new migration trajectories in less than half of a year (see Gladwell & Elwyn, 2012). Deportation for them will not put an end to the migration cycle but rather be only another phase of recirculation. They belong to what Peter Nyers (2003) has termed *deportspora,* an "abject diaspora," whose members are rejected asylum seekers, undocumented and irregular migrants, stateless people, and deportees who have been turned into "transnational corridors of expulsion."

My decade-long ethnographic fieldwork among travelers without paper (see Khosravi, 2010) has been full of migrants living a life shaped by a dialectical interplay between deportation and remigration. Young Afghan men are stuck on one side of a powerful transnational apparatus that forcibly excludes and expels them from the Global North, and on the other side the circumstances and forces that push them toward emigration from the Global South. Although the former attempts to impose a petrifying immobility on them, the latter forces them toward an incessant mobility in the shadows and through the cracks of the global order of borders (Hage, 2014). The dialectical positionality, affected by opposing forces, turns them into both object and subject of the national order of things, and at the same time. Several of these Afghan men have been subject to multiple deportations. Others were deported to a country they had never been to. In the course of only a few days, one ended up on another continent with no time to pack or say goodbye to friends. They spend a lot of time in one country waiting to find a way to the next one. They speak several languages and have good geographical knowledge about cities, borders, legislations, and transport systems. They are forced cosmopolitan subjects, not by choice, class, or ethnic privileges but by the deportation regime, stuck in a mobility in search of citizenship rights.

One afternoon in late June 2014, I was sitting with Hamed in a café in central Tehran. Hamed was born 1990 in Tehran to undocumented Afghan parents. He, like his brothers and sisters, grew up in a condition of deportability. The first time he was deported was at the age of 21. After one month in the notorious Asgarabad detention center south of Tehran, he was taken to the border of Afghanistan and forced to cross on foot. He came back to Iran the day after, with the help of *daldals* (literally brokers, human smugglers) for whom every deportee is a new client. While back in Tehran he decided to liberate himself from *deportspora* by seeking asylum in Europe, unaware that his destiny is interwoven with deportability. His applications for asylum were rejected in the Netherlands and then in Sweden. During the past three years he had been deported four times. The most recent one was from Sweden to Afghanistan in February 2014. He crossed the border to Iran again, to join his family, as the first step of his new journey toward

Europe. While talking about his asylum process first in the Netherlands and then in Sweden, he described the urban landscapes of Malmö and Amsterdam in detail. Between one rejection and the next, he lived with a lesbian couple in Copenhagen for a short time. In our conversation he threw in now and then Swedish words and idioms while speaking Persian with a Tehrani accent. His cultural identity could not be territorialized, fixed in one single nation-state. Hamed's body is like those of many other Afghan deportees, exposed to a cycle of deportation by the forces of nationalism; their narratives, however, disclose the multilayered relationship between space and identity or between territory and belonging (cf. Zilberg, 2011). For many Afghan deportees stuck in a circle of deportation, the relationship with geography is expressed not in the standard question "Where are you from?" but rather in "Where are you deported from?"

Walls

Because of the harmonization of migration and asylum policy within the European Union, the relatively generous Swedish policy toward asylum seekers gradually became more restrictive over the opening years of the new century. Accordingly, the penalty for immigration, exclusion and expulsion of undesired noncitizens, has become a central part of the asylum regime in Sweden (Khosravi, 2009). Immigration penalty arose as a result of the current security panic associated with migration, in the early 1990s, but was dramatically radicalized after the 9/11 terror attacks. Consequently, immigration policies are regularly criminalized, and immigration control is governed more and more through techniques and discourses used to regulate, control, and above all emphasize crime. The justification for immigrant penalty is to protect citizens from the threats of *anti-citizens* (Inda, 2006), regarded as threats to the well-being of the social body. Immigration penalty "constitutes and enforces borders, polices non-citizens, identifies those deemed dangerous, diseased, deceitful, or destitute, and refuses them entry or casts them out" (Pratt, 2005, p. 1). What makes immigration penalty in Sweden different is that it adopts the general welfarist discourse of "caring" and "saving," emphasizing concern for the well-being of detainees. As a migration officer put it in an interview, "many EU countries overlook deportation but we don't. If one is here she or he should have food and shelter."

The removal policies are justified by ideas of Swedish welfarism: the detainees should be excluded (deported) today, because they are ineligible to be included tomorrow. The Swedish self-image of being a prominent humanitarian society does not tolerate the presence of the excluded. Thus as the clocks on the wall indicate, the deportees' "tomorrow" belongs somewhere else. Accordingly one major principle in preremoval detention is to rob detainees of any hope for having a future in Sweden. For instance, Swedish language programs are not allowed at the detention centers. In the documentary *Förvaret* (*Detained*, 2014), directed by Anna Persson and Shaon Chakraborty, a female caseworker in a detention center, trying to comfort a depressed young detainee, told him, "There is still hope. You are not put in an airplane. You are not deported yet." Afterward we can see that the head of the detention center criticized her for working against the interest of her employer. Detainees should not be given hope that they have a chance to stay in Sweden. The clocks on the wall in another detention center, showing other time zones, display the same rationale. The detainee's body is related to a temporality other than that of Sweden. He or she is out of sync with Swedish time. He or she is displaced spatially as well as temporally.

Thus the idea of deportation is to restore the displaced, out-of-place people to their "natural" place of life, their "home-land." In the Swedish welfarist discourse a fundamental right is the right to be at home. In April 2011, the Migration Board in collaboration with a private company started an information campaign for the children of asylum seekers about the asylum process in Sweden. The popular children's cartoon character Bamse was used in a special issue of a comic book on migration. Bamse, "the world's strongest bear," who stands for justice and equality, was hired as a migration board officer to rationalize, naturalize, and depoliticize deportation of asylum seekers from Sweden. In one scene the deportees, all in animal figures, arriving back "home" are welcomed by family members and friends. In defense of using the children's cartoon hero, the Migration Board stated that the children "have rights to know about their rights." In this information campaign what is meant by "rights" for children of asylum seekers is the right to "return home." The notion of home is based on a botanical ideology that naturalizes the border regime and is built on the uncritical link between individuals and territory, making border crossing pathological (Malkki, 1992, p. 34) and "uprootedness" an "unnatural" mode of being. Deportation would restore the "broken" link between "nativity" and nationality. The link between life/birth and the nation becomes obviously naturalized in language. The terms *native* and *nation* have the same Latin root as the word for birth, *nascere*.

Although Sweden has a restrictive approach to migrant detention and the Migration Board claims it is used as "the last resort," the number of migrants confined for removal has risen in past years. The number (not including police detentions) of migrants confined in preremoval detention has increased 66 percent (from 1,742 to 2,893) between 2009 and 2013. There are currently five permanent detention centers in Sweden with capacity for 235 detainees. All are located close to international airports. In 2007 about 95 percent of the detainees were rejected asylum seekers, whereas in 2013 the rate was only 50 percent. During the same period detainees subject to the Dublin proceedings rose as a consequence of harmonization of EU asylum policies. This change of categories is related to a drastic decreasing of the average length of detention, from 18 days in 2005 to 13 days in 2009 and to 5 days in 2013. This is primarily because of an easier and faster removal of so-called Dublin cases from Sweden to other EU countries. Generally, persons under the Dublin procedures spend less time in detention than rejected asylum applicants.

According to the Migration Board, "the purpose of the confinement is not to tend [*vårda*] or to treat [*behandla*]. . . . It is to keep an alien accessible [*tillgänglig*] for investigation or deportation" (MAL111, 2006-346, p. 6). Not surprisingly, migrant detention centers in Sweden are called *förvar,* which literally means "warehouse." The bureaucratic rationality of "warehousing" deportees demands impersonal and emotionless relationships that reduce the deportees to merely body-objects, thinglike, "maintained" as transportable. The directives explicitly emphasize "professionalism," i.e., emotions should be kept at a reasonable level in the interest of bureaucratic efficiency. As in the relationship between prison officers and prisoners (Crawley, 2004), the deportees should be regarded as merely bodies. To show too much hospitality and care is discouraged. As the documentary *Förvaret* reveals the staff in a detention center are explicitly ordered to suppress their emotions. Two workers who showed "too much" emotion (through hugging, touching, and celebrating an old female detainee's birthday) faced warnings and sanctions for causing a disturbance in the work environment. The inmate as body-object becomes an abstraction, reduced merely to a thing to be stored. The experience of objectification is expressed by a young Iranian man who in an interview described his deportation in terms of dehumanization: "They did not treat me like a human." Not only were his human needs such as eating and using the toilet in privacy rejected and disrespected; he was not allowed to behave like a human.

> In the airplane I sat in the middle with one officer on each side. The pilot came to us. He looked at me and smiled. Then he said something in Swedish. I got up to salute him and to shake hand with him but the officers pushed me down aggressively. I said I just wanted to be polite and say hello to the pilot. The officers laughed and said that there was no need for such things.

Bodies

The bodies of deportees become the battlefield where the struggle for removal and resistance is going on. Antideportation campaigns are now using medical documents of illness emphasizing physical suffering as humanitarian reasons and evidence for unremovability of the deportees. As Didier Fassin (2005) correctly shows, the right to life has moved from the arena of political rights to the humanitarian. It is not surprising that deportees' resistance to deportation at airports and inside airplanes often happens in the form of stripping naked to display their human bodies, and in the form of screaming words to express their human voices. Naked bodies and voices—signs of humanity—are acts of resistance against the dehumanization and objectification of deportees. In Jacques Rancière's meaning (2004), it is political action, since it disrupts the rules and orders that determine what is visible and invisible, sayable and unsayable, audible and inaudible. By showing their naked bodies in airports and in airplanes, deportees make visible the double violence they are exposed to: first, what forces them to cross borders as asylum seekers, and then what sends them across the same border as a deportee. As Fassin states it, government operates not so much *on* the body as *through* it (in Lemke, 2011, p. 89).

This hostile hospitality is illustrated in a scene in the documentary *Förvaret* when the head of the detention center rejects detainees' request for having a longer lunchtime. For his decision he refers to the directive from the Public Health Agency of Sweden, which says that food should not be allowed to sit in open containers longer than 30 minutes. Although this person is diligent about the bodily health of the detainees, he is frank that the detainees should not feel comfortable. The significance of bodily health can be seen in encouragement of physical training. In the words of a caseworker, "exercise is good for detainees so they don't think about bad things." What the caseworker referred to as "bad things," i.e., deportation, is the rationale for the existence of the detention center. There are gyms in every section of the Märsta detention centers. A caseworker showing me around the gyms once said, "Did you know that in prison there is a limit in building muscle with body-weight exercises? The inmates should not become too strong. But here there is no limit. The detainees can build as huge muscles as they wish."

Multiculturalism

Rather than operate in the form of physical violence, biopolitical relationships between the body of the detainees and the state are organized around health and corporeal integrity (Lemke, 2011). The detention apparatus adopts a discourse of hospitality that emphasizes the safety, dignity, and comfort of the detainees. To create a hospitable atmosphere, staff with non-European background (first-generation immigrants or children of immigrants) have been recruited, mainly as caseworkers, on the assumption that their ethnic background gives them cultural competence and language skills that facilitate communication with the detainees.

Comparing the detention center with his previous workplaces, all of which were in public service, the head of the Märsta detention center proudly said, "Here is the most multicultural workplace I can imagine. More than 50 different languages are spoken here." Indeed, no other Swedish workplace encourages cultural diversity as do detention centers.

Interestingly, potentialities of migrants' cultural competences are recognized and valued only in service of expulsion of other migrants. The hostile hospitality embedded in the detention apparatus uses multiculturalism to make deportations faster, less painful, and less complicated. Furthermore, although not openly expressed in the interviews, the transnational ties of staff are calculated in facilitating the deportation procedure. The head of a detention center had an example:

> One of my staff is Iraqi. He just returned from visiting his family in northern Iraq. He can describe the situation for the detainees who will be sent to Iraq and reassures them that there will be no danger for them.

Personnel regularly visiting their homeland, where detainees would be deported to, causes tension in detainee-staff relations, expressed for instance by an Iranian detainee this way:

> These people have no problem going back. They go to their families and enjoy their time over there. They are not arrested or harassed. The migration officers here see that and tell us that Iran is safe for me too. They see Iran Air flights take Iranians back and forth twice a week and say, "Look: Iran is safe." The Migration Board doesn't want to understand we are here for different reasons.... These immigrants who work here have become more Swedish than Swedes themselves.

The "hospitable" multicultural personnel create familiarity, but also alienation and anxiety.

The hospitality discourse, endorsing the "good feeling" comfort and dignity of inmates, is not shared by the detainees. Amin, a young Afghan confined for more than four months said, "Here they cut your throat with cotton. They say nice things to us but their job is to send us back to where we have escaped from." Amin experienced his time in detention as constant exposure to humiliation: "They treat us like if we are kids ... [as] if we can't understand what is good and what is not good for to us."

The detention apparatus applies a child-making approach to detainees, who are regarded as minors in need of guidance by the Swedish detention apparatus. Comparing detainees and children was once clearly expressed by the head of a detention center who, in response to my question about inmates' activities, said, "They sit in front of computers all the time, just like what my kids used to do."

The paradox is that whereas the detainee is treated as an ignorant child who should be guided through conversation toward what is the best option for her or him—going back home—the detainee is seen at the same time as responsible for his or her situation.

One officer at the Migration Board said:

> We tell them that they have a choice. If you go through this door you go home with dignity and even get some money [the cash grant given to voluntary returnees], but if not, you should go to the other door and there the only thing waiting for you is the police. . . . We can't force people to accept our help. We can help when the person wants to be helped.

The detainee is regarded simultaneously as a child unable to understand what is in his or her interest and as an adult responsible for deeds and choices. The pedagogical aim is to make the detainee realize accepting the deportation decision is the best option, and to collaborate in his or her own deportation. Another officer put it this way: "They don't collaborate to buy time. It is their own fault. They can go home when they want. . . . We want to help them to look for alternatives and what they can do with the rest of their lives."

To make detainees believe they have a choice and have control over their own lives is to make them responsible for their confinement. The verb *deport,* after all, means to behave oneself. In the eyes of the migrants, long-term detention is generally used to tire them out and force them to collaborate.

Waithood

The etymology shows that the word *deport* in Old French meant "to be patient" and "to bear."

Waiting is a particular experience of time. In detention centers, waiting is inescapable. For the inmates, waiting is expecting something to come from others, e.g., officials' decisions, help from advocacy groups, or miracles saving them from deportation. Keeping others waiting is a technique for regulation of social interactions. It is a manipulation of other's time and "part of the domination" (Bourdieu, 2000). The "punitive" aspect of waithood in preremoval detention is when a person is "kept ignorant as to how long he must wait" (Schwartz, 1975 p. 6).

In the documentary *Förvaret* a female caseworker told an inmate, "You are not deported yet" in order to cheer him up. "Not yet" hints at the uncertainty and arbitrariness of waithood, i.e., keeping him waiting without giving him any hope. A consequence of waiting is the feeling that one is not fully in command of one's life. For detainees, lack of information on how long they have to wait makes their lives unpredictable and uncertain. To be kept waiting for a long time "is to be the subject of an assertion that one's own time (and therefore, one's social worth) is less valuable than the time and worth of the one who imposes the wait" (ibid. p. 11). Prolonged waiting for deportation means "not being in-time with others." For many people, Mondays represent "moving forward" (indicating mobility), the first day of a meaningful week of work; in contrast, for detainees Mondays mean "remaining at the same point" (indicating immobility). Mondays or other days are not experienced by detainees in the same way as for people outside the detention center. So how can we say that they exist in the same day? Exposing detainees to prolonged waiting is to expel them from simultaneity. Not unusually, detainees use terms like "dead time" or "a time of death" when talking about their lives kept waiting. But waiting can be an act too, a strategy of defiance on the part of detainees. Waiting does not have to mean passivity, and can be an element in a strategy for migrants to improve their situation, as, for instance, by not collaborating they try to postpone deportation in hope of a new chance to stay.

Bargaining

The removal system is based on a distinction between those whose lives are useful/legitimate and those whose lives are wasted/illegitimate. Afghans are regularly sent to Kabul, while the Swedish Foreign Department persistently warns Swedes to avoid traveling to Afghanistan owing to security risks. The removal operation is a transnational enterprise involving authorities from different states, transport companies, private security companies, deportation escorts, international networking, and private expert companies.

In the case of detainees who have no travel documents and whose identities in the eye of the Swedish authorities are indeterminate, the caseworkers and the Swedish police are in regular contact with foreign authorities, e.g., the embassy and police in the countries the detainees are believed to have come from. The primary purpose is to verify the identities of deportees who lack official documents. However, it is a bargaining process between deporting and receiving countries. Some countries do not accept deportees if they lack travel documents, such as Iran. To my question about why they keep sending deportees when the Iranian authorities do not let them come in, the chief of the migration division at the National Police Board said, "we will get them in through bargaining" (*vi snackar in dem*). Bargaining means an exchange of information about the deportees. Documents and information about them are handed over to various persons, e.g., the embassy, a pilot, or border guards in a destination country. Consequently, the safety and security of the deportees are systematically neglected and migrants, particularly the rejected asylum seekers, are put in even more danger after deportation than before they arrived in Sweden. The main protagonist in the documentary *Förvaret* is a failed asylum-seeking Chechen woman. She hid herself from the

Chechen authorities for more than 15 years, until the Swedish police contacted the Chechen authorities in order to verify her identity. The Chechen police officers visited her sister's home with a picture of her and other information they had received from Sweden. The deportation procedures often pose high risks for deportees, particularly in countries where seeking asylum is itself a punishable offense.

In the case of Afghanistan, Swedish authorities have been successful in "bargaining deportees in" even when they lack travel documents or identity cards. Lack of transparency in the deportation process creates a risk of corruption. In fall 2013, there was a national story about wide-ranging financial corruption in the ministry of Refugees and Repatriation in Afghanistan. In Sweden, public outrage erupted in fall 2014 over how tax money had been used to reward officers who follow deportees to the receiving countries with vacation days at luxury hotels and business-class flights after successful deportations. Furthermore, the sections in the Migration Board that are successful in deportations receive more money, about $500 for each deportee.

Involving private companies in the asylum investigation has also created a high vulnerability to corruption in Sweden. For instance, the Swedish language analysis company Sprakab has provided services to the Migration Board (and even to the Home Office in UK and the Australian Department of Immigration) since the early 2000s. They have analyzed audio recording interviews with the asylum seekers to determine their country of origin. The company has been criticized for systematically falsifying its language experts' qualifications. It is thus not surprising that many have been deported to the wrong country—Somalians to Kenya, Iranians to Iraq, Syrian-Yazidis to Armenia. Testimonies from young Afghans show that being deported to the wrong country is not uncommon.

Deportspora

Deported Afghans have an experience of "double abandonment" (cf. Lecadet, 2013), being a deportee from Sweden and an outcast in Afghanistan. Unlike voluntary returnees, Afghan deportees are abandoned and left with no support from the moment of their arrival. I recurrently heard them commenting on their arrival, "No one was there." For many, deportation often means forced return to a situation worse than prior to the initial departure, politically, financially, and socially. Consequently, adjustment and re-integration into the home country is usually uncertain and difficult. Opposite to what the Migration Board attempts to show, deportees do not go back *home*, but rejoin an abject diaspora, a deportspora (Nyers, 2003). They enter a transnational space of expulsion, oscillating between redeparture and redeportation. While in Kabul in search of information and a network, deportees find each other through social media. One active community network of deportees in Kabul is Kabulblog, established by a young Afghan man who himself was deported from Norway in April 2013. For him as a Hazara, a journey through Taliban-dominated areas in southern Afghanistan to Pakistan where he grew up and where his family lives is suicide. While stuck in Kabul, he started a support network for deportees. He gives them information, warns them of swindlers and bogus human smugglers, and helps them reestablish contacts with advocacy groups in the countries they have been deported from in the hope of initiating a new asylum process. In this small community of deportees the customary question "Where are you deported from?" (*diporti koja hasti?*) hints at their sense of belonging together, not to a territory but to deportspora, in which they are exposed to a continuing sequence of of expulsion.

There are multiple factors that make adjustment and re-integration difficult, if not impossible, for the deportees. First, many Afghan deportees cannot return to their hometown or village because of armed conflict. Three decades of civil war, foreign occupation, and disastrous environmental degradation have resulted in not only destruction of homes as physical places but also torn-apart families. Facebook pages of Afghan deportspora, such as *Khatrat-e talkh-e Afghanha dar younan* (bitter memories of Afghans in Greece) or *Panahjooyane andonezi* (Refugees in Indonesia) are full of appeals incorporating photographs and names to trace missing family members or friends en route between one border and another.

The majority of the Afghan deportees belong to the Shiia Hazara ethnic minority, who have historically been exposed to racial harassments by the powerful Sunni Pashto majority. Furthermore, many of the Afghan asylum seekers in Europe (including Sweden) were born and grew up in Iran or Pakistan. Afghanistan is for them a foreign country. Deported to Kabul, they have nowhere to be integrated, no one to reunify with. Accordingly the majority of them have to cross borders irregularly to Iran or Pakistan to go home. Interestingly, there is a dialectical interplay between deportation and human smuggling; every Afghan deportee is a new client for human smugglers.

Second, the cost of the initial migration, many times in the form of debt, is often not refunded. Deportation means also deletion of remittances, i.e., the source of livelihood for many poor families. Therefore, the whole household economy is affected by deportation. Generally, deportation affects negatively both the deportees and the receiving communities. Thus financial insecurity and unpaid debt force them to leave again, in the hope to "achieve goals thwarted by deportation" (Schuster & Majidi, 2013, p. 224). Deportation has a deep impact on relations between deportees and their country of origin.

Third, as my own study and others show, a common postdeportation experience is stigmatization from the failure of the migratory project common among deportees (Khosravi, 2009; Schuster & Majidi, 2013). One of the few studies on postdeportation shows that deportees experience cultural estrangement, stigmatization, a high level of violence, and little access to basic material needs

(Plambech, 2014). *Ekhrajee* (ejected) deportees are regarded as "polluted and polluting" (see Khosravi, 2009). "Double abandonment" is experienced by being regarded as a "failed citizen" in the host country and a "failed migrant" in the country of origin. Many mentioned feeling shame for the failure of their migratory project. In the case of Afghan deportees, stigmatization takes on a cultural aspect as well, in terms of being "culturally contaminated" by the foreign cultures. They are stigmatized and harassed for their accent, clothing, and behavior. Deportees who grew up in Iran face harassment and derision by being called *iranigak* (acting Iranian). Furthermore, being associated with the West worsens their vulnerability. Deportees are objects of suspicion and may be regarded as spies (Gladwell & Elwyn, 2012). Some have been exposed to suspicion and even violence just for having a foreign name and telephone number in the contact list of a cell phone. Moreover, being associated with the West makes them easy prey for swindlers and robbers who believe they have foreign currency.

Fourth, another issue that makes reintegration difficult and serves as a pull factor for remigration is that strong social ties remain through relatives or friends in the deporting country (Majidi, 2011). Furthermore, during their time in Sweden, deportees learned the language, made friends, maybe fell in love, and grew accustomed to the lifestyle in Europe. The desire to reunify with friends and family members and the desire for a missed lifestyle push them to start migration again toward what deportation deprived them of. Going through postdeportation suffering, i.e., dealing with unpaid debts, vanished remittances, the shame of failure, and stigmatization, outweighs the risk of being caught and deported once again. Deportation rarely deters further migration (Hiemstra, 2012). A UNHCR report (Gladwell & Elwyn, 2012) shows that up to 80 percent of the people forcibly removed to Kabul attempt a new migratory adventure within a short time after their arrival. Despite all efforts to deter and remove Afghan migrants, Afghanistan is still the second-leading country of origin of refugees, and among the top four source countries of asylum seekers in Sweden. So if deportation does not deter Afghan migrants, what then justifies these deportation policies?

The limited knowledge we have on postdeportation tells us two things:

1. There is no sustainable return for many deportees, and the aforementioned factors make adjustment and reintegration of deportees very challenging.
2. Deportation is not the end of the migration cycle but rather just a phase of recirculation.

Deportation thought of as a disciplinary measure that will deter migration fails because the structural realities behind why people leave are ignored. Therefore deportation, rather than stopping aspirant migrants, contributes to "the perpetuation of cycles of global inequality and human mobility" (Hiemstra, 2012, p. 307). For Afghans en route, deportation is absorbed into their cycle of migration and into the history of Afghanistan (Schuster & Majidi, 2013). For members of the Afghan deportspora, deportability has become a way of life. They do not imagine themselves in terms of *where they are from*, but *where they are deported from*.

References

Bourdieu, P. (2000). *Pascalian meditations*. Stanford, CA: Stanford University Press.

Crawley, E. (2004). *Doing prison work: The public and private lives of prison officers*. Cullompton, Devon, UK: Willan.

Fassin, D. (2005). Compassion and repression: The moral economy of immigration policies in France. *Cultural Anthropology, 20*(3), 362–387.

Gladwell, C., & Elwyn, H. (2012, November). Broken futures: Young Afghan asylum seekers in the UK and on return to their country of origin. *UNHCR's New Issues in Refugee available at:* http://www.refworld.org/docid/ *5142dc952.html Research*.

Hage, G. (2014, Jan. 26). Globalization and its borders. *Allegra*. Retrieved from http://allegralaboratory.net/globalisation-and-its-borders-by-ghassan-hage.

Hiemstra, N. (2012). Geopolitical reverberations of US migrant detention and deportation: The view from Ecuador. *Geopolitics, 17*(2), 293–311.

Inda, J. X. (2006). *Targeting immigrants: Government, technology, and ethics*. Malden, MA: Blackwell.

Khosravi, S. (2009). Detention and deportation of asylum seekers in Sweden. *Race and Class, 50*(4), 38–56.

Khosravi, S. (2010). *The illegal traveler: An auto-ethnography of borders*. Basingstoke, UK: Palgrave.

Lecadet, C. (2013). From migrant destitution to self-organization into transitory national communities: The revival of citizenship in post-deportation experience in Mali. In B. Anderson et al. (Eds.), *The social, political and historical contours of deportation* (pp. 76–97). New York: Springer.

Lemke, T. (2011). *Biopolitics: An advanced introduction*. New York: New York University Press.

Majidi, N. (2011). Urban returnees and internally displaced persons in Afghanistan. *Middle East Institute–Fondation pour la Recherche Strategique, 6*.

Malkki, L. (1992). National geographic: The rooting of peoples and the territorialization of national identity among scholars and refugees. *Cultural Anthropology, 7*(1), 24–44.

Nyers, P. (2003). Abject cosmopolitanism: The politics of protection in the anti-deportation movement. *Third World Quarterly, 24*(6), 1069–1093.

Plambech, S. (2014). *Points of departure: Migration control and anti-trafficking in the lives of Nigerian sex worker migrants after deportation from Europe*. Dissertation. Department of Anthropology, University of Copenhagen.

Pratt, A. (2005). *Securing borders [Elektronisk resurs] detention and deportation in Canada*. Vancouver: UBC Press.

Rancière, J. (2004). *The politics of aesthetics: The distribution of the sensible*. London: Continuum.

Schuster, L., & Majidi, N. (2013). What happens post-deportation? The experiences of deported Afghans. *Migration Studies, 1*(2), 221–240.

Schwartz, B. (1975). *Queuing and waiting: Studies in the social organization of access and delay*. Chicago: University of Chicago Press.

Zilberg, E. (2011). *Space of detention: The making of a transnational gang crisis between Los Angeles and San Salvador*. Durham, NC: Duke University Press.

15

Immigration Detention in South Africa

The View from Inside Lindela

REBECCA SUTTON

In Abdulrazak Gurnah's *By the Sea,* Tanzanian refugee Saleh Omar muses, "I am an involuntary instrument of another's design, a figure in a story told by someone else" (2001, p. 68). Of Saleh's decision to feign inability to speak English when claiming refugee status, his friend says, "You're just a condition, without even a story" (ibid., p. 143). This exchange serves as a backdrop to a discussion of how undocumented migrants experience immigration detention in South Africa.

South Africa's deportation regime has been run by the African National Congress since the mid-1990s, but it is undergirded by an enforcement and penal structure that was created by the apartheid government (Sutton & Vigneswaran, 2011; Segatti & Landau, 2011). Hundreds of thousands of individuals are deported from South Africa annually, with many of these deportations involving procedural irregularities (Amit, 2010) and sometimes human rights abuses (Sutton & Vigneswaran, 2011). The Lindela Repatriation Center, which can house 4,000 individual detainees, is located in Krugersdorp, west of Johannesburg. Lindela, which literally means "place of waiting," is the only dedicated facility in South Africa where undocumented foreign migrants are sent pending deportation. A number of formal legal challenges have been successfully brought regarding treatment of detainees at Lindela in recent years. In 2014, litigation reached the Gauteng High Court, and an investigation by the South African Human Rights Commission (SAHRC) took place. The High Court's ruling and the SAHRC investigation call for important changes to how Lindela is run, but there is still value in directing the gaze inside Lindela. As Lawyers for Human Rights (LHR) has noted, the problem is not the legal regime as such but rather the implementation of rules at Lindela: "The law is clear but it is ignored" (2014).

In the following discussion I explore four specific topics from the vantage point of individual detainees: how they make sense of the "illegal foreigner" label, whether they experience Lindela as prisonlike, how they interact with officials at Lindela, and implications of their stay in Lindela for their "life outside." This ethnographic study draws on a series of semistructured interviews and life histories I conducted with individual detainees at Lindela in 2009, as part of a wider study by the African Center for Migration and Society. My modest aim is elucidate the views and opinions shared by individual detainees in all their ambiguity, nuance, complexity, and ambivalence. In doing so, I hope to illuminate aspects of South Africa's deportation regime that are often out of sight and therefore out of mind.

A Note on Life Histories, Narrative, and Agency

The personal narrative (Lyotard's *petit recit*, 1979) is often equated with an account of an individual's experience. This can be contrasted with the grand narrative (*grand recit*), which is a global explanatory scheme that upholds institutional practices by appealing to abstract entities such as the State, or Reason (Herman, Manfred, & Mari-Laure, 2005). To conduct life history research is to engage with personal narratives, which can evoke the complexity of people's feelings in a way that the historical record cannot (James, 1997; Omidian, 1994). Life history research invites the perspectives of individuals "located at different places in the social and historical world towards objects of knowledge" (Runyan, in Crapanzano, 1984). It is a purposeful move away from the universal and toward the particular and the autobiographical (Boyden & de Berry, 2004). Life histories can draw us into the world of an individual and help us see through their eyes (Powles, 2002).

Lewin finds the process of telling one's story enabling: it allows one to mediate reality, to show how one's present self was constituted in the past, and to impose a sequence on what might otherwise be a chaotic experience (1992). Ricoeur makes the interesting point, however, that one may detract from one's own agency in the very act of narration; that is, the account may have a lack of agency as its subject matter (in Brown, 1997). These tensions are relevant in the context of immigration detention; there are concrete limits to the extent to which the *petit recit* of an individual detainee can concretely challenge the *grand recit* of South Africa's detention and deportation regime. What is perhaps most important, though, is not *whether* detainees at Lindela have agency with regard to their deportation, but rather *how* they have agency in the myriad things they do while detained, including imagining their future.

Detainee Experiences at Lindela: The "Illegal Foreigner" Label

How do individual detainees at Lindela make sense of their ascribed identity as "illegal foreigners"? For one Malawian detainee I spoke with, Lindela is connected to the widespread xenophobic violence that took place in South Africa in 2008. In his view, the cause of the violence was that South African nationals believed foreign migrants were taking their jobs: "The problem is, here in [South Africa] they give free food and houses for workers, whereas if you work in Zimbabwe or Malawi you don't get that kind of assistance." He understands that the South African government built Lindela because "they want to control the population."

I spoke with three Chinese detainees who had very recently arrived at Lindela, and the issue of economic reasons comes up again. Two of them are brothers, and they were in South Africa for only one day when they were caught at the Department of Home Affairs (DHA) at the airport. They said they didn't exactly understand what went wrong, or why they had been detained. They speculated that now was a bad time for Chinese people in South Africa, as locals fear the economic success of Chinese migrants. The DHA simply does not want anyone from China to come; it just wants to send them home without giving a reason.

A number of detainees understand the objective facts of their situation but seem to distance themselves from shame or acceptance. They deflect blame onto others, admit only to mistakes of a technical nature, or think in terms of practical outcomes. One such detainee from Pakistan, who had been at Lindela for a year and a half when we spoke, understands he made a tactical error by showing the immigration officer who stopped him a fake driver's license. A young woman from Liberia acknowledged that the police found her without the proper documents, but she viewed this as the fault of her baby's father, who she said hid her documents to keep an eye on her. She was adamant that "I am not a criminal, I have not done anything wrong. Except a man chose to take advantage of me, keep my child." A Kenyan detainee explained he is not so interested in what is illegal about his stay in South Africa. Rather, his main concern is simply whether he is going to be able to stay in the country and work.

It is common for detainees to insist they are at Lindela as the result of some technical or administrative error. Such individuals feel they could reverse their fortunes if given the opportunity. Their stories often begin with the words "If only. . . ." As one Zimbabwean individual maintained, "If only I had the chance to show the police my passport." I spoke with a Malawian detainee who had already been in South Africa for four years at the time of his arrest. Initially, he was adamant about needing a chance to prove to the officials that his papers were real and he was a legitimate resident. Yet he subsequently admitted that his documents "might be fake" because the police said they were. For some detainees, though they do not expect release they at least hope that officials will be lenient if they have an opportunity to show some further documentation or make their case once more. One Namibian detainee explained that his papers were expired when he was arrested, but only for "a short while." He expects that once someone takes a closer look at his case, there might be some reprieve. Others feel there is little point in having an official take a second look at their documents. As a Malawian detainee said, "They don't even care if your papers are real, they just say you are illegal." He told me that when he asked police why they needed his fingerprints upon arrest, they simply said, "We will send you back home, you are *Makwala*" (foreigner).

Some detainees appear more active in their attempts to circumvent or subvert the "illegal foreigner" label. When a detainee from Pakistan first outlined his story for me, he depicted himself as just sitting on a bench at the airport in South Africa and suddenly being arrested. As we talked more, however, it emerged that he had two sets of documents. He knew that one set of documents was illegal, because he was arrested for fraud several years ago. He pled guilty to those charges, spent time in prison, and was later released. The DHA was supposed to cancel these documents but failed to do so. He blames the officials for this, yet he also said it was his mistake to show the official who stopped him the wrong, fraudulent, license. He added, "So many other people keep four or five IDs, it's what foreigners do." The issue of multiple identities comes up often throughout these interviews, the most extreme case being where I spent an hour speaking with a man who claimed to be Zimbabwean (and is recorded on the Lindela daily status list as Zimbabwean) but had told previous researchers he was American and born in Hollywood. Another detainee, who was currently at Lindela for his third stay when I met him, explained that he sometimes presents himself to officials as Sudanese, other times Tanzanian. He chooses his country of origin according to the level of conflict or security in each place and the likelihood of deportation to either place at a particular time.

A minority of detainees seem to have internalized South Africa's broader deportation discourse, viewing themselves through the eyes of the state as the soon-to-be excluded (Sutton & Vigneswaran, 2011). They view their current predicament as being of their own making, their present detention as a reflection of their mistakes or culpability for past actions. A Congolese man who had only been at Lindela for three days, for example, appeared to have quite thoroughly absorbed the state's decision to deem him deportable. As he explained to me, he accepts the state saying he is an illegal person: "They gave us the opportunity to be here legally, but we broke it." In his view, he was sent to Lindela to be punished, and the only freedom he can aspire to will be his eventual deportation. The shame and embarrassment he expressed was reflected in conversations with other detainees, some of whom elected not to make contact with friends and loved ones in their country of origin, even when they were granted access to a phone.

Lindela as Prison

According to South Africa's Department of Home Affairs, Lindela's official purpose is administrative, rather than punitive. It is a center where people are held until their case is reviewed and a decision is made with respect to their status in

South Africa. During one of my visits to Lindela, I was sitting in a corner, writing, when one of the officials at Lindela approached me and said without prompting:

> This place is *not* a detention center. Keeping people contained, it's not good, but what can you do? I would prefer to keep people here just a day or two, but it's not possible. We try to ensure that people who are deportable get deported quickly, that they don't stay.

He told me he is worried that we (researchers) will portray Lindela in a bad way, perpetuating stereotypes. I ran into him later in the courtyard, and I could tell he hoped I would observe how nicely he treats the detainees he is interacting with. He turned to one of them and asked, "You are Rwandan?" "Yes," The official then glanced at me, and asked the detainee, jokingly, "Is there government in Rwanda?"

Individual detainees hold a wide range of views about whether, and to what extent, Lindela feels like a prison. One common thread is that most detainees seem to care little about the symbolic or ostensible purpose of Lindela. They are instead preoccupied with more tangible or physical implications, such as whether they can go outside and how long this detention is going to last. Some detainees feel that spending time in a "regular" prison offers certain advantages over Lindela. They note that in a regular prison one can at least know a firm charge, and usually be informed of a clear sentence with a specific end date. As a detainee from Namibia explained to me, on his arrest in South Africa he was put in a holding cell for 24 hours and then taken to Pollsmoor Prison, where he was "kept with criminals" for two months. Following that, police simply called his name one day and sent him on a bus with a group of others to Lindela. In his view, Lindela is essentially a prison: "We have TVs, but even in prison they have TVs. They lock us six to six, what's the difference? No difference." At the same time, he seemed to see a distinction between those whose company he shared at Pollsmoor and Lindela: only the former are criminals.

A 30-year-old detainee from Kenya who has been at Lindela for two weeks tells me that he has not yet informed his wife that he is in Lindela. He knows that if he ends up being in here for a long time she will wonder where he is, but he does not want anyone to know he is "in prison." For him, Lindela is a prison "because you cannot go outside, there is no freedom. It is very hard." He says his time at Lindela has been particularly difficult for him because he was never arrested before this, was never "in prison" before. A Sudanese detainee, recently returned to Lindela without explanation after a number of his fellow nationals were released, was despondent. "You're supposed to be out," he said. "How long you gonna stay inside. You don't see far. Anyone would like to be free. I feel like I'm in jail."

In some of the most fascinating exchanges I had at Lindela, detainees draw my attention to the paradox of being deemed "deportable" yet being kept inside South Africa for an interminable period. A 24-year-old Liberian woman who told me her father was a rebel leader with Charles Taylor said: "It's a prison here. They put us in the TV room. We are supposed to stay there all day. Then we go to the [cell]." She explained that her brothers were child soldiers, and for her Lindela is like the training camps in Liberia they described to her:

> They told me about the training. They are doing the same thing here. It is a real prison. You can imagine all this only for papers! If they think we are so bad, they should release us.... It's a process, I believe, but why keep us? You keepin' cows in a place and you just leave them there.

A Sudanese detainee said he just feels pain: "It's like you are sentenced [in prison] but I didn't do any crime. OK, they can deport you. But to keep you!" He would do anything to go out, even if it means to be deported: "It would be better, just to be free." One Kenyan detainee simply could not fathom what the purpose of keeping him at Lindela might be: "We have been here for one year, after being rejected the first time. Why don't they deport you?" Another Kenyan detainee who has been at Lindela for 18 months simply said: "This place, they lock you and leave you."

A Zimbabwean detainee admitted to being in South Africa without proper papers, but was adamant that other, criminal charges of abuse brought against her by her stepdaughter were false. It was those criminal charges that led to the discovery by police of her lack of documentation. She said of Lindela, "It's not good for human beings to be here. We are treated like prisoners, it's even worse. To be arrested for something you didn't do and to be locked, it makes your mind not work properly." She maintains of Lindela, "I can see it's a daylight robber. I paid the fine, but I'm not released, at the end of the day. I'm in prison again, they should have sentenced me."

I discussed the presence of video cameras and surveillance at Lindela with a number of detainees. For one Namibian detainee, these things amplify the feeling that Lindela is prisonlike: "They lock us, watch us, it is not a free place. It's hard, not good, not nice, to have guards everywhere." He raises the possibility of escape.

> You can escape, jump over the wall, but there's no point in doing this if you think you are getting out anyway. There are cameras, not in the cell, but all around. And if you get caught trying to escape you will get punched.

A Congolese man who had been there for three days said of Lindela, "Tout est permit, sauf la liberté." (Everything is allowed, except freedom.) He tells me he has no problem with the surveillance: "We need security because of the type of people here." A 31-year-old detainee from Pakistan also thinks the cameras can be helpful, for example, if someone else steals. He sees Lindela not as a prison but rather as a "foreigner's place." In his view, "It is more open, it is less strict, you don't have to stay in rooms for 24 hours a day, you can go where you want to go as long as it is in Lindela." A Zimbabwean detainee who has spent time in Pollsmoor prison told me that Lindela is better than a prison in a number of ways: "Here, you can walk around, in prison you can't, the rooms are smaller. Here you have access to go stretch your legs." After telling him that our interview was ending, I asked him if he had anything to add. "Nothing," he said, "except I have to wait."

Regardless of whether they view Lindela as prisonlike or not, all detainees agree on two key features of Lindela: it is a place they cannot leave and also a place where they have to wait.

Getting Information, Interacting with Officials

As Vigneswaran and I have noted, detainees at Lindela are often kept "on their toes" by officials. Approximately half of the detainees arrive at Lindela without formal notification they will be deported; fewer than 17 percent of detainees are notified of this after their arrival; fewer than 6 percent of detainees are informed of their rights relating to the deportation process, and even fewer understand they are allowed to appeal (Sutton & Vigneswaran, 2011).

A Bangladeshi detainee who spent seven days in prison before being brought to Lindela said he arrived without a clue as to what Lindela was or what it is for: "No, they told me nothing about Lindela." A Namibian detainee who has been at Lindela for five months said he sometimes gets nervous here, wondering "why I am here, what's going on, what's happening." He has little interaction with officials at Lindela, and no one has officially explained to him how Lindela works. Despite this, he said he feels that he knows what his rights are, in Lindela and more broadly, "because I am always asking questions, and won't stay dumb."

Making guesses about one's legal case appears to be a particularly popular pastime for detainees. A 30-year-old Kenyan who has been at Lindela for two weeks knows another Kenyan detainee who has been at Lindela for a year and a half. The Kenyan detainee I spoke with feels he will not be here so long because he has a passport and the other detainee from Kenya did not. A number of detainees told me that once they hear word a minister or ambassador from their home country has visited Lindela, they know they will soon be released.

With a lack of reliable information available, detainees thus look for cues and develop their own codes to make sense of the differing outcomes they face. One widely held belief is that some individuals pay bribes to get out. A 23-year-old detainee from Rwanda told me that before the police put him in a van to take him to the police station when he was arrested, they asked him for a bribe. He explained that it is the same at Lindela: "People are corrupted. Sometimes people at Lindela pay." I asked him what they pay for. "So that they get released," he replied. The Tanzanian detainee who was on his third stay at Lindela told me, "There is some scandal inside, yes. People, especially from India, China, Pakistan, bribe to get out." I inquire about the others, those who don't pay, and he told me, "Those ones are staying for long." I asked him if he was worried he might be one of them, one of those who stay for very long. He replied, "Yes, that's the thing." Lindela has indeed been described at times as a place for "those without money" ("Lindela Deportation Center . . . ," 2005).

The young detainee from Liberia told a different story. In her experience, they would not accept bribes at Lindela. She explained that she knows this because she tried hard to offer one: "My boyfriend said he would pay. How much did they want? The woman from Home Affairs heard me on the phone and took the phone from my hand, saying to my boyfriend 'we don't take bribes'."

A 31-year-old detainee from Pakistan said he finds it difficult to approach officials in Lindela.

> They don't treat you like humans. You try to talk to them and they don't listen like you are a person. They treat you like animals. It hurts when they don't care that you want to express yourself or are in trouble. They use their power.

Generally, he got information from other detainees, and sometimes from security people. He said he has not personally experienced corruption at Lindela, but others tell him "if you want to go out, get things done quickly, you can pay a bribe." His perspective on formal justice mechanisms at Lindela is that "there is a system, but it is a little bit slow because [people in the head office] are lazy." He says it is important to identify and approach the right official if you want to report a problem: "Some try to bullshit us. They don't want to listen to your story."

A Kenyan man told me that he was actually re-arrested almost immediately after being officially released from Lindela. He said of his relationship with the guards: "No, they leave me alone. When they re-arrested me I realized we are not friends." For him, there is no difference between DHA officials, street police, and the guards at Lindela.

Perhaps alone in many of his views, the Congolese detainee who had been at Lindela for only three days spoke highly of the officials he interacted with at Lindela: "The guards are nice, they respect you, they are not violent with us, they are helping us." I was curious about how he managed to have such a positive experience in contrast to his fellow detainees, and I asked him what he thought of the rules at Lindela. He summarized them as "soit vigilant de soi-meme" (look after oneself), "protégé sa vie" (protect oneself), "keep clean," and "don't escape because the cameras are watching." Although he is aware of and abides by these survival rules, he confided he has no idea what is happening with his own legal case.

Implications for "Life Outside"

As Vigneswaran, Wells, and I explored in "Waiting in Liminal Space: Migrants' Queuing for Home Affairs in South Africa," Lindela is essentially the "end of the line" in South Africa's status determination process. Release, or granting of legal status permitting one to remain in South Africa, is very unlikely (Sutton, Vigneswaran, & Wells, 2011). Prior to their arrest and detention in Lindela, many individuals do everything in their power to evade deportation. They procure false identification documents, they evade immigration officials by lying low (or as a detainee from Zimbabwe calls it, "playing hide and seek"), and some visit Home Affairs relentlessly in an attempt to legitimately renew their permits. Once an individual is brought to Lindela, however, deportation often emerges as a preferred solution.

That being said, some detainees do cling to the possibility of a release, and such individuals tend to maintain some claim (valid or otherwise) to asylum or refugee status. For a Burundian man who said he will face violence if sent back home, for example, the possibility of deportation keeps him in a state of constant anxiety. He told me he worked as a hairdresser in South Africa before his arrest, and cutting hair had previously earned him enough money to pay his rent and buy food and clothes. He worries that in the month he has been at Lindela his brush, combs, and other salon equipment have probably been stolen. When people see he is not at work, they will take his things. He had already paid the deposit for his room when he was arrested, so that is gone. An issue that looms larger for him is the fact that he has a failed refugee status claim and feels deeply afraid of being returned to Burundi, where he says the people who killed his family still live: "Life will go down. I think too much. If they will deport me, I will die." A Rwandan man who says he has been at Lindela for a full two years tells me: "It is so sad for me to go home. No home. No parents." Having watched the recent release of some of his friends from Lindela, he said: "When you see your friends are gone and you are coming back, it's very pitiful. You could just kill yourself." I asked a Sudanese detainee what he would do if he is released. He answered: "I'm just looking for a better life. I would like to be free. Maybe I can push my life." And what if he is deported? "I don't want to go back to Sudan. I have no parents. I'm done in my life." For all three of these detainees, their detention at Lindela is a devastating event that is forcing them to think about building a new life from scratch after they leave Lindela.

Other detainees know full well they will be deported and find ways to incorporate the fact of their detention into their broader life plans. Some are adamant they will simply return to South Africa once deported. While I was interviewing a Namibian detainee, a large group of Malawian detainees queued near where we were sitting, and we watched them being processed for deportation. Many smiled at the Namibian detainee as they pass by, saying goodbye. "It doesn't matter," the Namibian said to me, scratching his leg, "they'll just come right back." When a Chinese detainee who had been caught with fraudulent papers explained to me what he would do differently next time, he said that he would never again pay a middleman to obtain his documents for him. It remains unclear whether this denoted acceptance of moral wrongdoing, a determination not to get caught again, or some mixture of both. I asked a Namibian detainee who has been at Lindela for five months about his life outside Lindela. He said he doubts he will be blacklisted from South Africa because his was just a case of his visa expiring. So, once he is deported, he intends to return to Cape Town in order to finish his studies. He told me that he is not particularly worried about deportation. He just wants to leave, to go out. What he is worried about is "being behind" at school and at work.

For a self-employed detainee from Pakistan, the one-and-a-half months he has spent at Lindela make him worry for his business. There is no one to cover for him in his absence. He told me he has been in South Africa for more than 11 years, and at one point he was married to a South African woman. She is now deceased, but he claims to have naturalized as a South African. He has two children with another woman, and maintains a relationship of some sort with them. A Chinese detainee who had owned a clothing shop in Johannesburg at the time of his arrest told me he is very worried about his shop. Some friends of his are watching it for now, but if he stays at Lindela for a long time, who knows what will happen? He said he wants to stay in South Africa because he has invested so much money here. A detainee from Bangladesh who ran two shops at the time of his arrest is also worried: "Now they are finished. I have no more. No nothing." A 26-year-old detainee, also from Bangladesh, has been at Lindela for 10 months and told me he was working in a grocery shop before he was arrested; "Now, I don't have a job. It's a long time left from work." On a lighter note, I spoke with a number of recently arrived detainees from China as a group, and the concerns of one man elicited knowing laughter from the others. He explained that his biggest fear of being deported is that he will have to return to China and spend time with his wife.

A Malawian detainee who has been at Lindela for three weeks told me that the hardest thing about Lindela is that "you forget your friends. And it stops you from succeeding in life." He is particularly worried about his property and possessions. The What he most wants back are his TV, his kitchen things, and his money. Now that he is at Lindela, he is worried people outside might think they can steal his things when they see he's not there for three weeks and is not at work. He is mostly concerned about his neighbors who don't work. If he could, he would phone someone to look after his things. He assumes that when he is eventually deported he will have nothing left, so he intends to make money back home in Malawi for a month or so and then return to South Africa.

After three months in Lindela, a Zimbabwean detainee speculated about his life outside, surmising that "work is maybe over, stopped. Even if you are released, the situation is difficult." He feels that he still has control of his destiny as long as he can get out, but he just cannot say whether that will happen. For him, the hardest thing about his experience is "taking your time. There is a decline. You have to start again." In the words of a Rwandan detainee: "They give us hope, but we don't know when [we will leave Lindela]. Today is Friday. Tuesday is gone. Wednesday is gone. Thursday is gone." I have heard others at Lindela speak this way, commenting on how each day spent at Lindela is one day they will never get back in their lives outside. A woman from Zimbabwe told me she is worried about what will happen to her children while she is at Lindela. They were taken away from her by Child Services, and she wondered whether the DHA will help her get them back when she gets out. For her, every day at Lindela is a day her children are looked after by someone other than her.

Finally, as is perhaps true of any group of people or population anywhere in the world, there are those detainees who manage to keep dreaming big about their future from inside Lindela. The young Liberian woman told me that although she is tired now, she wants to follow her dream of being a singer. She is adamant that when she gets out of here, "I want to make a name for myself." In what is perhaps the most memorable statement I heard while at Lindela, she confided, "I'm an atheist. But I think God has a plan for everyone."

Conclusion

In this discussion I have explored the *petits recits* of undocumented migrants in South Africa in a specific place and at a specific moment in time: during their stay as detainees at Lindela. In doing so, I hope I have offered a glimpse into the world of immigration detention in South Africa, a milieu that is typically mysterious and rather inscrutable to the average observer of global and transnational migration dynamics.

We might consider here again Gurnah's character Saleh in *By the Sea*, who is described by his friend as being in "a condition without even a story." The individual detainees at Lindela have indeed been assigned a condition, that of being "illegal foreigners" who are deportable. This has drastic, concrete implications for their migration trajectories and their lives more broadly. As I have endeavored to demonstrate, however, this does not mean individual detainees are without a story. Quite apart from the specific content of a given individual's narrative and his or her ability to challenge the *grand recit* that deems these people deportable, the experiences of individual detainees and the stories they tell simply matter in their own right.

References

Amit, R. (2010). Lost in the vortex: Irregularities in the detention and deportation of non-nationals in South Africa. Johannesburg: African Center for Migration and Society.

Boyden, J., & de Berry (Eds.). (2004). *Children and youth on the front line: Ethnography, armed conflict and displacement.* New York: Berghahn.

Brown, D. (1997). On narrative and belonging. In J. Morny (Ed.), *Paul Ricoeur and narrative: Context and contestation* (pp. 125–148). Calgary, Alberta: University of Calgary Press.

Crapanzano, V. (1984). Life histories. *American Anthropologist, 86*(4), 953–960.

Gurnah, A. (2001). *By the sea.* London: Bloomsbury.

James, W. (1997). The names of fear: Memory, history, and the ethnography of feeling among Uduk refugees. *Journal of the Royal Anthropological Institute, 3*(1), 115–131.

Herman, D., Manfred, J., & Mari-Laure, R. (2005). *Routledge encyclopedia of narrative theory.* London: Routledge.

Lawyers for Human Rights (LHR). (2014, Oct. 10). Waiting for change at Lindela. Retrieved from http://www.lhr.org.za/news/2014/waiting-change-lindela.

Lewin, C. (1992). The Holocaust: Anthropological possibilities and the dilemma of representation. *American Anthropologist, 94*(1), 161–166.

Lindela Deportation Center is for those who do not have money. (2005, Feb. 10). *IRIN News.* Retrieved from http://www.irinnews.org/report/52979/south-africa-lindela-deportation-center-is-for-those-who-do-not-have-money.

Lyotard, J. F. (1979). *The postmodern condition: A report on knowledge.* Manchester: Manchester University Press.

Omidian, P. A. (1994). Life out of context: Recording Afghan refugees' stories. In L. A. Camino, A. Linda, & R. M. Krulfeld (Eds.), *Reconstructing lives, recapturing meaning: Refugee identity, gender, and cultural change.* Amsterdam: Gordon & Breach.

Powles, J. (2002). Home and homelessness: The life history of Susanna Mwana-uta, an Angolan refugee. *Journal of Refugee Studies, 15*(1), 81–101.

Segatti, A., & Landau, L. (Eds.). (2011). *Contemporary migration to South Africa: A regional development issue.* Washington, DC: World Bank.

Sutton, R., & Vigneswaran, D. (2011). A Kafkaesque state: Deportation and detention in South Africa. *Citizenship Studies, 15*(5), 627–642.

Sutton, R., Vigneswaran, D., & and Wells, H. (2011). Waiting in liminal space: Migrants' queuing for Home Affairs in South Africa. *Anthropology Southern Africa, 34*(1&2), 30–37.

16

"They Cut Your Wings over Here . . . You Can't Do Nothing"

Voices of Children and Parents Held in Immigration Detention in Canada

RACHEL KRONICK, CÉCILE ROUSSEAU, AND JANET CLEVELAND

In Canada approximately 9,000 persons are held in immigration detention centers every year, according to the Canadian Border Services Agency (CBSA, 2011). Approximately half of these detainees were either asylum seekers or failed refugee claimants awaiting deportation. Detention takes place in Immigration Holding Centers (IHCs) in 65 percent of cases and also in provincial jails (35 percent; ibid.). The three IHCs, located in Toronto, Montreal, and Vancouver, function like medium-security prisons and are surrounded by razor wire fences and staffed by guards (Cleveland & Rousseau, 2013).

Approximately 650 (im)migrant children are detained every year in Canada, again according to the CBSA. This is likely a significant underestimate of the actual numbers of children held in immigration detention, however, because children are often not issued detention orders themselves and are in detention accompanying parents who have chosen to stay with their children rather than relinquish their care to provincial children protection services (Kronick, Rousseau, & Cleveland, 2015; "Detention . . . ," 2009). In these cases, children are statistically and legally invisible as detainees. They are detained with their mothers in a mother-child section (separate from the women's section), and separated from fathers or older male relatives, who are held in a separate men's section. In Canada asylum seekers' mean detention length is approximately one month, though families may be detained for anywhere from 48 hours to many months.

This chapter examines the research looking at (im)migrant children and parents who have been detained in Canada. We draw on research conducted between 2011 and 2012, investigating the lived experiences of 20 detained families

(Kronick et al., 2015). As an ethnographic study, the investigation sought to understand children's and parents' daily detention experiences, as well as their perceptions of and reactions to the immigration detention system in Canada (ibid.). In this chapter we use the in-depth interviews as well as participant observations and discussions with key informants of the study to illustrate the experiences of detained families. We look first at the pre-migratory experiences of families, and then explore the day-to-day lives of children and families in detention, including their experiences of being arrested and navigating the legal processes of immigration detention. Next we examine the experiences of families who have been separated in the context of detention, as well as those mothers who are parenting in detention. Finally, we address detainees' own perceptions of immigration detention in Canada.

Pre-migratory Contexts: Trauma, Separation, and Complex Migratory Trajectories

Families who had experienced detention in Canada described significant prior trauma and persecution. They described histories of physical assault, rape, and torture; threats or harassment by an organized group; murder or disappearance of family or friends; witnessing murder; religious persecution; domestic violence; and forced separation of family members and of parents and children (Kronick et al., 2015). Some participants had also experienced significant stress and even trauma during the transnational migration process (ibid.). There were families who had lived with precarious status in another country. One family had already been detained as migrants in a Central American immigration prison prior to their arrival in Canada. Several families had endured long, dangerous journeys by boat or on foot, in some cases traveling through multiple continents. These findings, suggesting a heavy burden of pre-migratory stressors and trauma, correlate with international literature (Steel et al., 2009; Ryan, Kelly, & Kelly, 2009). Children and families arrived in Canadian detention centers already having lived through trauma, and often having already faced marginalizing immigration practices in other countries.

Living in Detention: Arrests, Reviews, and Daily Life

Arrests. Families initially arrive in detention on the basis of a decision of a Canadian Border Services Agency (CBSA) officer, who is invested with the power to arrest and detain migrants. (Im)migrants and asylum seekers are detained primarily for three reasons: (1) a person's identity has not been established; (2) a person is deemed unlikely to appear for an examination, admissibility hearing, or removal from Canada (i.e., a flight risk); or (3) someone is deemed a threat to public safety or inadmissible on security grounds (Nakache, 2011). Importantly, fewer than 6 percent of detainees are deemed a risk to public safety (Cleveland & Rousseau, 2013).

For many parents and children, the experience of arrest was described as frightening and humiliating. One mother, arriving by plane with her two teenage children and a six-year-old, described 10 hours of interrogation by CBSA officials at the airport after making an asylum claim. The interrogation was followed by their arrest:

> We just arrived and we didn't know what was happening. . . . I didn't understand that they were taking me to a detention. . . . It was horrible, I was crying. "Why are we in a jail? Why are we detained?". . . We didn't know what to do, what was happening. Actually they said they weren't through with us, so they said we could stay [in detention] or they can send us back. (Case 12)

As this mother described, families were often flanked by uniformed officers during their arrest, who accompanied them to the van transporting persons to the IHC:

> Yeah, that was the most undesirable thing also. They didn't put us into handcuffs, but there were three to four policemen. Of course one was ahead—in front of us. The other ones were behind us. Two at our sides . . . . it was security for us to . . . to take us into the car. (Case 12)

Parents reported how humiliating this experience was for them—to be seen in public appearing as criminals—and how frightening these experiences were to their children. In one case a child of five years had to be forced into the van by officers when he tried to flee in fear.

Three families told us that their children had been witness to their parents in shackles and handcuffs:

> INTERVIEWER: They handcuffed you in front of the kids?
>
> MOTHER: Yes. In front of the kids. And . . . we were all crying, you know? My kids were crying. They were like: "Mom what happened? Why are they doing this?" (Case 17)

Participants also noted the experience of being searched in front of their children. A mother of a 21-month-old boy described arriving at the detention center, having her personal belongings confiscated, and then being searched in front of her toddler. When security guards attempted to search him he cried, frightened, refusing to enter the small room.

Some families reported that during long periods of interrogation and waiting for transport, they were left without food for themselves or their children. One mother was arrested in her driveway while holding her infant in her arms (Kronick et al., 2015). She was separated from her infant—who was still breastfeeding—for four days in provincial jail until she was transferred to the IHC when space became available.

In summary, for the families we interviewed, arrests evoked feelings of terror and shame and were in some cases made more trying by long interrogations, lack of food, the intimidating presence of officials in uniform, and detainees' lack of knowledge of the process and their rights. Children are witness to their parents being searched and sometimes being handcuffed.

Review hearings. Once families have entered detention facilities, their imprisonment is reviewed before an administrative tribunal of the Immigration and Refugee Board (IRB) at 48 hours, 7 days, and then every 30 days after detention. Families are typically represented by legal counsel, though they may represent themselves. A decision maker from the Immigration Division of the IRB determines if someone is to be released or detained further after hearing arguments from the detainee or representative and the lawyer representing the CBSA. Families in our study described these hearings—particularly unsuccessful ones—as painful and frustrating experiences. Parents spoke both of a failure to take into consideration the presence and best interests of their children, and of a sense that the proceedings were arbitrary and unfair.

In several cases, children's well-being was not taken into account by decision makers at detention review hearings. During one hearing, the decision maker stated aloud that he was "taking into consideration the best interests of the child" but proceeded to give a decision that did not mention the children. In other cases, parents attempted to make the decision maker aware of their children's interests (or in this case a pregnant spouse) and were ignored during the hearing:

> They just stopped and I said "please, I need to talk to somebody. Help me." My wife was pregnant. We started to have problems with that pregnancy. . . . The baby basically stopped growing. . . . She wasn't in good condition. She was having trouble here by herself. Basically they didn't care about that. We provided them with some letters from my family doctor and everything. . . . And they didn't care. (Case 18)

One mother noted that the only time her children—ages six and four years—were invoked in the hearings or arrest (despite the children being present) was when the decision maker cited the parents' desire to make a good life for their children as evidence that they were a flight risk:

> Yes, that was the only time [they mentioned the children]. Not even when we were arrested . . . even when we said that we want to be together. They say: "It's not a big deal." . . . The way that they treat you is . . . it's not nice, it's not fair and it's not respectful at all. (Case 17)

We also observed avoidant reactions to children in a detention review hearing. An IRB member did not look at the two young children who were present throughout the hearing; nor did the member appear to notice when the eldest child, age 11, wept as the decision was announced. The child left the hearing room and vomited soon after, according to her mother, as a consequence of her enormous distress at returning to detention.

While families noted the invisibility of their children in the detention review hearings, they also felt that hearings were often unjust and arbitrary. One father who was separated from his family described the process as a kind of farce:

> [The detention review hearing] was a theater: this guy talks, I am supposed to respond, he talks again then the judge makes his part. That's it. Every single time was the same thing. Even when I got released it was the same thing. (Case 18)

Key informants also explained that during some detention hearings CBSA lawyers had sometimes used medical records from the detention center without patient consent, thus breaching patients' (i.e., detainees') confidentiality.

Rules of daily life. While children and parents are in detention, their daily life is dictated by rigid schedules, surveillance by guards, and minimal stimulation. Despite children's right to access education (Citizenship and Immigration Canada, 2007; UNHCR, 2012), schooling provided within the IHCs is onsite and described by children and parents as inadequate (Kronick et al., 2015). Although spaces are clean and physically safe, there is sometimes a lack of space and often children are deprived of age-appropriate toys and stimulation. The difficulties of daily living, combined with pervasive understimulation and lack of freedom of movement, make life in immigration detention feel degrading, overwhelming, and distressing for children and their parents.

The following vignette, witnessed by our researcher, underlines restrictive regulations governing children's activities in detention. In one IHC the family yard, which children could access at the discretion of the guards, was adjacent to the yard for the men's holding section. We observed an 11-year-old girl, detained for approximately two weeks with her mother and younger sister. The child entered the family yard—having not been able to go outside previously, because she did not have adequate winter clothing—and noticed her father across the barbed wire fence separating the men's yard. The girl ran toward the fence, smiling and waving hello, visibly delighted to see her father, from whom she and her mother and sister were separated. The guard quickly yelled at the child to stop, insisting that she not acknowledge her father. The child, shocked and frightened, backed away from the fence (ibid.).

Even meals and wake-up times were strictly regimented, making the mundane act of getting up and breaking bread trying. In one IHC, meals required families to exit the family areas accompanied by guards to travel to another building. "At five in the morning a woman came to tell us 'get yourselves ready, you're going downstairs. We're going to eat.' At five in the morning!" (Case 19) This mother explained that she would sometimes have to wait forty minutes outside in the snow with her two children before they reached the cafeteria (Kronick et al., 2015).

The institutional norms and regulations were upheld even while appearing absurd when applied to young children. For example, after an interview was completed with a mother and a 21-month-old toddler in a conference room, the guards tried to contain the family in the room until permission was given for them to leave. In general, guards were careful to open doors and release families from specific rooms only when permission was given by the central guard desk. While waiting, the toddler sang songs with his mother for several minutes to pass the time. A guard then arrived and opened the door, explaining that they must still remain in the room until an order was given. The toddler, laughing delightedly, quickly ran out of the room as if playing a game of chase. The guard pursued him with seriousness, attempting to block the child's path with his knees and forcing him back into the room with his mother.

In contrast, guards often enacted a dual role: that of jail keeper, but also of caregiver for the children. We observed a five-year-old run to a guard who was arriving on shift and who picked him up and spun him around playfully. Similarly, guards were often attentive to mothers' well-being, and would sometimes tell us during our interviews that they believed the mother was depressed, in one case adding that she (the guard) could not imagine being detained herself. They were also attentive to children's needs, for example pointing out to a mother that a child had lost a sock, or commenting on how sophisticated a drawing done by a five-year-old was for his age. In this sense, guards acted so as to resist collusion with the oppressive practices of detention (ibid.), while at the same time their actions appeared to almost deny the harsh reality of children's circumstances in detention.

In short, detainees, including children, are the objects of near-constant surveillance in the IHC and have limited freedom of movement. Security personnel's interaction with children and families is characterized on the one hand by mothering and nurturance, and on the other by power and authority. These ambivalent actions toward detainees point to the difficult position of guards, as they are tasked both with *protecting* migrant children and *protecting us from* the presence of certain migrant children.

Health Care and Psychosocial Supports in Detention

Parents described limited sources of support in the IHCs. There are primary care medical services, which include nurses who are available during the day and a doctor who visits the IHC every three or four days. Key informants also told us that a previous family doctor working in one of the IHCs had been fired because of his advocacy work on behalf of detainees. Another doctor hired on private contact by the CBSA was nicknamed "Doctor Tylenol" because he provided such minimal treatment.

Families can sometimes access support from nongovernmental organizations that are permitted to visit the IHCs in Toronto and Montreal. These organizations typically help families access legal representation. They also may furnish clothing, toys, and books to detained families. In one IHC, an NGO provides volunteer therapists who lead a support group for detained adults, but there were no regularly available social workers or psychologists in either IHC. Significantly, many of these services would be offered by the state in a prison, but they are not in the IHCs.

Frightening Separations in Detention

Separation of children from their parents because of detention was an important and common experience for families in our study (Kronick et al., 2015). Children may be separated from fathers or older male siblings when they are detained, or parents may be detained without their children in some cases. Sometimes parents are given the *choice* of having their children accompany them in detention, or separate from them, leaving them in the custody of provincial child protection services ("Detention . . . ," 2009).

Children appeared highly distressed by separation from a father within detention. One 11-year-old child, detained for nearly three months, spoke to her mother frequently about her father, asking where he was and if he was OK. As the detention progressed she began to refuse meals, asking that the food be saved and given to her father (Kronick et al., 2015). Several mothers reported that when children were able to visit their fathers they would cry on reunion. It appeared that despite opportunities to meet fathers a few times a day, children were extremely anxious about the absent parent. This high level of anxiety may point to the retraumatizing effects of separation and detention following multiple pre-migratory traumas.

For children who were separated from their parents during the latter's detention, there were opportunities to visit the detention center. However, as we learned from participants, these visits were often very stressful for children and parents. For example, one parent described the experience of having his three-year-old child and pregnant wife visit him in detention. Because they were not Canadian (as some detainees' children are), they were required to meet in a visitors room, speaking to the father/husband behind glass:

> These other Canadian kids could come in, but my son—because he was [non-Canadian]—couldn't get in. They are so mean [. . .] It is up to the mood of the judge, the guard. It's up to everyone's moods. (Case 18)

The same father noted the strict rules surrounding contact with visitors. He told us that after meeting with his wife and child in the visiting room behind glass he would go to his cell to watch them leaving the IHC from his barred window:

> Sometimes they didn't treat us like humans. . . . I'd go as fast as I could to my room just to say bye to her [my wife] every single day. Once one of those guards just came to me and said ". . . Don't say 'hi'. Don't salute people." I told him "Hey it's my wife! It's my family. What are you talking about?" "You are not allowed to do it." I couldn't even respond to that. I was just brought to tears. (Case 18)

Children who were spared detention but separated from one or both parents frequently appeared to fare poorly during the parent(s') detention. After his mother was detained alone, a five-year-old's school noted social difficulties, regression in academic milestones, and inability to separate from the female teacher from whom he was seeking comfort and "affection." As his father described:

> I think that he is scared. He is scared for his mother. Is she in danger—he knows that she is here [in Canada], but why isn't she coming home? He's already asked me the question "Tell me, papa, tell me the truth." I cried when he asked me that. . . . I don't know what to say. . . . I have to reassure him before he'll be calm and not ask more questions. "She's going to come, she's going to come." It's as if he doubts that she will come home. (Case 20)

The detention of his wife and the resultant family separation also appeared to affect the children's father, who reported insomnia, loss of appetite, weight loss, and suicidal ideation:

> I got angry and I said to myself "I prefer to go and die in my country. I prefer to be imprisoned in my country than my wife should be in prison for something that she didn't do. . . . Why are they keeping her there [in detention]? For nothing! I say that it is shameful. It's a shame on Canada. (Case 20)

One family who had chosen to separate from their two children, ages six and four, in order that they not face imprisonment, reported how anxious their children were about their parents' absence. To try to console the children, the parents had told them they were merely working overtime to help pay for a vacation.

> FATHER: They are always asking "When do you come back? When do you come back?"
>
> MOTHER: Yes. They cry. Sometimes they get really upset, you know? They tell us: "Why are you taking so long? Why do you need a lot of money to take a vacation? . . . Mom, why do you say 'soon'? 'soon' never happens, Mom." (Case 17)

The children's grandmother, who was caring for the children while the parents were detained, also reported to the parents that their children's behavior had changed, suggesting they were more aggressive and irritable and would cry more easily since being separated from their parents. The mother noted:

> Of course it is a stressful situation for them. We never, never separate. Never. We are always together. They have on their minds what happened [when parents were arrested and handcuffed in front of the children]. . . . I just can't wait to be with them, to have them, to smell them. I can't wait. (Case 17)

We also documented separation experiences of families who were detained as part of a specific mass arrival of Tamil asylum seekers from Sri Lanka aboard the *Sun Sea* (Cleveland, Dionne-Boivin, & Rousseau, 2013; Cleveland, Rousseau, & Kronick, 2012). In that case, 25 mothers arriving with children were detained in a separate facility from fathers who were detained in provincial prisons. The family we interviewed reported that for a period of two months the mother and children were permitted no contact with the father. After two months, phone contact of 10 minutes per week was allowed, and after three months children and mother could visit father in jail every 7 to 10 days for 15 minutes to one hour. As in other cases, the family reported children's high anxiety at being detained and separated: "Why aren't we getting released? When do I get to see my father? Is father coming to take us?" (Case 11) the children frequently asked. These children had experienced a high level of pre-migration trauma, including witnessing the violent deaths of children or adults (including extended family members) and enduring months of shelling, in addition to the difficulties entailed in migration (Cleveland et al., 2012).

We also met with parents who were detained without their children in provincial jails. The detentions in jail occurred because there was no more room in the IHCs. In all of these cases, children were necessarily separated from their parent because children are not permitted in provincial prisons. One father told us he was unable to reach his wife and children, having been permitted only one phone call, which had not gone through, so for two weeks his family did not know where he was. Two mothers were held in jail and forcibly separated from their breastfeeding infants until they were permitted a transfer to the IHC (Kronick et al., 2015).

Overall our research suggests that families are affected not only by detention, but also by the family separations that are caused by immigration detention (ibid.). Separating children from their parents—often with the intention of protecting children from the harmful experiences of detention—severs children's secure attachments (even if only temporarily), leading to severe distress and psychological maladjustment.

Children and Parents in Detention Together

Several parents, especially mothers of infants, noted how difficult it was to parent under the IHC rules. Parents were not permitted to let children out of their sight. For example, the mother of a four-week-old who had been detained for nine days when we met her complained how difficult it was to use the bathroom, given she had to carry the baby with her in his car seat—a weight she had been advised not to lift after her caesarean section.

Parents we interviewed disclosed significant distress manifesting as sleep difficulties, nightmares, anxiety, suicidal thoughts, weight loss, and feelings of shame and humiliation. Parents spoke of their loss of confidence in detention. One father remarked: "Detention, for me, it demoralizes you. And then you even start to doubt yourself" (Case 19).

The mother of a four-week-old described her lack of confidence caring for a newborn as a first-time mother cut off from all social supports in detention. Several parents were also adamant that the IHC was not an appropriate place to parent their children: "I don't think this is a place you can take care of children" (Case 14).

Yet despite the inherent challenges of parenting in detention, many parents demonstrated significant resilience in caring for their children. One mother would use the few picture books in the IHC to tell traditional stories from her country of origin to her children. Another mother spoke of using traditional lullabies and songs to soothe her distressed children. Multiple families devised stories about detention to try to protect their children from the frightening and uncertain reality of their status; for example, parents often denied that they were in detention, or if they were detained without their children they told them they were hospitalized, "studying English" (Case 17), or working overtime.

Despite parents' capacity for resilience and their determination to protect their children from the deprivation of detention, the evidence suggests high rates of psychiatric symptoms in adult asylum seekers who are detained in Canada. Compared with nondetained asylum seekers with equivalent premigratory trauma experiences, both women and men held in brief detention (average 31 days) are significantly more likely to have symptoms of posttraumatic stress disorder, anxiety, and depression (Cleveland & Rousseau, 2013). This suggests that parents' mental health may be strongly affected by detention. There is considerable evidence suggesting that parental depression has an impact on children's well-being in multiple domains (Weissman et al., 2006a; Weissman et al., 2006b). Thus, children in detention may face not only the adversity of the detention experience, but the effects of parental mental illness.

Perceptions of Detention: Children's Perceptions

In our study, many children were keenly aware of being in detention, and even younger children struggled to understand what it means about themselves and their future. Older children also perceived the experience of detention as having a negative impact on their well-being.

A four-year-old returning by van to the detention center after a detention review hearing said to her mother while looking out the window: "Those kids are lucky, they get to play in the park. I don't want to stay [in the IHC]" (Case 6). Even a toddler, age 21 months, was described by his mother as knowing "that [the family's circumstance] was not normal" (Case 5). A key informant described being in the outdoor yard with a child who asked how to spell "help." He explained that he wanted to write "help" in the dirt so that airplanes above might come and rescue him.

Older children questioned why they were detained. One 11-year-old asked: "we are not bad people. Why are we here? We don't do bad things" (Case 2). A brother and sister, aged 13 and 12, describe an experience of confinement in detention:

> SON: I feel trapped. I want to ride my bike, to see my friends. That's all.
> DAUGHTER: I feel like I am in jail.
> S: It's basically jail.

Children also responded to detention with prominent psychological distress and psychiatric symptoms (Kronick et al., 2015), suggesting that detention likely has harmful psychological consequences. Further, though many children experienced relief of symptoms on release from detention, several children in the study demonstrated ongoing psychological effects even long after brief detention (ibid.).

Adult's Perceptions

Parents spoke strongly about feelings of disappointment at being detained on arrival in Canada:

> Canada, with its values as a so-called developed country, it's shameful. I would say that it is really unacceptable. . . . I say that it is criminal . . . and you don't even want to take into account children who are suffering. . . . No. I would rather die with dignity than be treated as a subhuman. (Case 20)

Some parents also noted how degraded and criminalized they felt in being detained: "They [CBSA officials and guards] didn't like immigrant people, illegal people. Sometimes they didn't treat us like humans or something like that." Another father noted:

> The moment we came here we were treated like crooks. . . . The moment we landed here, the treatment, the detention—we were really disappointed and we never expected this. . . . We were under oppression there [in our country of origin], so we came here. . . . So that was very painful that after suffering there we come here and we are treated as being part of a terrorist organization.

Overall, parents denounced the practice of detention and emphasized how inappropriate imprisonment was for their children.

Conclusion

Children who come with their parents to Canada seeking asylum are regularly held in immigration detention. According to the UN Convention on the Rights of the Child, detention should used only as a measure of "last resort" and only when children's *best interests* are given primary consideration (UNHCR, 1989). Far from considering children's best interests, current immigration policy and practice in Canada opens the door to (im)migrant child and family detention.

Our research suggests that experiences of detention are frequently traumatizing to children and may result in traumatic family separations even when children are not incarcerated themselves. Although detention in Canada is relatively less harsh and briefer than it is in other countries, children speaking out in our study made clear that detention was profoundly distressing. Children often live through frightening arrests and detention review hearings, and experience deprivation, understimulation, lack of psychosocial support, parental distress, and harsh surveillance during their day-to-day life in detention.

(Im)migrant children in Canada should be protected from the harmful experiences of detention *and* from separation from their primary caregivers in cases where parents are detained alone. Policy makers, advocates, and health professionals have an obligation to shape Canadian immigration practice and legislation to ensure that children and parents are not detained for immigration purposes.

References

Canadian Border Services Agency (CBSA). (2011). Detentions at a glance. In CIC Data Warehouse (Ed.). Candian Border Services Agency, Ottawa, ON: Author.

Citizenship and Immigration Canada. (2007). Enforcement manual (ENF-20): *Detention*. Retrieved from http://www.cic.gc.ca/english/resources/manuals/enf/enf20-eng.pdf.

Cleveland, J., Dionne-Boivin, V., & Rousseau, C. (2013). L'expérience des demandeurs d'asile détenus au Canada. *Criminologie, 46*(1), 107–129.

Cleveland, J., & Rousseau, C. (2013). Psychiatric symptoms associated with brief detention of adult asylum seekers in Canada. *Canadian journal of psychiatry, 58*(7), 409–416.

Cleveland, J., Rousseau, C., & Kronick, R. (2012, Feb. 2). The harmful effects of detention and family separation on asylum seekers' mental health in the context of Bill C-31. Retrieved from http://www.csssdelamontagne.qc.ca/fileadmin/csss_dlm/Publications/Publications_CRF/brief_c31_final.pdf.

Detention and best interests of the child. (2009). Canadian Council for Refugees. Retrieved from http://ccrweb.ca/files/detentionchildren.pdf.

Kronick, R., Rousseau, C., & Cleveland, J. (2015). Asylum seeking children's experiences of detention in Canada: A qualitative study. *American Journal of Orthopsychiatry. 85*(3), 287

Nakache, D. (2011). *The human and financial cost of detention of asylum-seekers in Canada*. Ottawa, ON: UNHCR. Retrieved from http://www.refworld.org/docid/4fafc44c2.html

Ryan, D. A., Kelly, F. E., & Kelly, B. D. (2009). Mental health among persons awaiting an asylum outcome in Western countries. *International Journal of Mental Health, 38*(3), 88–111.

Steel, Z., Chey, T., Silove, D., Marnane, C., Bryant, R. A., & Van Ommeren, M. (2009). Association of torture and other potentially traumatic events with mental health outcomes among populations exposed to mass conflict and displacement: A systematic review and meta-analysis. *JAMA, 302*(5), 537–549.

UNHCR. (1989). Convention on the Rights of the Child. New York, NY: Author.

UNHCR. (2012). Detention guidelines from United Nations High Commissioner for Refugees. New York, NY: Author.

Weissman, M. M., et al. (2006a). Remissions in maternal depression and child psychopathology: A STAR*D-child report. *JAMA, 295*(12), 1389–1398.

Weissman, M. M., Wickramaratne, P., Nomura, Y., Warner, V., Pilowsky, D., & Verdeli, H. (2006b). Offspring of depressed parents: 20 years later. *American Journal of Psychiatry, 163*, 1001–1008.

INDEX

Note: Page numbers followed by italicized letters indicate *f*igures or *t*ables.